MICROCOMPUTER KEYBOARDING AND FORMATTING

SECOND EDITION

JO ANN E. SHERRON, ED. D.
J. Sargeant Reynolds Community College

RONALD H. SHERRON, PH. D.
Virginia Commonwealth University

PARADIGM

Editors Sonja Brown and Eileen Slater
Consulting Editor Dennis Gladhill
Text Designer Joan Silver
Illustrator Larry M. McGowan
Cover Designer Pam Belding
Desktop Production Brad Olsen and Kathleen Oftedahl

ISBN 1-56118-630-9

TEXT + 3.5" DISK: ISBN 1-56118-626-0
Order Number: 36142

TEXT + 5.25" DISK: ISBN 1-56118-627-9
Order Number: 31142

Published by **EMC**Paradigm
875 Montreal Way
St. Paul, MN 55102
(800) 535-6865
E-mail publish@emcp.com

Printed in the United States of America

4 5 6 7 8 9 10 XXX 99 98

Contents

Introduction

Need for Keyboarding Skills

The rapid growth of technology, the data explosion, and the expanded use of computers in the workplace, schools, and home have increased greatly the need for keyboarding skills. Everyone is directly or indirectly influenced by computers. The person who can keyboard effectively will have an advantage both occupationally and personally in adjusting to the age of computers.

Program Purpose

This program teaches keyboarding through computer-assisted instruction. The instruction is provided by a microcomputer software program that controls your interaction between the computer and the text. It is a self-paced program.

Learner Outcomes

After completing this program, you will be able to:

1. Use the complete microcomputer system keyboard, monitor, disks, disk drives, and printer.
2. Demonstrate proper keyboarding techniques.
3. Key straight-copy alphabetic material for three minutes at a minimum of 40 words a minute (wam).
4. Key copy with top-row numbers using proper touch techniques at a minimum of 25 wam.
5. Key copy containing frequently used symbols at a minimum of 25 wam.
6. Key numeric copy using correct touch techniques on the ten-key numeric keypad.
7. Use selected microcomputer special function keys.
8. Develop keyboarding composition skills.
9. Understand computer terminology.

Program Design and Features

This software can be used with an IBM Personal Computer or IBM compatible. The program teaches keyboarding through individualized computer-assisted instruction using a textbook, learner disk, instructor's guide, and teacher management disk. Optional enrichment lessons offer an introduction to formatting letters, reports, and tables.

Coordinated Software and Textbook

The computer-assisted instruction of this program is coordinated with textbook instruction to provide an interactive, self-paced environment. Learners receive instruction on the screen; their input is met with either prompts, reinforcement, drill-and-practice, or word-processing screens. Speed drills also are a feature of the program. In addition to prompts and reinforcements, learners receive feedback on their performances in the form of computed speed rates and errors. The learner may enter or exit the program at will.

Computerized Recordkeeping and Grade Calculation

The Teacher Management disk is designed to assist in student recordkeeping and grade calculation. It allows teachers to assign speed and error limits. Other grading factors also can be entered—the teacher can decide what constitutes an "A" grade, a "B" grade, and so on for each exercise as well as how the different scores will be weighted in calculating final grades. Student progress can be monitored through "Measure Progress" scores, which are automatically registered on the learner record.

The Instructor's Guide gives complete information on how to operate the program and use the Teacher Management disk. It also provides suggestions for course organization, instructional procedures, and evaluation.

Research Based

This program is based on a comprehensive review of the research related to keyboarding skill acquisition and computer-assisted instruction. New concepts incorporated into this program have been field-tested with learners from a variety of backgrounds and are based on a dissertation completed by the senior author.

Individualized

This self-paced program allows the learner to move forward or backward within the lessons and to enter and exit the program when desired. The program is personalized with prompts and individual records. Minimum goals are set for each lesson. However, learners are encouraged to set higher goals for themselves as appropriate.

Flexible

This program is designed for use with the IBM Personal Computer and compatible equipment. The techniques, skills, and knowledge acquired in this program are transferable to all standard keyboards. The program can be used individually or with groups in a variety of instructional settings, such as:

1. Microcomputer keyboarding/typewriting courses.
2. Microcomputer laboratories.
3. Business and industry training.
4. Self-instruction.
5. Computer literacy courses.
6. Data entry courses.

Interdisciplinary

By using related terminology and vocabulary, the program complements other content areas such as data processing, business management, computer literacy, word processing composition, and computer science.

Emphasis on Techniques

Correct techniques are stressed throughout the program, both in the textbook and on the microcomputer screen. Prompts and technique checks are repeated periodically along with "Get Ready" checklists.

Skill Building

Keyboarding skill is increased and reinforced in each lesson through review of previously learned keys, presentation and practice of new keys, and straight-copy skill building drills. In "Measure Progress" sections, minimum performance goals are established for each lesson. These performance goals are gradually increased as the learner progresses through the program until a minimum goal of 40 wam is reached.

Performance Based

This program is goal-oriented. The program sets minimum performance goals on straight-copy material throughout the lessons. Learners have the option of increasing the goals and are encouraged to exceed these minimums. Learners progressing sequentially through the program will attain the minimum goal of 40 wam for three minutes on straight-copy material. At the end of each activity, learners are informed of their progress.

Computer-Assisted Instruction

The program uses the computer to perform a variety of instructional functions, such as:

1. Analyzing speed and indicating errors.
2. Recycling based on performance.
3. Providing prompts, reinforcements, and drill and practice.
4. Personalizing performance for each learner.
5. Maintaining learner records.
6. Providing a copy of lesson output for the learner and the teacher.

Learning Principles

This program incorporates the following research-proven learning principles.

Goal Setting

Learning is enhanced by clearly stating each lesson's objective. Minimum performance goals are given for each lesson. The learner has an option of increasing the goal for each lesson.

Drill and Practice

Each new skill and understanding is repeated and practiced until the learner reaches a selected performance level.

Immediate Feedback

Learners get immediate feedback during lessons and assessment activities. When learning new keys, misstrokes are immediately identified so the learner can key the correct response. This prevents the learner from repeating a wrong response that must later be unlearned, which can interfere with new learning.

Reinforced Learning

Reinforcement is provided in the speed drills and "Measure Progress" sections. Immediate knowledge of results is provided in the drills.

Small Increments and Spaced Practice

The program presents new material in small increments and allows for spaced practice and review of new skills and understandings. At no time is the learner overloaded with new concepts and psychomotor skill demands. This allows learners to proceed at their own pace and to experience success.

Work-related Vocabulary

The program uses examples related to the real work world. A fringe benefit of the program is the attainment of basic computer literacy.

Microcomputer System

Study the photograph to familiarize yourself with the components of a computer.

IBM Personal System 2, Model 30

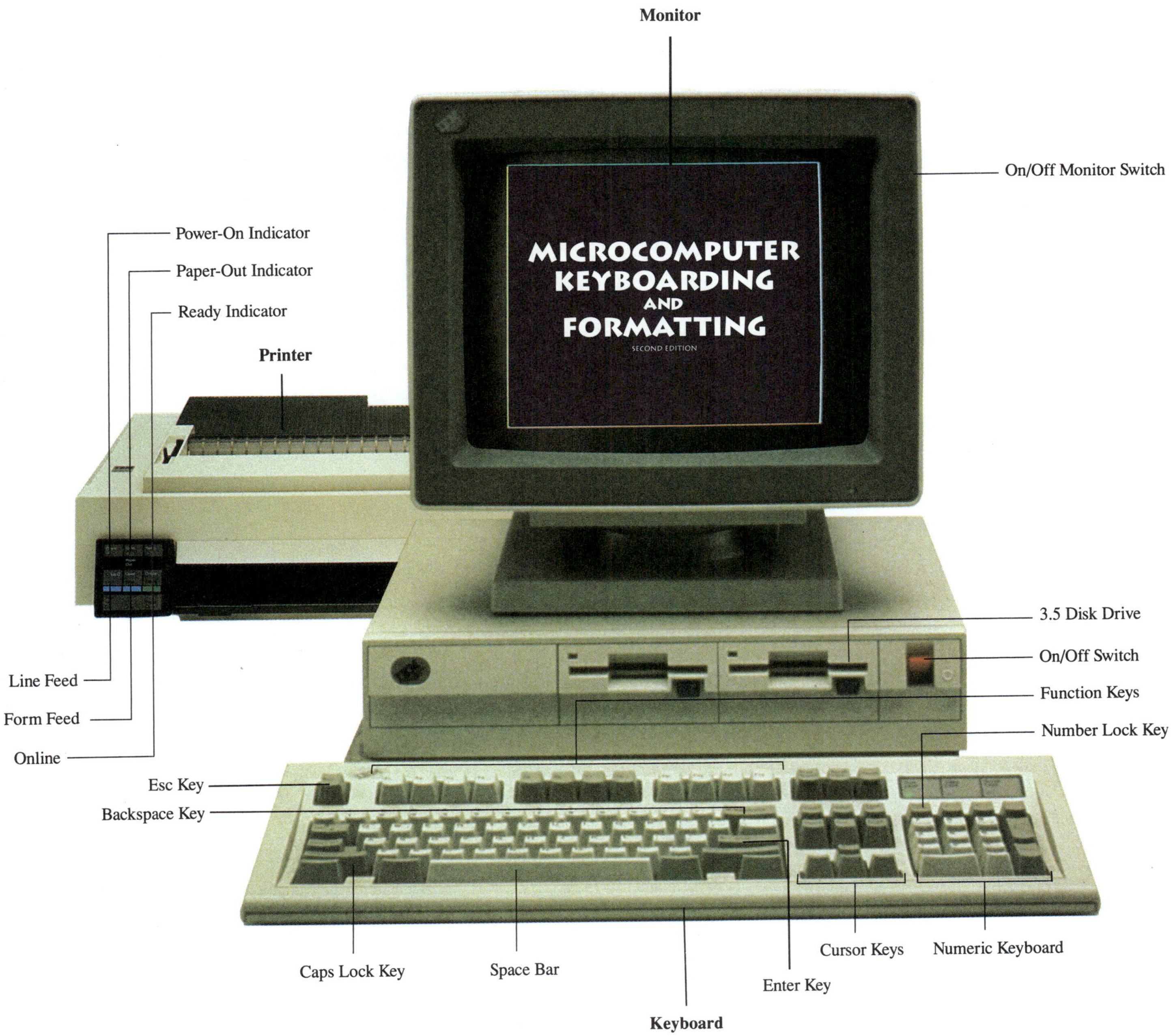

Microcomputer Operation

In order for a microcomputer to operate, whether to create original programs or to run various application programs, it must have an operating system. This Disk Operating System (DOS) is usually provided when the computer is purchased. Two common operating systems are MS-DOS and PC-DOS.

DOS tells the computer how to run software. When you "boot" your system, you are loading the DOS program. This enables the system to run any software program compatible with the DOS system. The DOS program also tells the computer how to respond to certain DOS commands entered by the user.

Once DOS is loaded onto the computer, a prompt appears on the screen. If the computer has a hard drive, a C> prompt appears. Dual or single "floppy" disk drives usually display an A> prompt. Either of these prompts indicates that the system is ready to run software programs and that the keyboard is ready to accept input.

The alphabetic and numeric keys on the microcomputer keyboard work just like a typewriter. Certain keys, however, perform functions that are unique to the software program in use. Some function keys are introduced and used in this program.

Software

The computer system will not operate without software. Software must be loaded and available to the computer system in order to perform special functions or to run a particular program.

Protect.

Do not bend or fold.

Insert carefully.

Never touch.

50°-125°

Never place near magnetic fields.

The software for a microcomputer system is contained on a magnetic disk—either a 3½-inch or a 5¼-inch size. Disks are sealed in a protective cover and then inserted in a removable cover. They should be held by the corner when removing them from the outer cover. When inserting a disk into a disk drive, care should be taken not to use force. The disk should be inserted slowly and gently.

When handling floppy disks, there are certain precautions you must take in order not to damage them:

1. Do not fold or bend a disk.
2. Do not touch the exposed surface of the disk.
3. Do not expose a disk to extreme temperature or moisture.
4. Do not insert or remove a disk when the "in use" light or a disk drive is on.
5. After use, always store a floppy disk in its protective cover in a vertical position in a disk holder or file.
6. Do not store a disk near any magnetic or electrical fields such as monitors, telephones, or magnets.
7. Do not write on the protective cover of a 5¼-inch floppy disk with a pencil or a ballpoint pen. Write on the label provided and then attach it to the disk, or use a felt-tip pen.

Computer Keyboard

Two standard IBM keyboards are widely used in business: the enhanced keyboard and the alternate keyboard. Look at the following illustration of the enhanced keyboard. If your keyboard is arranged somewhat differently, it does not matter. The function of the keys remains the same no matter where they are located. Throughout this textbook, the "enhanced" keyboard is used for illustrations.

The "enhanced" microcomputer keyboard consists of four groupings of keys:

1. The function keys
2. The typewriter keys (alphabetic/numeric keyboard)
3. Cursor movement or editing keys
4. The ten-key numeric keypad

Most of the keys on either keyboard are typematic. That is, they continue to repeat their function as long as you hold them down. However, many function and editing keys act as toggle keys: pressing once turns them on, and pressing them again turns them off.

Getting Started

Equipment Required

You will need the following equipment in order to run the program provided with this textbook:

1. An IBM PC, XT, AT, PS/2 or compatible computer
2. PC-DOS or MS-DOS version 2.0 or higher
3. A monitor set for 80-column mode
4. A student program disk
5. A student data disk (blank disk for your files)
6. Access to a printer

Starting the Software

To run the software program that accompanies this textbook, you must initialize the program for your personal use. Determine which of the following systems is similar to the one you are using and then read the instructions.

Dual-Disk Computers

1. Insert the DOS disk in disk drive A.
2. Turn on the monitor and the computer.
3. When the date prompt appears, press Enter.
4. When the time prompt appears, press Enter.
5. The A> prompt should appear. (If it does not, consult your instructor.)
6. Once you have the DOS system installed on your computer, insert the student program disk in drive A and a blank formatted disk to use as a student data disk in drive B. Now key **A:** and press Enter.
7. At the A: prompt, key **MKF**. A title screen will appear; press any key to continue. The first time you run the program, you will be asked to enter your full name and your I.D. number. Your instructor will assign you an I.D. The computer will mark your disk as belonging to you, so you will not need to fill in the information each time. All of your timings and scores will be saved on your data disk. In the future, continue to insert your student data disk in drive B.

Hard-Disk Computers

1. Turn on the monitor and the computer.
2. When the date prompt appears, press Enter.
3. When the time prompt appears, press Enter.
4. The C> prompt should appear.
5. At the C> prompt, key **cd** and the name of the directory in which the student program is installed. For example, you might key **cd micro**. Insert a formatted data disk into disk drive A.
6. When the name of the prompt switches to the keyboard directory, such as C:\MICRO, key **MKF**. A title screen will appear; press any key to continue. The first time you run the program, you will be asked to enter your full name and your I.D. number. Your instructor will assign you an I.D. The computer will mark your disk as belonging to you, so you will not need to fill in the information each time. All of your timings and scores will be saved on your data disk. In the future, continue to insert your student data disk in drive A.

Network System

Consult your instructor to run this program on a network system.

After Initial Booting

Once the program disk is personalized for your use, you will not have to enter your name and I.D. number again. Simply insert your data disk at the appropriate prompt and key **MKF**. When the title screen appears, press any key to continue. A screen similar to the following should appear. Check the information to be certain that you have the correct disk. If you have someone else's disk by mistake, press ESC to exit and locate your disk before you continue. If all of the information is correct, press Enter to continue.

```
Please verify that this is your name and ID number:

Student Name: JO ANN SHERRON

ID Number    : 5

Data Drive   : A

Date (m/d/y): 02/28/96

     Press ENTER if the information is correct.
     Press F9 to modify the information.
     Press ESC to exit the program.
```

Main Menu

The *Microcomputer Keyboarding and Formatting* program is organized around a series of simple "menus" that let you select what part of the program you want.

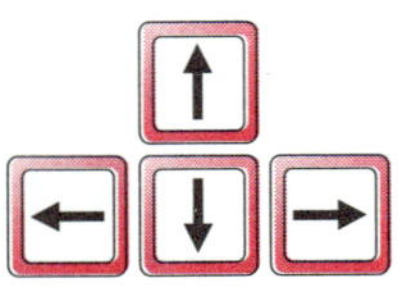

The Main Menu lists five choices, one of which is always highlighted. If you wish to begin with the highlighted choice, press Enter. To select a different choice, use the Up- and Down-Arrow keys to move the highlight. When the choice you want is highlighted, press Enter.

```
M A I N   M E N U

Lessons
Word Processor
Options
Print Activities
Exit to DOS
```

On your screen, the Main Menu looks similar to the previous illustration. Only one choice can be highlighted at a time. Selecting one of the choices will take you to one of the possible activities. A description of each activity appears below.

LESSONS

This selection allows you to work with specific lessons. It is the option you will select most often. When selected, a menu similar to this appears.

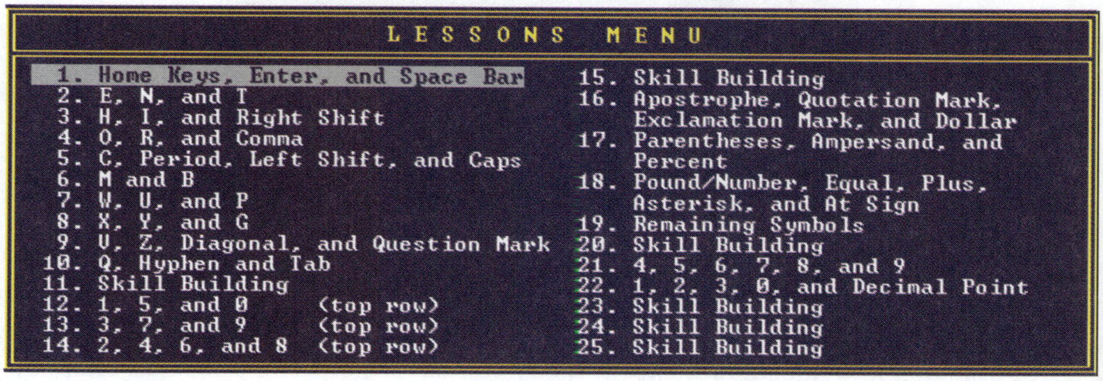

Again, one option is highlighted. Use the Up-, Down-, Left-, or Right-Arrow keys to select a specific lesson. When your choice is highlighted, press Enter. The program will take you to that lesson. Once there, follow the directions for that lesson.

WORD PROCESSOR

Many lessons in *Microcomputer Keyboarding and Formatting* contain composition and document production exercises (required or optional). In addition, your instructor may assign some special activities or timings that are not included in the textbook. These exercises usually are completed in the Word Processor option.

When Word Processor is selected, the following menu appears on the screen.

All word-processing exercises already completed appear within the box. If you wish to return to one of those documents, use the Up- and Down-Arrow keys to highlight your choice and press Enter. If you wish to create a new document, press Enter, then key the file name for the new document.

When using the Word Processor, you will be able to use the editing keys to make corrections to existing or newly created documents. Material keyed using this option can be scored for speed only. Errors will not be highlighted on the screen. Production work keyed directly from the text lessons will be graded by the computer

Options

When a computer is booted, the software program loads default (preset) instructions for running the program. These selected settings within the program can be controlled on the options menu. When this choice is selected from the Main Menu, you can set the printer option to be compatible with the one you are using.

If the listed settings are appropriate for your hardware and for the lesson activities that you plan to complete, press ESC to return to the Main Menu. If changes are needed, press the appropriate function key listed at the bottom of the screen to change a setting. For example, if you change from a dot matrix printer to a laser printer, select F8.

Print Activities

When you select Print Activities from the Main Menu, the following screen appears.

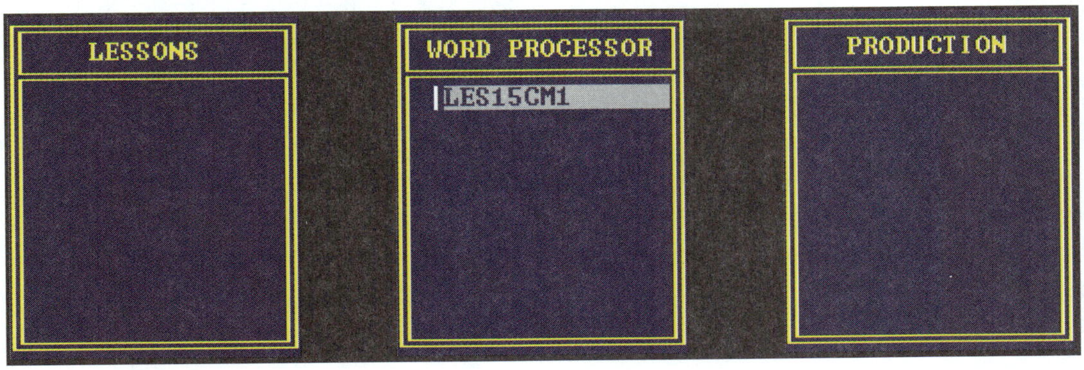

Three boxes list the document names of the last ten activities that you completed in three categories. Use the Up-, Down-, Left- and Right-Arrow keys to move the highlight to the name of the document you want to print and press Enter. If you select from the Lessons box, you will have the option to print the entire lesson or only the "Measure Progress" exercise.

If you do not have a printer connected to your computer, you can still obtain printouts of your work. When at the Main Menu, exit from the program. Remove your disk and take it to a computer connected to a printer. Boot and run your disk in the normal way. Then select Print Activities from the Main Menu. After printing, be certain to bring your disk back to your computer.

Print size is determined by the pitch setting of the printer. Pitch refers to the number of characters or spaces printed per inch. The most common pitch sizes are 10 (10 characters per inch), 12 (12 characters per inch), and 15 (15 characters per inch.) The higher the number, the smaller the print. *Microcomputer Keyboarding and Formatting* defaults to 10 pitch. All exercises and word-processing documents are in 10 pitch.

Exit

The Exit option in the Main Menu allows you to leave or stop running the program at any time. If you desire to quit the program during a lesson, press ESC until the Main Menu appears and select the Exit option. When prompted, verify your intent by selecting "Yes."

Special Function Keys

Refer to page 7 for position of the function keys.

Depending on the keyboard you are using, a series of function keys is located either in a single row across the top of the keyboard or in two columns to the left of the alphabetic keyboard. Except for the ESC key, these keys have an F and a number printed on them (F1- F12 on some keyboards; F1- F10 on others). These keys "inform" the software to perform special functions according to the programmed instructions. In the *Microcomputer Keyboarding and Formatting* software, certain function keys perform special actions within specific portions of the program. Some are used only while working with drills and exercises within a lesson, and others are used only when completing activities using the word processor.

The prompt line at the bottom of each screen informs you which keys are available for use at any time. If the key is not "active" and you press it, nothing will happen.

Functions keys used in the lessons of *Microcomputer Keyboarding and Formatting* include:

ESC Automatically takes you back to the last menu from which you made a selection. For example, if you are working in a lesson, ESC would take you back to the Lessons Contents Menu. Each time you press ESC, you will go back one more menu until you arrive at the Main Menu.

F1 Allows you to go back to the immediately preceding activity or to repeat the present activity. An "activity" is one part of a lesson such as "Review," "Increase Keying Speed," or "Improve Keying Accuracy." If you press this function key before starting an activity, you will return to the beginning of the previous activity. If you press this function key anytime after starting a particular activity, you will return to the beginning of that same activity.

F2 Allows you to skip ahead to the next activity in the lesson. If for some reason you do not wish to complete the activity presently on the screen, press this function key to move to the beginning of the next activity in the lesson sequence.

F10 Allows you to skip lines within a particular type of activity. A "line" is an individual item within a drill or exercise. This option cannot be used in "Measure Progress" or word-processor activities.

Examples of the function keys used in the word processor include:

ESC Allows you to save your document and/or have the computer check your work and score it electronically.

F3 Displays the help screen that lists all the function keys and shortcut keys available while using the word processor. The F3 key is a toggle key.

F5 Toggles the line spacing to single-, double-, or triple-spacing.

F7 Allows you to change margins and set or remove tab stops.

The word processor's function keys are explained and practiced when they are introduced in the textbook. For a complete listing, press F3 in the word processor.

Prepare for Lesson 1

If you have not loaded the *Microcomputer Keyboarding and Formatting* disk, please do it now and proceed to Lesson 1. Follow the directions on the screen.

Organize Your Work Environment

A well-organized and comfortable work environment is essential to efficient keyboarding. Your work station should be uncluttered and contain only those items essential for working on the lesson. As you start each lesson, check the following:

1. Position the keyboard so it is even with the desk's front edge and slightly off-center to the left of your body.
2. If your work station is adjustable, center the monitor screen at eye level.
3. Place your book (when used) at the side of the keyboard and elevate it so that it can be clearly read.
4. If possible, adjust the monitor screen position to eliminate glare. Adjust the contrast and brightness controls for ease of viewing.

Assume Proper Posture and Correct Finger Position

Proper posture and correct finger position help prevent keying errors and fatigue. At the beginning of each lesson, do the following:

1. Place your feet flat on the floor with one foot slightly in front of the other.
2. Sit up straight with your back supported by the chair.
3. Sit the correct distance from the keyboard: drop your arms straight down by your sides and then place your fingers on the keys. If you are in the correct position, your elbows will be straight down by your sides.
4. Place your fingers on the keys in a curved position.
5. Slant your forearms at the same angle as the keyboard.
6. Keep your wrists low, but do not rest them on the keyboard.

S The sacred scroll was a scientific spoof about some super species.

T The total trip turned to tolerance of tight scheduled trivia.

U It was urgent until the usage of the unit made it unable to unload.

V The value of a good valve became evident as the vapor rose from the vat.

W What woman would wish to work in worse conditions?

X The group text exploited and became excited when they were excluded from the expansion.

Y The yearly trip to see the yoga was nearly canceled.

Z The zebra was one of the dozen shipped to the zoo.

Paragraphs—All Letters

❶ Computers, like any piece of equipment, will need some maintenance. If you do not have the computer checked on a regular basis, then it will surely break down. When the computer is down, the work flow will not be up to par. So good maintenance plans do pay!

❷ In the near future, many more business transactions will be done via computer. When computers are linked with home systems, many people will work at home. This will change many lifestyles and reduce traffic problems. Many new cottage jobs will emerge.

❸ Every clerk needs to know how to set up a set of files. The files need to be arranged in an order that anyone can understand. A filing system that only the person who created it can use is not a good system. Many types of files can be categorized in logical sections. These sections need to relate to the type of business that is conducted.

UNIT 1

ALPHABETIC KEYBOARDING

Specific Key Drills

A An ad announcing the annual assembly was advertised in American public announcements section.

B Business buys goods and brings better bounty to citizens.

C Careless cars careening across the concrete could cause accidents.

D Did the demise of Dameron Doolittle dampen the party?

E Every easy entry eventually costs in the end.

F Foundations find funds frequently. Funding fads is false and foolish.

G "Good gracious," greeted Gary. Get the garbage off the grate.

H Hassle the harried housewife. How many husbands has she had?

I I will find it. Will it be filled? The dill will fill the pickle with a thrill.

J Justice just joins the jobs. Junior Jackson just jeers jauntily.

K To know how to knot the kite tail without kinks is essential.

M The military wants mastery of the marine and other main markets.

A machine can match the main and major manners of mischief makers.

N The nurse nurtured the neck nerves with new techniques.

O The original ornate object offended the officials.

P Pamela paid the prize for pleasing purple.

Q The quaint queens quickly quoted Quo Vadis and Quintus.

R Ronald roasted the round roll of rare rabbit.

1

Home Keys, Enter, and Space Bar

GOALS

- Learn Home Keys, Enter, and Space Bar

Get Ready

Check the following:

1. Place your feet flat on the floor with one foot slightly in front of the other.
2. Sit up straight with your back supported by the chair.
3. Sit the correct distance from the keyboard: drop your arms straight down by your sides and then place your fingers on the keys. If you are in the correct position, your elbows will be straight down by your sides.
4. Place your fingers on the home keys in a curved position.
5. Slant your forearms at the same angle as the keyboard.
6. Keep your wrists low, but do not rest them on the keyboard.

Lesson 11

1 The well-known quacks told some very stupid jokes.
2 Once upon a time a quiet lamb lived on a big farm.
3 The up-to-date story was told with a quick finale.
4 The accounting teacher lives in the near East End.
5 Philosophically, I do not know how to answer them.

Two-Letter Word Drills

1 he in on so or of it at if be by ti do ha la it or
2 if it is or no an si in as at no up me en an of on
3 of at or in an it if is to te ti do id di my fa go
4 an is he at me go bo as of it an am co to if at it
5 to no on in or so up fa go am em be ex by me my do

Three-Letter Word Drills

1 how cut big put hot ten lie was per its eve cab
2 too for bag him did gas get out fly old bug cat
3 say day aim big way hat dim sit sin bet did war
4 won all bar eat did cat ton saw tar vat was zip
5 art but cat did eat far gut had ill fog sap tow

Four-Letter Word Drills

1 half mail gear roll must site mark plea good line
2 cold here went open pain toll past tore site dues
3 must want true area quit rely room move dove love
4 sale must take here list hall want mark head take
5 lain cook boys mind pear faze tear vote fade have

LOCATE THE HOME KEYS

Locate the home keys (A S D F J K L ;) and place your fingers on them lightly as follows.

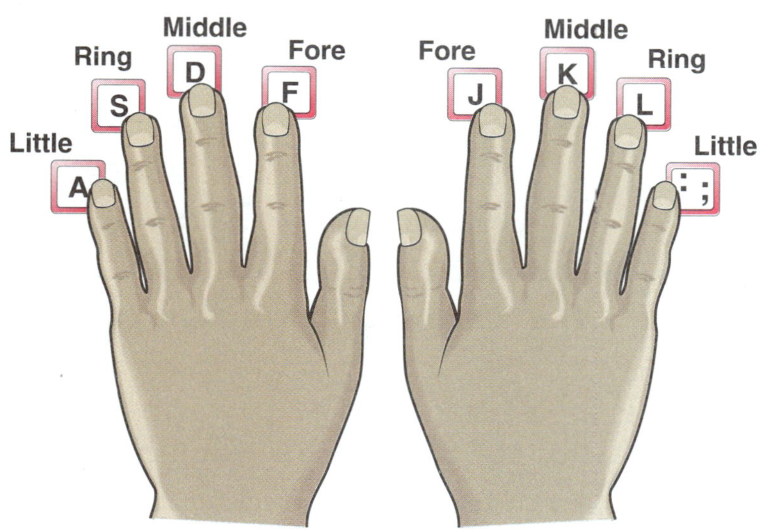

Assume proper body, hand, and finger position

Left hand:

- Little finger on the A key
- Ring finger on the S key
- Middle finger on the D key
- Forefinger on the F key

Right hand:

- Forefinger on the J key
- Middle finger on the K key
- Ring finger on the L key
- Little finger on the ; key

Practice striking the keys several times with your fingers in the proper position. Look at the screen while you key the following line.

```
asdfjkl;asdfjkl;asdfjkl;
```

Lesson 5

1 Cel felt that she cared; Joe said he did not deal.
2 Rest safe; no one called Ta and Rickie, I said no.
3 Le said that the docks are closed, no one listens.
4 CARLOS and JANE closed the closet doors hard, Rae.
5 Les O. said that the credit classes were canceled.

Lesson 7

1 Marcie: I do need to see the cats, fish, and rat.
2 Boats are safe. Mine is not. A car is safe. Hi.
3 NASA leases land to: Karl, Jane, Mark, and Marci.
4 Ask Mat and Chris to assist. The tent sales fell.
5 The trashes ashes landed on docks B, and M, and D.

Lesson 8

1 Mr. and Mrs. Wallace told the tale about two fish.
2 William wants the rainfall to be in the mountains.
3 I must tell the truth to the auditor of be jailed.
4 Chocolate pies are the best; lemon pies are third.
5 The three purple clocks were placed on the mantel.

Lesson 9

1 Go to the Xerox machine and make ten copies of it.
2 You can do anything, if you think you can and try.
3 Xanaxe is a medicine and is prescribed by doctors.
4 Women had been working for many years. Good work.
5 Six sassy sailors raised taxes on the large ships.

Lesson 10

1 The phone number was two zero two one two one two.
2 Can you go to the Zodiac Club with me tomorrow Jo?
3 Was it advisable to pick up the available waivers?
4 Can you go to or come from the stores immediately?
5 Will you be stopping by the party at a frat house?

LOCATE THE Enter KEY

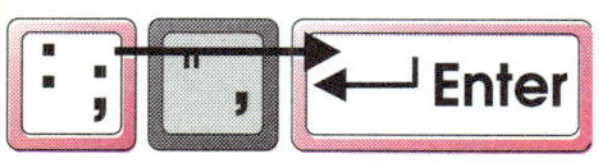

When you reach the end of a line, the Enter key is used to return the cursor to the beginning of a new line. Strike the Enter key with the little finger of your right hand.

1. Locate the Enter key.
2. With your fingers in the home key position, strike the Enter key with the little finger of your right hand (the ; finger).
3. Keep your other fingers over the home keys so that you don't lose your place.
4. Tap the Enter key quickly. Immediately return your finger to the semicolon key.

While watching the screen, practice this reach several times (; then Enter and return your finger to ;).

```
1 ;(Enter)
2 ;(Enter)
3 ;(Enter)
```

Key the following lines so that each one begins on a new line. Tap the Enter key quickly at the end of each line.

```
1 asdfjkl;(Enter)
2 asdfjkl;(Enter)
3 asdfjkl;(Enter)
```

Strike the keys quickly as if the keys were hot.

Appendix C
Supplemental Drills

These drills can be used for extra practice. The drills labeled Lessons 1-11 should be practiced only after the appropriate lesson has been completed. The drills following Lesson 11 contain all letters of the alphabet; practice on these drills should be delayed until Lesson 11 has been completed.

Lesson 1

1 ded fad flask ask lad; ask dad jak flak as; falls;
2 salsa lass lad asks fall; add sad dads dak; as alf
3 a sad lad falls as a fad adds a flask salad; asks;
4 a sass sad dad adds lads asks; ad jaks add salads;
5 alas; a lad adds salsa; fad flasks fall salads add

Lesson 2

1 tends; attends; lends leases dent lent as kent end
2 a fad flask attends; jade ants lend sands; last as
3 dent a tent; lent a jade; jade lends and adds fads
4 lakes dealt attends leaf deaf fan ale sale need as
5 ease kent sand end ants; ten tees tested ten leafs

Lesson 3

1 The hit health ahead hate shall shell slant leash;
2 The kid said knit instead; The lite kite aided Ede
3 Ted and Dad hit it; Tad had said hi; Elsie failed;
4 Al added Teds jade and said hi; The knife fell at;
5 Tell Ella and Ted and Tad and Fae and Ded and Elsi

Lesson 4

1 The net losses told the tale to all those near Ed;
2 Rafe, Teri, Ted, and Sissie joined Elsi and Father
3 Take an order for ten trees and tents, Terrie Fae;
4 The old elf stole, so did the old kites, tie knot;
5 A flat train did it, too; She hit the fastest fans

Locate the Space Bar

To leave spaces between letters or words, use the Space Bar.

1. Strike the Space Bar with your right thumb. If you are left handed, you may find it easier to use your left thumb.
2. Strike the Space Bar with a down and in motion of your thumb.
3. Look at the screen and practice keying the following:

```
asdf (space) jkl; (space) asdf (space) jkl; (space)
```

Practice the Home Keys, Enter, and Space Bar

Practice the following lines. All drill lines in all lessons should be keyed at least two times. Where indicated, use the Space Bar. At the end of a line, a ↵ appears on the screen. When you get to this symbol, strike the Enter key.

You will learn the location of the keys faster if you say each key as you strike it.

```
1 aaa ;;; sss lll ddd kkk fff jjj asdfjkl; asdfjkl;a ↵
2 ff jj dd kk ss ll aa ;; fj dk sl as las; asdf jkl; ↵
3 fj dk sl a; a ad sad fad lad fad asd as ask fad as ↵
4 all fall dad jal jad jas jaf lass flak falls flask ↵
5 jak sad fad dad jal lad fad add ask fall lass flak ↵
```

Develop Keying Skills

Do not space before a semicolon; space once after it.

Key each line two times.

```
1 adds a sad salad; asks a sad lad; a sad lass adds;
2 all dads fall; a lass asks a dad; add a fad flask;
3 a sad lass falls; all salads fall; fall dads; asks
4 ask fall lads; a lass adds; a lad falls; dad falls
5 as a fad; as all ads; as a lad asks; a salsa salad
```

```
/* MileKilo */
#include (stdio.h)
void MilesToKilometers(void)
{
         float Miles;
         printf("Miles to Kilometers Conversion\n\n");
         printf("Enter miles to convert: ");
         scanf("%f", &Miles);
         printf("Kilometers: %5.2f\n, Miles * 1.6093);
}
void KilometersToMiles(void)
{
         float Kilometers;
         printf("Kilometers to Miles Conversion\n\n");
         printf("Enter kilometers to convert: ");
         scanf("%f", &Kilometers);
         printf("Miles: %5.2f\n", Kilometers / 1.6093;
}
main()
{
         char ch;
         printf("Miles/Kilometers Conversion
Program\n\n");
         printf("(1) Convert Miles to Kilometers\n"n;
         printf("(2) Convert Kilometers to Miles\n");
         printf("Enter option number: ");
         ch = getch();
         printf("%c\n", ch);
         if (ch == '1')
          MilesToKilometers();
         else
          if (ch == '2')
               KilometersToMiles();
          else
               printf("Bad option entered.\n");
```

End-of-Lesson Procedure

At the end of each lesson, you will have the following options:

1. To restart the same lesson, press the F1 function key.
2. To return to the Lessons Menu, press ESC. This action automatically will save the completed lesson.
3. To proceed to the next, or any other lesson, highlight your choice on the menu and press Enter.
4. To return to the Main Menu, press ESC again.
5. To print the lesson, select Print Activities.
6. To exit the program:
   a. Select the Exit option and press Enter.
   b. When the DOS prompt appears on the screen, remove your data disk.
   c. Turn off the monitor. (Your instructor also may ask you to turn off the computer and printer.)

```
C        PROGRAM TO COMPUTE THE VOLUME OF A RIGHT CIRCULAR
CYLINDER
C
C        PROGRAM USES NESTED DO-LOOPS TO INCREMENT DATA
C
         PI=3.141593
         PRINT 5000
  5000   FORMAT ('1')
  50     FORMAT (12X,'HEIGHT',13X,'DIAMETER',13X,'VOLUME')
         DC 100 J=1, 12
         H=FLOAT9J*10)
         PRINT 5C
         PRINT 6C
60       FORMAT (3(10X,10('*'))/)
         DC 110 I-1,15
         D+FLOAT (i*12)
         V+PI**2/4.*H
         PRINT 200,H,D,V
200      FORMAT(3F20.0)
110      CONTINUE
         PRINT1000
1000     FORMAT (//)
100      CONTINUE
         PRINT 5C00
         STOP
         END
```

Format a C Program

The following program is written in C language, which is used primarily with microcomputers. Its primary applications are in science, mathematics, engineering, and business.

Learning Activity 6

1. Key the following C program. Proof your copy carefully to be sure that every space, punctuation mark, and character is correct. Any error could cause the program to run improperly.
2. Set 1-inch side margins. Begin at the left margin and set a tab nine spaces from the margin.
3. Print a copy and compare it with the model. Mark any uncorrected errors on the printout.

2 E, N, and T Keys

GOALS

- Reinforce Previous Learning
- Learn New Keys E, N, and T
- Use Proper Keyboarding Techniques
- Develop Keying Skills

Get Ready

Check the following:

1. Place your feet flat on the floor with one foot slightly in front of the other.
2. Sit up straight with your back supported by the chair.
3. Sit the correct distance from the keyboard: drop your arms straight down by your sides and then place your fingers on the keys. If you are in the correct position, your elbows will be straight down by your sides.
4. Place your fingers on the home keys in a curved position.
5. Slant your forearms at the same angle as the keyboard.
6. Keep your wrists low, but do not rest them on the keyboard.

Review

Key each line two times.

Keep your fingers curved and upright.

```
1 asdfjkl; aa ;; ss ll dd kk ff jj fdsa ;lkj asdfjkl
2 asks a dad; add a salad; all dads fall; ask as dad
3 ask a dad; all lads; ask a lass; all fall; dad all
```

```
3000-REPORT SECTION.
3010-REPORT-CONTROL.
    PERFORM 3020-INITIALIZATION.
    PERFORM 3030-REPORT-BODY.
    GOTO 3040-REPORT-TERMINATION.
3020-INITIALIZATION.
    OPEN OUTPUT PRINT.
    MOVE 0 TO EOF-FLAG.
    MOVE 57 TO MY-LINE-COUNTER.
    RETURN SORT-FILE AT END MOVE 1 TO EOF-FLAG.
3030-REPORT-BODY.
    IF MY-LINE-COUNTER > 56
        WRITE PRINT-LINE FROM SUBHEADING AFTER PAGE
        MOVE 1 TO MY-LINE-COUNTER.
    MOVE CALL-NUMBER-SR.
    MOVE AUTHOR-SR.
    ADD 2 TO MY-LINE-COUNTER.
    RETURN SORT-FILE AT END MOVE 1 TO EOF-FLAG.
3040-REPORT-TERMINATION.
    CLOSE PRINT.
```

Format a FORTRAN Program

The following program is written in FORTRAN, which is used with mainframe and microcomputers. Its primary applications are in science, mathematics, and engineering.

Learning Activity 5

1. Key the following FORTRAN program. Proof your copy carefully to be sure that every space, punctuation mark, and character is correct. Any error could cause the program to run improperly.
2. Set 1-inch side margins. Begin at the left margin and set a tab seven spaces from the margin.
3. Print a copy and compare it with the model. Mark any uncorrected errors on the printout.

Locate the E Key

The E is keyed with the D finger. Place your fingers on the home keys. Look at your hands and practice the reach to E.

```
ded ded ded ded
```

Then look away and practice.

```
ded ded ded ded
```

Practice the E Key Reach

Key each line two times.

```
1 ded ded deed sees keels lakes seal seeds dells ded
2 ded desks lease fakes jaded seal see leak ease fee
3 dead deaf added fled leeks sales leaf fees del ded
4 a fake; desk sales; a jaded elf asked; a deeded ad
5 see a lease; fake a seal; see a leak; eases a seal
```

Say each key as you strike it. Remember: Right little finger strikes Enter.

FORMAT A COBOL PROGRAM

COBOL is a popular language for business applications software. The line identifying labels have been omitted from the following program. The computer usually adds these automatically in a COBOL program.

LEARNING ACTIVITY 4

1. Key the following excerpt from a COBOL program. Proof your copy carefully to be sure that every space, punctuation mark, and character is correct. Any error could cause the program to run improperly.
2. To format a COBOL program, begin at the left margin and set tabs every four spaces.
3. Print a copy and compare it with the model. Mark any uncorrected errors on the printout.

```
IDENTIFICATION DIVISION.
PROGRAM-ID. PRACTICE COBOL.
AUTHOR. UNKNOWN.
ENVIRONMENT DIVISION.
INPUT-OUTPUT CONTROL.
FILE CONTROL.
    SELECT INFD ASSIGN TO READER.
    SELECT BOOK-FILE ASSIGN TO DISK.
    SELECT SORT-FILE ASSIGN TO SORT DISK.
    SELECT PRINT ASSIGN TO PRINTER.
DATA DIVISION.
FILE SECTION.
FD INFD
    DATA RECORD IN INPUT-RECORD.
01 INPUT-RECORD.
    02 CALL-NUMBER-IR.
    02 AUTHOR-IR.
    02 TITLE-IR.
    02 DATE-IR.
    02 ITEM-NUMBER-IR.
    02 PRICE-IR.
    02 DISCARD-CODE-IR.
FD BOOK FILE
    DATA RECORD IS BOOK-RECORD.
2030-BUILD-EXIT.
    EXIT.
```

LOCATE THE N KEY

The N is keyed with the J finger. Place your fingers on the home keys. Look at your hands and practice the reach to N.

```
jnj jnj jnj jnj
```

Then look away and practice.

```
jnj jnj jnj jnj
```

PRACTICE THE N KEY REACH

Key each line two times.

```
1 jnj jnj fan and land sand nan den jen ned end lend
2 ned dens ends an dan jan allen fallen fan land jan
3 nell nan and sands; dean dan; land fan; an nan and
4 fallen fan; lands and sand; land end; fall and fan
5 need all ends; and a den; and a deed; end all fads
```

Fingers are curved and upright.

2. Begin the numbers at the left margin. Begin the text five spaces from the margin at the first tab.
3. Print a copy and compare it with the model. Mark any uncorrected errors on the printout.

```
10  HOME: PRINT "PRACTICE"
20  PRINT "COPYRIGHT (C)"
30  PRINT "IBM-PC"
40  PRINT
45  PRINT "THIS PROGRAM ALLOWS YOU TO KEEP"
50  PRINT "STOCK RECORDS"
60  PRINT "YOU CAN LIST ALL OF YOUR STOCKS"
100 PRINT "GAIN OR LOSS, AND THE"
210 PRINT "TOTAL IN YOUR PORTFOLIO."
220 GOSUB 410
230 IF CP = 5 THEN CM = 225
240 IF CP = 3 THEN CM = 18
250 IF CP = 1 THEN CM = 6
270 IF CP <1 OR CP >5 THEN 190
280 PRINT
290 PRINT "ENTER THE REQUIRED AMOUNT"
300 INPUT P
320 PRINT "ENTER THE INTEREST RATE (%)"
330 INPUT X
340 PRINT
350 ON CP GOTO 400
360 FOR T = 1 TO 10
370 NEXT T
380 RETURN
390 REM DAILY INTEREST
400 HOME
410 PRINT "WEEK # ";N;" : STOCK PRICE=$";BA
420 GOSUB 459
440 PRINT :GOSUB 580
450 PRINT "DO YOU WISH A PLOT?"
460 PRINT "1-YES 0-NO"
470 INPUT T
480 IF A = 1 THEN 370
490 END
```

Locate the T Key

Do not rest your wrists on the keyboard.

The T is keyed with the F finger. Place your fingers on the home keys. Look at your hands and practice the reach to T.

```
ftf ftf ftf ftf
```

Then look away and practice.

```
ftf ftf ftf ftf
```

Practice the T Key Reach

Keep your other fingers on the home keys as you make the reach to T.

Key each line two times.

```
1 ftf ftf ta tans tall tale take teak teal left sets
2 tad tell at tat nest test let tee ten sat nets tan
3 ten ales; net sales; let test; tan teaks; as a lad
4 tells a tall tale; settle nest at left; ask at lad
5 tend all lakes; set a tee; lent a kale; end an elf
```

Develop Keying Skills

Say each key as you strike it.

Key each line two times.

```
1 tan lads take ten tall lasses salads; as all dads;
2 fallen sand settles; a fake desk sale; sales tale;
3 feds lend land fees; net sales; and ten sad teens;
4 fat ned sat; fallen sand lands; as last tests sat;
5 all ants eat kale; ease all lakes; sale fell flat;
```

17	ZENO R MS	ROUTE 5 BOX 2	
		SAN JUAN PR	00911-9832
18	HARROD Z MR	58972 BULL RUN	
		ST ALBANS VT	05478-9821
19	CLEMONS T DR	APT 7 INNSBROOK	
		SEATTLE WA	98143-9832
20	DOWNS P MR	OUTPOST 6	
		FAIRBANKS AK	85621-9432

Learn Computer Applications

In order for a computer to perform specified functions, it must have a program to run. Programs are written in various languages. The central processing unit of a computer understands machine language which is numerical (binary). Since it is most difficult to write programs in a code of unique number combinations, languages were created that use words and other symbols to construct programs. Commonly used high-level programming languages include the following:

BASIC (Beginner's All-Purpose Symbolic Instruction Code)
COBOL (Common Business-Oriented Language)
FORTRAN (Formula Translator)
PL I (Programming Language I)
ALGOL (Algorithmic Language)
RPG (Report Program Generator)
Pascal (Named after Blaise Pascal)
C (Child of B Language)

Often, a programmer creates programs at the keyboard. At other times, the programmer writes them out and someone else may enter them at the keyboard. Most programs have to be edited many times. This requires hard copy and reentry of the changed program using the keyboard.

Format a BASIC Program

In order to acquaint you with the various languages and to further develop your keyboarding skills, several programs are presented in different languages for you to enter at the keyboard. The first program is written in BASIC, which is a popular programming language for writing instructions or programs for the microcomputer.

Learning Activity 3

1. Key the following excerpt from a BASIC program. Proof your copy carefully to be sure that every space, punctuation mark, and character is correct. Any error could cause the program to run improperly.

Measure Progress

Each Measure Progress exercise in this text presents a minimum goal for words-a-minute (wam) performance. In all these timed drills, the software automatically will compute your keying speed. In computing keying speed, the software counts every five strokes (including spaces and punctuation marks) as a word. Keying speed is reported as an average of words keyed in one minute (wam).

A prompt will appear on the monitor before starting the exercise. You may either accept the stated minimum goal or set a higher speed goal. If you do not want to change the minimum goal, enter N at the prompt. If you wish to set a higher goal, enter Y at the prompt and enter the higher goal. You are encouraged to set a higher goal to challenge yourself.

Take two 1-minute timings on the following group of lines. Read the copy from the book and key the lines on the computer. The computer will calculate the speed, record the score, determine if your goal was met, and indicate the next activity. If you complete the drill before time runs out, begin again.

Minimum goal: 10 wam

Key quickly.

```
a fallen desk lands; tan lass falls; send as fast;
tan lasses talked; ten teak desks; dads lend; asks
daff lads sass dads; fallen tasks; takes ten; lads
```

End-of-Lesson Procedure

At the end of each lesson, you will have the following options:

1. To restart the same lesson, press the F1 function key.
2. To return to the Lessons Menu, press ESC. This action automatically will save the completed lesson.
3. To proceed to the next, or any other lesson, highlight your choice on the menu and press Enter.
4. To return to the Main Menu, press ESC again.
5. To print the lesson, select Print Activities.
6. To exit the program:
   a. Select the Exit option and press Enter.
   b. When the DOS prompt appears on the screen, remove your data disk.
   c. Turn off the monitor. (Your instructor also may ask you to turn off the computer and printer.)

2. Print a copy of the exercise.

Employee No.	Name	Address	ZIP
1	SMITH J MR	147 EAST BLVD	
		RENO NV	89525-4832
2	JENKINS R MS	519 BAKER ST	
		ELMIRA NY	14932-9842
3	O'MALLEY J DR	SUITE 7 92 PARKWAY	
		ALBUQUERQUE NM	87102-3394
4	HARRISON B MS	5916 BROAD CT	
		RICHMOND VE	23261-4039
5	SHERIDAN L MR	ROUTE 2 BOX 47	
		KNOXVILLE TN	37916-9834
6	PETERS J DR	ROUTE 1 BOX 598	
		ABERDEEN SD	57401-8928
7	BROCK S MS	4219 SOUTH PLACE	
		BOZEMAN MT	59715-4921
8	BORAX N MR	10 PARK PLACE	
		NEW YORK NY	10121-3929
9	WILLIAMS B MR	123 PINE ROAD	
		OREM UT	84057-1229
10	LOVELL A MS	14876 PLAZA CIRCLE	
		LEBANON PA	17042-9876
11	REGESTER A MS	527 CHARLES RD	
		GREENVILLE SC	29611-2394
12	HALL L DR	19 LONG PINE ROAD	
		BURLINGTON NC	27215-9843
13	WEIS J MS	ROUTE 98 BOX 24A	
		CHARLESTON WV	25319-0293
14	FOISE B MS	5917 GREY RUN	
		CALGARY AB	
		CANADA	J8M 4T2
15	MEESE R DR	17 KNOTT PLACE	
		ST JOHNS NF	
		CANADA	9S 4R6
16	SMOTHERS L MR	59 HILLTOP	
		DURANGO CO	81301-8943

3

H, I, and Right Shift Keys

GOALS

- Reinforce Previous Learning
- Learn New Keys H, I, and Right Shift
- Develop Keying Skills

Get Ready

Check the following:

1. Place your feet flat on the floor with one foot slightly in front of the other.
2. Sit up straight with your back supported by the chair.
3. Sit the correct distance from the keyboard.
4. Place your fingers on the home keys in a curved position.
5. Slant your forearms at the same angle as the keyboard.
6. Keep your wrists low, but do not rest them on the keyboard.

Review

Remember to key all drill lines two times.

```
1 asdfjkl; aa ;; ss ll dd kk ff jj ded jnj ftf asdfj
2 task all dads; fallen desk lands; ask all tan lads
3 lasses ask daff lads; dad sets nets; a flask; ants
4 a fake desk sale; a jaded elf asked; all deaf lads
```

Strike each key quickly as if it were hot.

Appendix B
Optional Computer Applications Lessons

Key these exercises using the word processor.

Learn Data Entry

Many software programs provide a series of prompts and menus that require the operator to enter data. The operator must then make responses to these prompts and enter them in the spaces provided. The following Learning Activities will simulate different types of data entry operations.

Learning Activity 1

Key the answers to the following simulated prompts. Begin each response at the left margin. Double-space between each entry. Print a copy of the responses.

```
1. Enter today's date.
2. Enter your name and social security number.
3. Enter your current address.
4. When did you start this course? ____ ____ ____
                                    MO   DA   YR
5. How would you describe your current keyboarding
ability?
6. How will you use your new keyboarding skills?
7. List the first and last names of five friends and their
approximate ages.  Start names at the left margin; for
ages, set a tab 25 spaces from the left margin.
8. List and number sequentially ten qualifications you
feel you have for a future job.
```

Learning Activity 2

1. Key the following addresses. Use the OCR envelope style. Double-space between entries. Do not key the column headings. Set the following tabs:

```
Employee No.    15
Name   20
Address    38
ZIP   60
```

(So that the numbers in column 1 will align on the right side, space in one time before keying the first nine numbers.)

LOCATE THE H KEY

H←J

The H is keyed with the J finger. Place your fingers on the home keys. Look at your hands and practice the reach to H.

```
jhj jhj jhj jhj
```

Then look away and practice.

```
jhj jhj jhj jhj
```

PRACTICE THE H KEY REACH

Key each line two times.

```
1 jhj jhj had halls has held she the that has dashes
2 that ahead hate had hal heal shell shed hat health
3 he shall lash that shaft at the sale; slant at ash
4 the fallen lash landed at that desk; has she asked
5 he has the shells; she has that shed; he had that;
```

Keep your fingers curved and upright. Keep your other fingers on the home keys. Strike Enter with your little finger.

delete In word processing, a key that tells the computer to remove data that has been input.

Enter The key that sends a message from the keyboard to the central processing unit. Also, in word processing, after keying a line of text, pressing Enter will return the cursor to the beginning of the next line. On some keyboards, Return and Enter have the same functions.

file A set of records that is stored under a specific name or label.

graphics The artwork, diagrams, pictures, charts, and graphs that are displayed on the screen or by the printer.

hard copy The paper copy of information stored in a computer or a document.

hardware All parts of the computer system except the software program. Hardware includes the CPU, the keyboard, the monitor, and the printer.

indent In word processing, a key or combination of designated keys that temporarily moves the left-hand margin of a screen or page.

input Adding data into the computer. Can be done from the keyboard or from a disk.

keyboard The input device for word processing. It has the alphanumeric, symbol, and function keys.

memory The area in a computer in which data is stored for processing.

output The data displayed, printed, or stored as the result of a specified process.

printer The computer hardware that makes printed pages from data.

software The programs and instructions that run the computer and allow the user to perform different functions.

store To hold data on a disk in memory or on a tape for future use.

turnaround time The amount of time from the input of data to the output or completion of the job.

word processing An automated system or procedure that provides for correspondence and composition functions.

word wrap A feature of most word-processing programs that moves a word that will not fit within the right margin to the beginning of the next line.

Locate the I Key

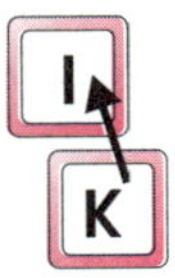

The I is keyed with the K finger. Place your fingers on the home keys. Look at your hands and practice the reach to I.

```
kik kik kik kik
```

Then look away and practice.

```
kik kik kik kik
```

Practice the I Key Reach

Key each line two times.

```
1 kik kik kits kite lite site lids diet slid fits ki
2 it sit sift list fit is aid said knit kit hit sits
3 kid slid; kite kits; site list; sift it; it is his
4 kids said knit; lite lit site; it said aid; hit it
5 that site did fit; she said that last tent failed;
```

Your J finger may lift slightly, but keep your other fingers on the home keys.

Appendix A
Computer Keyboarding Glossary

The following terms are used throughout this textbook and in most word processing and computer application books.

alphanumeric Letters of the alphabet, numbers, and/or symbols used to refer to the keyboard, as in alphanumeric keys.

arrow A key on some computers that you use to move the cursor or to delete something you have keyed. Arrows move the cursor backward, forward, up, or down.

author The person who writes a document.

backspace A key on some computers that moves the cursor back one space to the left and deletes keyed characters at the same time.

BASIC Beginner's All-Purpose Symbolic Instruction Code. A popular language for micro- and minicomputers.

binary Consisting of two parts. In mathematics, the binary system has two numbers: 0 and 1.

bit Binary digit of either 0 or 1. The smallest unit that computers read. In computer programs, most bits are arranged in groups of eight to represent letters, numbers, or symbols.

boot To load all the instructions that your computer needs to start and run a specific program.

break On many computer keyboards, a key that will stop the action of a program or process.

bug A mistake or error in a computer program or in the design of a computer.

byte A string of eight bits that stands for a letter, number, or symbol.

cancel In word processing, a key that is designated to stop a previous command or instruction.

catalog A command to the computer to list all the files stored in a software source.

character A symbol, letter, or number on the keyboard.

command An order that the computer processes.

control key (CTRL) A key that interrupts a computing process. It usually is keyed with another key.

copy In word processing, a key or process that will move data from one location to another.

cursor A small line or square that appears on the screen to indicate where the next keystroke will appear. The cursor can be moved around the screen with the arrow keys.

data The information, numbers, letters, and symbols that you input into the computer for processing.

data processing The work the computer does to input material into a specific program.

LOCATE THE RIGHT ⇧Shift KEY

Use the Shift keys to make capital letters. To capitalize left-hand letters, use the Right Shift key. When you operate the Right Shift key, use a three-step procedure:

1. Press the Right Shift key with your right little finger and hold it down. (Keep your J and K fingers on the home keys.)
2. Strike the letter you want capitalized with the correct left-hand finger.
3. Release the Shift key and return your little finger immediately to the ; key.

Look at your hands and practice the following:

```
Al; Al; Al; Al;
```

PRACTICE THE RIGHT ⇧Shift KEY REACH

Remember:
1. Depress Right Shift key.
2. Strike key with left-hand finger.
3. Release Shift key and return to home position.

Key each line two times.

```
1 Ada Ella Dad Eli Edna Dale Elsa Sandi Ella Fae Alf
2 Desk Dad Ten Dad lends Ella a desk; Did the sales;
3 Take ten ales; the fallen desk lands; Dad asks Ali
4 Dad did kid Ella; Tadd asks dad; Tan teak sets she
5 Ella asked Ted and Tina; The desk fell and hit Eli
```

DEVELOP KEYING SKILLS

Strike each key quickly and sharply.

Key each line two times.

```
1 an is if it hi fi tea sea tan fat dad had sad has;
2 net set let all tall fall hens had a desk ask dad;
3 A jaded elf asked; Ten tan lads; Takes salads; Fan
4 Dad had a fat hen; The lads had ten hits; Ask Til;
5 Tell Ed ask Tad; did sell; Talie and Elese failed;
```

of my other references, please let me know.

Will you please allow me a personal interview? If you wish, you may call me at (216) 555-9843 after 4:30 p.m.

Sincerely yours,

Timothy I. Beddingfield

Enclosure

Learn to Compose an Application Letter

1. Create a new document, which is LES60CM1. Use one of the brainstorming activities described in the previous lessons to compose a draft of a cover letter to accompany your resume. Decide on a specific job you are applying for and state how you received the information about the position. Possible sources are local newspapers, school placement services, or information obtained from your relatives or friends.
2. Save the document. Print a copy and read it for content. Indicate needed changes using proofreader's marks.
3. Retrieve the document and make the content changes indicated.
4. Proofread your letter again for grammar, spelling, and punctuation. Make revisions and print a final copy.

End-of-Lesson Procedure

At the end of each lesson, you will have the following options:

1. To restart the same lesson, press the F1 function key.
2. To return to the Lessons Menu, press ESC. This action automatically will save the completed lesson.
3. To proceed to the next, or any other lesson, highlight your choice on the menu and press Enter.
4. To return to the Main Menu, press ESC again.
5. To print the lesson, select Print Activities.
6. To exit the program:
   a. Select the Exit option and press Enter.
   b. When the DOS prompt appears on the screen, remove your data disk.
   c. Turn off the monitor. (Your instructor also may ask you to turn off the computer and printer.)

Increase Keying Speed

Now you will have a chance to race against the computer. Key the following sentences quickly. Strike the Space Bar at the end of each word. Do not space at the end of a line; strike the Enter key quickly. Try to beat the computer. If you finish before the moving light bar gets to the end of the line, you win! Key each line twice. Try to improve your speed the second time.

Snap your finger toward your palm after each stroke. Key quickly.

```
1 As it is;
2 See if it and
3 Tea is fit as ale;
4 Tall let ask set tin
5 At all is lad feel till
```

Key the lines again. Try to key them in less time.

Measure Progress

Take two 1-minute timings on the following group of lines. Read the copy from the book and key the lines on the computer. The computer will calculate the speed and record your score. If you complete the drill before time runs out, begin again.

Minimum goal: 11 wam

```
1 Ten tall tan lads sent dad a teak desk; As it has;
2 Tad lends Dela a tent; if it is inside the salads;
3 A jaded elf asked a fat lad; Tell Ella Fae a tale;
```

End-of-Lesson Procedure

At the end of each lesson, you will have the following options:

1. To restart the same lesson, press the F1 function key.
2. To return to the Lessons Menu, press ESC. This action automatically will save the completed lesson.
3. To proceed to the next, or any other lesson, highlight your choice on the menu.
4. To return to the Main Menu, press ESC again.
5. To print the lesson, select Print Activities.
6. To exit the program:
    a. Select the Exit option and press Enter.
    b. When the DOS prompt appears on the screen, remove your data disk.
    c. Turn off the monitor. (Your instructor also may ask you to turn off the computer and printer.)

a favorable impression on the employer. It should lead the employer to your resume by making a reference to it. If you are applying to an employment ad, mention the advertisement in your application letter and indicate when and where it appeared.

Learning Activity 1

1. Start a new document, LES60DC1. Key the following application letter in an acceptable format for a personal business letter (review Lesson 35 if necessary).
2. Proofread the copy on the screen. Use the editing keys to make corrections.
3. Have the computer check the document. Print a copy. Note any uncorrected errors on the printout.

```
4306 Norview Road
Cleveland, OH  44092
June 1, 1998
Ms. Zaritha Emory
Personnel Manager
Micro-Systems, Inc.
3097 W. Main Street
Cleveland, OH  43217
Dear Ms. Emory:
Please consider me an applicant for the Microcomputer
Specialist position that you advertised in the May 25
issue of the Evening Register.  My enclosed resume
supports my qualifications for the position.
I will graduate from Midlands Community College on
August 1, 1998, and will be ready for full-time
employment anytime after that date.  I have
maintained a 3.2 grade point average while working
part-time at DATASystems.  My duties include using
WordPerfect and Lotus software on a regular basis.
My exposure to many different microcomputer software
packages has provided me with a strong background in
microcomputers.
As you will note from my resume, I have participated
actively in student organizations.  As president of
Future Business Leaders of America, I was able to
lead the chapter in raising $2,000 for Project Ask.
Teamwork and responsibility are very important to me
as a result of my professional activities.
Mr. Edgar Woo, CIS manager for DATASystems, has given
me permission to use his name as a reference.  Please
feel free to contact him for additional information
concerning my work experience.  If you need the names
```

4

O, R, and Comma Keys

GOALS

- Reinforce Previous Learning
- Learn New Keys O, R, and Comma
- Develop Keying Skills

GET READY

Check the following:

1. Place your feet flat on the floor with one foot slightly in front of the other.
2. Sit up straight with your back supported by the chair.
3. Sit the correct distance from the keyboard.
4. Place your fingers on the home keys in a curved position.
5. Slant your forearms at the same angle as the keyboard.
6. Keep your wrists low, but do not rest them on the keyboard.

REVIEW

Key each line two times.

Space quickly. Do not pause.

```
1 asdf jkl; aa ;; ss ll dd kk ff jjj ded ded jnj jnj
2 ftf ftf jhj jhj kik kik tent hill heat hidden heel
3 desk sea see leak ease a fake title sale as if has
4 Tad lends Annie ten tan sandals; Takes ten stands;
```

Measure Progress

Minimum goal: 3-minute timing—40 wam with six or fewer errors; 5-minute timing—35 wam with ten or fewer errors

Take two 3- or 5-minute timings.

Ancient Greece has been called one of the world's finest civilizations. The Greeks had an appreciation of new ideas. Some famous people who lived in ancient Greece include Homer, Aesop, and Hippocrates.

Homer was blind. He wrote poems that were recited to music. Homer wrote long narratives (called epics) that convey a story of a hero. A couple of his famous epics are the "Iliad" and the "Odyssey." These works can give the reader information about the Greeks' lifestyle including their religious practices, customs, and history.

Aesop was famous for writing fables. Fables are tales that teach lessons. Animals were the main characters. Perhaps you are familiar with the tale of "The Goose that Laid the Golden Egg."

Hippocrates was a famous Greek medical doctor. He was one of the first people to study and document how medicine affected certain diseases. Prior to his time, priests were the medical professionals and hospitals were housed in temples. Hippocrates taught his findings to others. The students swore a vow, known as the Hippocratic Oath, in which they pledged to do all in their power to help the sick regain their health.

Learn to Format an Application Letter

When you send your resume to a prospective employer, it should be accompanied by a letter of application, or cover letter. This cover letter tells the prospective employer which job you are applying for, highlights your qualifications for the job, and includes any relevant information for that particular job. The cover letter is your chance to make

LOCATE THE O KEY

The O is keyed with the L finger. Place your fingers on the home keys. Look at your hands and practice the reach to O.

```
lol lol lol lol
```

Then look away and practice.

```
lol lol lol lol
```

PRACTICE THE O KEY REACH

Keep your J and K fingers on the home keys. Your ; finger may lift slightly.

Key each line two times.

```
1 lol lol look old told do does of so done doll fold
2 to do so of foods jot dots oaks sold loads off ton
3 does doses took nose toes foes also floss dole nod
4 not lost son ton tod off old too sod oaks odd oils
5 done told joke host loan knot look loss also stood
6 load food folks noise toast lesson stole to one of
7 Do old folks also do the salad; Sold one old food;
```

Key each of these sentences, choosing the correct form of the verb or the pronoun.

1 Sarah and Chris (live, lives) on this street.

2 Either of the coats (look, looks) good on him.

3 Most of the members (is, are) avid skiers.

4 Each of the car drivers (change, changes) lanes on the curve.

5 One of the books has a photo on (its, their) cover.

6 Neither Christina nor Stephanie wants to spend (her, their) time weeding the garden.

7 Several of the students did not turn in (his or her, their) homework assignment.

IMPROVE KEYING SKILLS

Take two 1-minute timings on each paragraph. Set a speed or an accuracy goal. If you complete the paragraph before time runs out, start over.

EXERCISE 1

Education is service oriented and not product oriented. Effective planning can eliminate the competition for resources and students. Most states have a planning agency within state government that assists higher education institutions in planning and budgeting. This agency looks at the overall picture to prevent undue competition for resources and eliminates costly duplication of programs.

EXERCISE 2

In some states, all education falls under the supervision of one agency. Other states have a separate agency for each division. For example, public schools report to one department, community colleges to another, and universities to another. This sometimes causes competition for funds and services. States appoint a coordinating board to oversee the activities of all educational agencies.

LOCATE THE R KEY

The R is keyed with the F finger. Place your fingers on the home keys. Look at your hands and practice the reach to R.

```
frf frf frf frf
```

Then look away and practice.

```
frf frf frf frf
```

PRACTICE THE R KEY REACH

Remember to keep your other fingers on the home keys.

Key each line two times.

```
1  frf frf forts rode rids rods or for jars risks red
2  areas first order after dears dare drain error ran
3  for rot roll are ear her ran rat jar tar far floor
4  tar ark era art rid rare rain dark order tree area
5  sir fir dear rear rake rest roast store other rate
6  dare dress stare horn torn front stair there their
7  fair risk after heart shirt their tired real there
8  letter are enrolled stern reasons desert steer tar
9  These Fords took a load of tar ore; toss a rose on
10 Take the order for trees; this note is not for her
```

60

Formatting an Application Letter

GOALS

- Build Language Arts Skills
- Improve Keying Skills
- Learn to Format an Application Letter
- Learn to Compose an Application Letter

Review

Key each line two times.

1 was the/are you/and the/was all/can she/let the/he

2 Senior scholar seeks serious, salubrious sentence.

3 Take Route 8 to 6 and turn left on 2; then try 15.

4 Travel arrangements are viable with your computer and modem.

Build Language Arts Skills

The subject and verb in a sentence must agree. That means if you use a singular subject, you need a singular verb. A plural subject requires a plural verb.

A pronoun antecedent and a pronoun in a sentence must agree. An antecedent is a word that comes before another word. A pronoun antecedent is a word that comes before the pronoun and means the same thing as the pronoun. A singular antecedent takes a singular pronoun. A plural antecedent requires a plural pronoun.

Study and key each of the example sentences.

Subject-Verb Agreement

1 She is the smartest person in class.

2 The car runs on unleaded gas.

3 None of the participants finds the game exciting.

4 Neither of the two students has completed the homework assignment.

Antecedent-Pronoun Agreement

1 Any one of the players could have bought his uniform today.

2 Everyone at the game rose to their feet.

Locate the , Key

Within a sentence, do not space before a comma; space once after it.

The , (comma) is keyed with the K finger. Place your fingers on the home keys. Look at your hands and practice the reach to , . Remember: Within a sentence, do not space before a comma; space once after it.

```
k,k  k,k  k,k  k,k
```

Then look away and practice.

```
k,k  k,k  k,k  k,k
```

Practice the , Key Reach

Your J finger may lift slightly, but keep your other fingers on the home keys.

Key each line two times.

```
1 k,k k,k Ron, Alf, Ann, deserts, letters, reason of
2 Stole a train ride for Eddie, Ronald, Ann, and Don
3 Send Annie roses, jade, jars, sand, tea, and tires
4 Files, letters, folders, and a list are in a desk;
5 The sandals, dress, and shoes fit Sheila and Terri
```

Develop Keying Skills

Say each key as you strike it. Key and space quickly—do not pause.

Key each line two times.

```
1 Take an order for ten trees, Teak desks are in it;
2 Send fees for Tad, Al, Te, and Ann, Feds sent land
3 Ask all sales lads to send net sales on rod deeds,
4 The order is for jars, teak, tests, tires, and sod
5 Slate the latest list of net sales, send the deed;
```

Learn to Compose a Resume

1. Create a new document, which is LES59CM1. Using the format suggested in Lesson 58, prepare a draft resume for yourself using your own personal information. Use one of the brainstorming techniques discussed in previous lessons. If your work experience is limited and you plan to receive additional education, you may include anticipated future experiences on your resume.
2. Proofread and edit your draft. Print a copy. Mark any needed content changes with proofreader's marks.
3. Retrieve the document and make the content changes. Proofread one last time for grammar, spelling, and punctuation. Make final corrections and print a copy.

End-of-Lesson Procedure

At the end of each lesson, you will have the following options:

1. To restart the same lesson, press the F1 function key.
2. To return to the Lessons Menu, press ESC. This action automatically will save the completed lesson.
3. To proceed to the next, or any other lesson, highlight your choice on the menu and press Enter.
4. To return to the Main Menu, press ESC again.
5. To print the lesson, select Print Activities.
6. To exit the program:
   a. Select the Exit option and press Enter.
   b. When the DOS prompt appears on the screen, remove your data disk.
   c. Turn off the monitor. (Your instructor also may ask you to turn off the computer and printer.)

MEASURE PROGRESS

Take two 1-minute timings on the following group of lines. Read the copy from the book and key the lines on the computer. The computer will calculate the speed and record your score. If you complete the drill before time runs out, begin again.

Minimum goal: 12 wam

Key quickly.

```
1 it is inside a load of lost ores on the old Fords;
2 Toss roses to lasses; Ask Don to lend Andi a tire;
3 Send fees for Tal, Ronald, Edna, and Sid; stole it
```

END-OF-LESSON PROCEDURE

At the end of each lesson, you will have the following options:

1. To restart the same lesson, press the F1 function key.
2. To return to the Lessons Menu, press ESC. This action automatically will save the completed lesson.
3. To proceed to the next, or any other lesson, highlight your choice on the menu and press Enter.
4. To return to the Main Menu, press ESC again.
5. To print the lesson, select Print Activities.
6. To exit the program:
   a. Select the Exit option and press Enter.
   b. When the DOS prompt appears on the screen, remove your data disk.
   c. Turn off the monitor. (Your instructor also may ask you to turn off the computer and printer.)

Measure Progress

Take two 3- or 5-minute timings.

Minimum goal: 3-minute timing—40 wam with six or fewer errors; 5-minute timing—35 wam with ten or fewer errors

Rome, the capital city of Italy, has lasted more than 2,500 years. Rome is the center for Italian government, education, and religion. Vatican City is an independent state within Rome and is the home of the pope. The pope is the official head of Vatican City and the head of the Roman Catholic Church. The pope lives at Vatican Palace, which is the largest palace in the world and contains numerous famous art treasures.

Saint Peters, the largest church in the world, also is located in Vatican City. The dome of the church was designed by the famous artist and architect, Michelangelo. Michelangelo also painted the ceiling of the Sistine Chapel, the most famous chapel in the Vatican Palace.

Florence is located north of Rome. Florence is known as the art center of Italy. In 1966, many famous paintings and statues were ruined by the flooding of the Arno River. Water and mud filled many famous galleries and churches and destroyed valuable works of art.

Venice is a port city located across the Italian Peninsula from Genoa. In Venice you may take a gondola, a long flat-bottomed boat, to travel about the city. If you are not interested in water travel, most places can be reached on foot. Because of the narrow streets and bridges, automobiles are not used for travel in Venice.

5

C, Period, Left Shift, and Caps Lock Keys

GOALS

- Reinforce Previous Learning
- Learn New Keys C, Period, Left Shift, and Caps Lock
- Develop Keying Skills

Get Ready checklist:

1. Feet flat.
2. Sit straight.
3. Elbows by side.
4. Fingers curved, upright.
5. Slant forearms.
6. Wrists low but not on keyboard.

REVIEW

Key each line two times.

```
1 asdfjkl; fdsa; lkj ded ded ftf ftf jnj jnj kik kik
2 jhj lol lol frf frf k,k k,k or, old sold told rode
3 A load of ore tested a tired lad; one fallen rose;
4 Ask De Ann to floss teeth often, lasses tossed it;
```

LOCATE THE C KEY

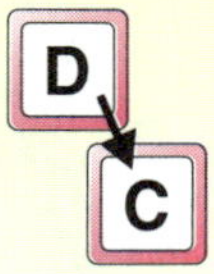

The C is keyed with the D finger. Place your fingers on the home keys. Look at your hands and practice the reach to C.

```
dcd dcd dcd dcd
```

Then look away and practice.

```
dcd dcd dcd dcd
```

Improve Keying Skills

Take two 1-minute timings on each paragraph. Set a speed or an accuracy goal. If you complete the paragraph before time runs out, start over.

Exercise 1

Budget crunches have had enormous effect upon smaller colleges. In seeking adequate funding, people must keep in mind the fundamental objectives. Successful financing must be committed to equal access to everyone. Eliminating the barriers of ability, finance, geography, and social class will contribute to equal access. In short, any person who can benefit should be allowed access.

Exercise 2

Institutions must share resources rather than compete and duplicate programs. High schools, community colleges, and universities will find that if they develop a joint plan to meet the needs of education, many resources can be saved. Many schools are developing articulation agreements to ensure these needs are met in an efficient manner. Each level of education, thus, can make realistic assumptions about the student's learning background.

Practice the C Key Reach

Key each line two times.

1 dcd dcd call cards credit can class office car cats
2 cakes cads casks calls decades scale cod docks cots
3 car can cell ace cake deck face cook coke case care
4 cask call cool cord coil cool cede cash cast decade
5 cane card cash calf since chase ancient chain scale
6 cease classes credit decease career corn calk notch
7 corn cook calk finance circle notice coin cook cane
8 cases jacks cease accord concern cad cost face coat
9 Cathi called the offices; the clock ticks, accessed
10 Cal can cook a cake, it is the circle in the field;

Your F finger may lift slightly, but keep your other fingers on the home keys.

Locate the > Key

Space twice after a period at the end of a sentence. Space once after a period in an abbreviation.

The . (period) is keyed with the L finger. Place your fingers on the home keys. Look at your hands and practice the reach to the period key. Remember: Space twice after a period at the end of a sentence. Space once after a period in an abbreviation.

l.l l.l l.l l.l

Then look away and practice.

l.l l.l l.l l.l

59

Composing a Resume

GOALS

- Build Language Arts Skills
- Improve Keying Skills
- Compose a Resume

Review

Key each line two times.

1 and can she/end the/all the/was the/for him/and it

2 As a rule, a receipt or canceled check is useable.

3 Jermaine's social security number was 826-77-0000.

4 Interactive software will be a superior skill-teaching tool.

Build Language Arts Skills

If a pronoun is used as a subject in a sentence, use one of these forms: I, you, he, she, it, we, you, they, who, whoever.

If a pronoun is used as a direct or indirect object, use one of these forms: me, you, him, her, it, us, you, them, whom, whomever.

Key each of the following examples.

1 Jona and I had a great time at the party.

2 Did you bake the cake for her and her brother?

3 She and Susanna took a trip to Montana last summer.

4 I'd like to congratulate your teacher and them.

Now key each of the following sentences, choosing the correct form of the pronoun.

1 Hassan and (I, me) went to the dance last night.

2 The music students and (I, me) like to listen to the bands.

3 The argument is between you and (I, me).

4 Can you give (her, she) and (I, me) a ticket to the game?

5 Between you and (I, me), I don't believe that story.

Practice the > Key Reach

Key each line two times.

Keep your fingers curved and your J and K fingers on the home keys.

Your ; finger may lift slightly.

1 l.l l.l Si is. Call Rae. Tell Candie. Ask Carl.
2 Dan Cane is in the A. R. S. in SD. Al is not ill.
3 El is late for dinner. The thief left the island.
4 Allen has landed the jet. Dennis failed the test.
5 Dona and Ted had an old clock at the sales office.
6 Dee had a class fan in the old jet dock for Salli.

Locate the Left ⇧Shift Key

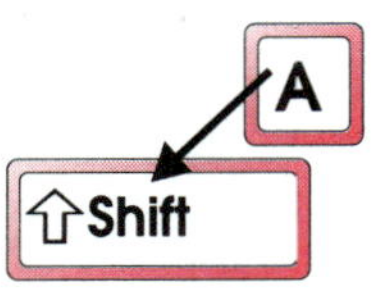

To capitalize right-hand letters, use the Left Shift key. When you operate the Left Shift key, use a three-step procedure:

1. Press the Left Shift key with your left little finger and hold it down. (Keep your F and D fingers on the home keys.)
2. Strike the letter you want capitalized with the correct right-hand finger.
3. Release the Shift key and return your finger immediately to the A key.

Look at your hands and practice the following:

Ja Ja Ja Ja

Line 13 → Timothy I. Beddingfield
4306 Norview Road
Cleveland, OH 44092
(216) 555-9843

1" margin
DS

Career Objective

Indent 5 → To secure a position that utilizes my microcomputer knowledge and skills.

Education

Midlands Community College, Associate Degree expected August 1998; majored in Computer Information Systems. Maintained a 3.2 grade average. President of Microcomputer Users Club, vice president of Phi Beta Lambda.

Cleveland High School, diploma, May 1996; graduated with honors. Vice president of Beta Club; president of Future Business Leaders of America.

Qualifications

Knowledge of COBOL, BASIC, C language, WordPerfect, spreadsheets, and accounting software.

Experience

DATASystems--part-time, while in school, from September 1996 to present. Work with software packages and perform accounting functions.

Hermitage Pool--worked as lifeguard during summers of 1994, 1995, 1996.

Special Skills

Fluent in Spanish.

References

References, including work supervisors and instructors, will be provided on request.

Remember:
1. **Depress the Left Shift key.**
2. **Strike the key with correct right-hand finger.**
3. **Release the Left Shift key and return to home position.**

Practice the Left Shift Key Reach

Key each line two times.

```
1 Jan Kal Hal Jack Lan Jeff Kitt Ken Joe Lea Les Kit
2 Kent and Joe see Jeff; Kal asks Les, Jo, and Lara.
3 Hank sells dads a teak desk son; Ken asked Leslie.
4 Order these:  Cartons, Jacks, Clocks, Dolls, Jars.
```

The colon in line 4 is the shift of the semicolon. Space twice after a colon used as punctuation.

Locate the Caps Lock Key

To key a series of letters or words in all capital letters, use the Caps Lock key. The Caps Lock key is located on either the left or right side of the keyboard. It is operated with the appropriate little finger. Locate the Caps Lock key on your keyboard.

Follow these steps when keying words or sentences in all caps:

1. Depress the Caps Lock key with the little finger.
2. Enter the letters to be capitalized.
3. Depress the Caps Lock key again. This releases the all caps feature. (The Caps Lock key is a toggle switch.)

When the Caps Lock key is on, only the alphabetic keys are affected. The shift key must still be used to key a colon or symbol.

Learning Activity 1

1. Start a new document, LES58DC1. Key the following resume in the suggested format. Leave a 2-inch top margin and use the 1-inch default side margins.
2. Proofread the copy on the screen. Use the editing keys to make corrections.
3. Have the computer check the document. Print a copy. Note any uncorrected errors on the printout.

End-of-Lesson Procedure

At the end of each lesson, you will have the following options:

1. To restart the same lesson, press the F1 function key.
2. To return to the Lessons Menu, press ESC. This action automatically will save the completed lesson.
3. To proceed to the next, or any other lesson, highlight your choice on the menu and press Enter.
4. To return to the Main Menu, press ESC again.
5. To print the lesson, select Print Activities.
6. To exit the program:
   a. Select the Exit option and press Enter.
   b. When the DOS prompt appears on the screen, remove your data disk.
   c. Turn off the monitor. (Your instructor also may ask you to turn off the computer and printer.)

Practice the Caps Lock Key Reach

Key each line two times.

1 THE CONTRACT CASE CONCERNED THE CONDO ORDER TAKER.
2 KARL and LINDA and CHRIS and CINDA and CATHE left.
3 The TEN ANCIENT RAKES is the title that JANE read.

Develop Keying Skills

Your fingers should not fly around but should be poised over the keyboard.

Let your fingers do the work—not your wrists.

Key each line two times.

1 Todd sold one clock; Jan sells docks and tan sand.
2 The cat ate the rat; Ten teals left the nest neat.
3 Tell Ken, Lara, Joel, Jeff, and Hank to call Jane.
4 Then HAL and JES tossed that fish on the old dock.
5 Dear Ron: Dear Carol: Dear Ted: Dear Catherine:
6 Janet told Rosanne to notice the financial losses.
7 The folks stood to stare at the area flood fronts.
8 The cash cards are essential for a finance career.
9 An ancient cane rake is their reason to notice it.
10 The credit classes are also the other cash lesson.

Measure Progress

Minimum goal: 13 wam

Key quickly.

Take two 1-minute timings.

1 Net sales for that first art soared for Lara Anne.
2 These Feds leased the trash lands for local areas.
3 Leslie said that local ore lands on the last dock.

End-of-Lesson Procedure

At the end of each lesson, you will have the following options:

1. To restart the same lesson, press the F1 function key.
2. To return to the Lessons Menu, press ESC.
3. To proceed to the next, or any other lesson, make your choice on the menu.
4. To print the lesson, select Print Activities.
5. To exit the program:
   a. Select the Exit option and press Enter.
   b. When the DOS prompt appears on the screen, remove your data disk.
   c. Turn off the monitor and/or computer.

Learn to Format a Resume

When you apply for a job, you will need a resume. A resume is a written summary of your personal qualifications for a job. It lists your personal experiences and skills as they relate to a job. A resume is your most important tool in promoting your abilities. Employers receive many resumes from people looking for jobs. Typically, a resume receives only three to seven seconds of review. As a result, it is important that it look good. Your resume must interest the employer in you. If your resume does not encourage the employer to learn more about you, you will not get an interview.

A resume is generally single-spaced with double-spaces between the main parts. A resume should be attractively arranged on the page. In general, leave a two-inch top margin. Try to keep the resume limited to one page. If necessary, decrease the top margin. Refer to the sample resume on page 362 as you read the following guidelines.

These are the parts of the resume:

1. **Name, address, and phone number**. In all capital letters and centered at the top of the page, key your name, complete address, and telephone number.
2. **Career Objective**. In this section list the type of job you would like to have and for which you believe you qualify. The heading, "Career Objective," starts at the left margin. Double-space after the heading. The career objective statement frequently begins with the word "To." Indent lines of the objective five spaces. Press F4 to use the indent feature.
3. **Education**. List your educational background in reverse chronological order starting with your present or most recent school. Anything before high school can be omitted. Emphasize courses taken, programs completed, or other activities that apply to your career objective. Follow the same formatting guidelines as for "Career Objective." Single-space within and double-space between each entry. Press F4 to indent.
4. **Qualifications**. In this section, list specific skills you have that would be helpful for the type of job you want. For example, if you want a job working with microcomputers, mention specific software packages and equipment that you have worked with and mastered.
5. **Experience**. List jobs that you held in reverse chronological order. If you have not held any formal jobs yet, list neighborhood or volunteer work that relates to your objective.
6. **Special Skills**. List any other skills you have that do not pertain directly to the job you are applying for but that will be of interest and helpful to the interviewer.
7. **References**. References are people who will tell employers about your character and quality of work. In most cases, do not list the references on the resume but state that they will be provided upon request. Before using a person as a reference, be sure to get his or her permission. People for whom you have worked are good references. Teachers, coaches, religious leaders, and club leaders are also beneficial.

6

Skill Building

GOALS

- Reinforce Previous Learning
- Increase Keying Speed

Get Ready checklist:
1. Feet flat.
2. Sit straight.
3. Elbows by side.
4. Fingers curved, upright.
5. Slant forearms.
6. Wrists low but not on keyboard.

Review

Key each line two times.

1 all dads fall; a lass asks a dad; add a fad flask;
2 a sad lass falls; all salads fall; fall dads; asks
3 ask all lads; a lass adds; a lad falls; lass falls
4 as a fad; as all ads; as a lad asks; a salsa salad

Develop Keying Skills

Key each line two times.

1 ask a dad; all lads; ask a lass; all fall; dad all
2 dead deaf added fled leeks sales leaf fees del den
3 see a lease; fake a seal; see a leak; eases a sail
4 need all ends; and a den; and a deed; end all fads
5 tells a tall tale; settle nest at left; ask at lad
6 tend all lakes; set a tee; lent a kale; end an elf
7 kid slid; kite kits; site list; sift it; it is his
8 Dad did kid Ella; Tadd asks Dad; Tan teak sets she
9 the fallen lash landed at that desk; has she asked
10 kids said knit; lite lit site; it said aid; hit it
11 Tad lends Annie ten tan sandals; Takes ten stands;

MEASURE PROGRESS

Take two 3- or 5-minute timings.

Minimum goal: 3-minute timing—39 wam with six or fewer errors; 5-minute timing—34 wam with ten or fewer errors

Italy is located in Europe. The country is about twice as large as Florida, and most agree that it's geographically shaped like a boot. Although today many Italians work in industry, farming continues to be very important. Even though there are many mountains and less than half of the country is level, wheat, corn, rice, olives, and grapes are grown. The Po Valley is the best farming area. The valley receives enough rainfall to allow the crops to flourish. Dairy cattle are raised in some regions. The milk they produce is used to make cheese. The chief grazing animals are sheep and goats.

There are some very interesting cities to visit in Italy. Naples is a great seaport. It has a beautiful bay and is located on the southwest coast. Not far from Naples is Mount Vesuvius, a famous volcano. Reportedly, Mount Vesuvius erupted during the early days of the Roman Empire. In 79 A.D., tons of red hot ashes and burning cinders erupted from its mouth. The town of Pompeii was buried in lava and lost for fifteen hundred years. Eventually archaeologists excavated the site of the ancient city by digging away layer upon layer of lava and ash. The archaeologists' discoveries have provided us with insight into the daily life of ancient Romans.

Increase Keying Speed

Key each line two times. Try to increase your speed on the second time.

Race to beat the computer.

1 Ted sets a date; all fish seek the seas and lakes;
2 look one thin foal sold; that fool told old jokes;
3 Ronn rakes rare red roses after the rain and hail;
4 Those letters on disk and data files are not rare;
5 dent a tent; last fat ant; tell tall tales to Ted,
6 Ella asked Ted and Tina; The desk fell and hit Eli
7 Desk Dad Ten Dad lends Ella a desk; Did the sales;
8 fallen fan; lands and sand; land end; fall and fan
9 all ants eat kale; ease all lakes; sale fell flat;
10 that ahead hate had has heal shell shed hat health
11 A faded elf asked; Ten tan lads; Takes salads; Fan
12 he shall lash that trash at the sale; slant at ash

Measure Progress

Take two 1-minute timings.

Minimum goal: 13 wam

1 fallen sand settles; a fake desk sale; sales tale;
2 that site did fit; she said that last tent failed;
3 Dad had a fat hen; The lads had ten hits; Ask Til;

End-of-Lesson Procedure

At the end of each lesson, you will have the following options:

1. To restart the same lesson, press the F1 function key.
2. To return to the Lessons Menu, press ESC.
3. To proceed to the next, or any other lesson, make your choice on the menu.
4. To return to the Main Menu, press ESC again.
5. To print the lesson, select Print Activities.
6. To exit the program:
   a. Select the Exit option and press Enter.
   b. When the DOS prompt appears on the screen, remove your data disk.
   c. Turn off the monitor. (Your instructor also may ask you to turn off the computer and printer.)

7 The testing program uses measurable objectives to evaluate performance.

8 Software programs save us a considerable amount of setup time in our accounting department.

9 Manual typewriters are considered obsolete.

10 Theodora's performance has been unsatisfactory.

Improve Keying Skills

Take two 1-minute timings on each paragraph. Set a speed or an accuracy goal. If you complete the paragraph before time runs out, start over.

Exercise 1

Some of the indicators of low morale are high absenteeism, high turnover rates, lower quality products, higher sick rates, and an increase in accident rates. It is, therefore, evident that low morale can be very costly to a company. On the other hand, high morale increases production and quality. Also, low turnover rates decrease training expenditures.

Exercise 2

One of the greatest assets for a potential employee is enthusiasm and willingness to learn new procedures. The rapid improvements and changes in the computer field make it essential that one be able to cope with numerous changes. New software and constant upgrading are characteristics of the word-processing field. As soon as you learn a new procedure, it is likely to be improved or even made obsolete by some new approach.

M and B Keys

GOALS

- Reinforce Previous Learning
- Learn New Keys M and B
- Develop Keying Skills
- Increase Keying Speed

Review the "Get Ready" checklist.

REVIEW

Key each line two times.

1 jnj jnj ftf ftf jhj jhj kik kik lol lol dcd dcd fr
2 cakes casks calf coat coach cocoa cocoon coed coin
3 The ashes of the trash landed on that one old dock
4 Ask Al, Kit, Jan, and Tod to access the CAD class.
5 NAL leases land to: Jeff, Ona, Ci, Carl, and Cil.

LOCATE THE M KEY

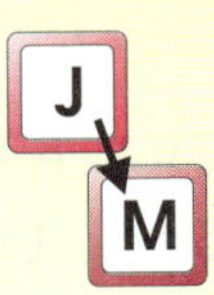

The M is keyed with the J finger. Place your fingers on the home keys. Look at your hands and practice the reach to M.

jmj jmj jmj jmj

58

Formatting a Resume

GOALS

- Build Language Arts Skills
- Improve Your Keying Skills
- Learn to Format a Resume

Review

Key each line two times.

1 Totally new furniture was situated in the library.

2 Having files properly named is a great time-saver.

3 Locate items #349, #755, and #52 in the warehouse.

4 Every once in a great while the earth aligns for an eclipse.

Build Language Arts Skills

A **synonym** is a word that has the same or nearly the same meaning as another word. For example, a synonym of *torrid* is *hot*.

Key each of the following sentences, replacing the underlined word with a synonym from the list. You do not need to key the underline.

Synonyms

accept	paltry	manage
criterion	industrious	antiquated
inadequate	substantial	rank
possible		

1 Buying new equipment is not feasible at this time.

2 Word-processing software allows users to manipulate massive text files.

3 Confidentiality is a requirement for a chief executive officer's secretary.

4 The sportscaster complained about her meager salary.

5 New employees must assume responsibility for learning about our products.

6 Ramona is a diligent worker.

Then look away and practice.

jmj jmj jmj jmj

Practice the M Key Reach

Key each line two times.

1 jmj jmj me mat met ham him tam make same fame home
2 dim aim mat same milk then them miss remit dreamed
3 elm jam Kim man mad dim time farm male metal admit
4 rim Mrs. Ms. farm main came cane them smile almost
5 arm mad mint seem harm make maid melts accommodate
6 mail come memo team ream seam mats meet mode small
7 Small teams made the main model memo come to fame.
8 Ask Matt to send me those metal milk cartons soon.
9 Fame comes to most men: Men met at the same time.
10 Admit as many teams as the memorial home may mass.

Keep your fingers curved and on the home keys.

Locate the B Key

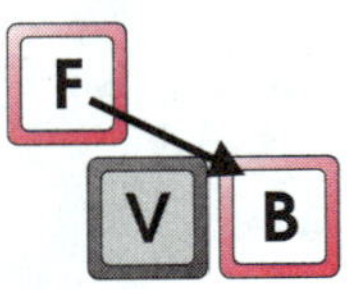

The B is keyed with the F finger. Place your fingers on the home keys. Look at your hands and practice the reach to B.

fbf fbf fbf fbf

Then look away and practice.

fbf fbf fbf fbf

UNIT 10

JOB-SEARCH SKILLS

Practice the B Key Reach

Key each line two times.

1 fbf fbf fibs lib rib bit be bat base ball baseball
2 bar herb debit ballet bet bald credit fiber border
3 bit bite ballot booklet black amber labor dab bell
4 Bob barb label bread remember blast job bear blast
5 Ben bare object alibi better mob belt harbor block
6 mob bee dab book back beef best debt bend bias ban
7 rob file better fiber object able debt booklet bar
8 bad beds black books blocks belts booklet boat bit
9 Cobie asked the Feds to bid on the old bank books.
10 N[illegible]ce a bank bid; a bank booklet boasts all jobs.

Use proper technique.

Develop Keying Skills

Key each line two times.

1 [illegible]d jnj ftf jhj kik lol frf dcd jmj fbf l.l k,k ;;
2 [illegible] be in on so do or it am if do ha ma to ti is as
3 [illegible] and for the not ten lie dim din too bid did rid
4 co[illegible] cake came back half roll mine site bake hates
5 he is in,so it [illegible] if he is,or he is or,be at,be me
6 can she see,an[illegible]r him,she had all,did not,bit it
7 Arnie; Fred; J[illegible]; Sam; Samantha; Dennis; Denise;
8 I can do it i[illegible]e all the hats in the old mall.
9 So the bold c[illegible]an for the rat on that cold mat.
10 Order these f[illegible]andi: coins, markers, and beads.

As you repeat each line, try to key it faster.

Measure Progress

Take two 3- or 5-minute timings.

Minimum goal: 3-minute timing—39 wam with six or fewer errors; 5-minute timing—34 wam with ten or fewer errors

During the reign of Charles II, the Spanish and English fought for control of the Bahama Islands. When independence was declared in the American colonies, Florida was awarded to the Spanish, and the Bahamas were returned to Britain.

In 1973, the Bahama Islands achieved independence. The Commonwealth of the Bahamas is governed by a two-house parliament. There is a ministerial cabinet headed by the prime minister and an independent parliamentary democracy.

Air travel and cruise ships continue to bring visitors who are ready for the tropical climate and atmosphere to the Bahama Islands. It is estimated that approximately 3.5 million people vacation in the Bahamas each year. The next time you are ready for some fun in the sun, fly or cruise your way to the Bahamas, because as the advertising slogan states, You're so close to so much.

Review Editing Compositions

1. Read your printed copy of the document LES55CM2 that you composed in Lesson 55. Read your report for content and meaning only. Do not worry about grammar, spelling, or punctuation changes at this time. Mark any needed content changes with proofreader's marks on the copy.
2. Retrieve the document and make the content changes. Print a copy.
3. Reread the document for grammar, spelling, and punctuation. Mark needed changes on the copy with proofreader's marks.
4. Make the final changes to the document, save it, and print a final copy.

End-of-Lesson Procedure

At the end of each lesson, follow the appropriate end-of-lesson procedure.

INCREASE KEYING SPEED

Key each line two times.

1 Most men limit times for comments. Bob made bits.
2 The last absences of both bosses are not abnormal.
3 The ten sales told the bankers to need that credit.
4 Madams and men make more comments than the lasses.
5 The time for sane comments is not before the meet.
6 Lease the land that has this oar. Take the books.
7 Both boats blocked the load of ore. Take her car.
8 The absence of the boss from her job left him mad.
9 Remember to accommodate the bank credit and debit.
10 The ballet dancer dreamed of a model dance career.
11 Admit a blast from the harbor jolted the main rim.
12 She is. It is. Ask Mark. Tell Bill. Call Bart.
13 Lt. Marke is a member of the A. M. B. in the A. F.

Try to beat the computer and improve your speed on the second try. Check your speed as noted by the computer.

MEASURE PROGRESS

Take two 1-minute timings.

Minimum goal: 14 wam

Key quickly.

1 Small fees make most banks mad. Send books to me.
2 The land leases left those men mad and then broke.
3 Lads send lasses red roses. That clock ticks Ben.

END-OF-LESSON PROCEDURE

1. To restart the same lesson, press the F1 function key.
2. To return to the Lessons Menu, press ESC.
3. To proceed to another lesson, make your choice on the menu.
4. To return to the Main Menu, press ESC again.
5. To print the lesson, select Print Activities.
6. To exit the program:
   a. Select the Exit option and press Enter.
   b. When the DOS prompt appears on the screen, remove your data disk.
   c. Turn off the monitor. (Your instructor may ask you to turn off the computer and printer.)

7 Many workers <u>succumb to</u> leaving the job early on nice days.

8 Software programs on our network are <u>unavailable</u> to all users.

9 The employees' actions <u>humiliated</u> their supervisors.

10 <u>Lenient</u> laws protect the consumers.

Improve Keying Skills

Take two 1-minute timings on each paragraph. Set a speed or an accuracy goal. If you complete the paragraph before time runs out, start over.

Exercise 1

Research on worker satisfaction has indicated that some environmental conditions may cause dissatisfaction if the conditions are absent, but may not create satisfaction if the conditions are present. Annual raises are an example of a condition that dissatisfies if they do not occur. If they do occur, but are considered too low, raises will not create satisfaction. A safe work environment is another example of this phenomenon.

Exercise 2

Isn't it amazing how many people do not plan in a systematic fashion? Setting goals and planning strategies to accomplish your goals are necessary for success unless you are willing to leave your progress to chance or luck. Most successful people have a definite goal in mind, and they plan a course of action for reaching that goal. Ideas plus no plan of action equal failure. Ideas plus a plan of action equal success.

8

W, U, and P Keys

GOALS

- Reinforce Previous Learning
- Learn New Keys W, U, and P
- Increase Keying Speed

Remember the "Get Ready" checklist.

Review

Key each line two times.

```
1 jkj kik lol frf dcd jmj jmj k,k fbf fbf l.l books.
2 Ask Al, Ted, and Ken to test the first sales kits.
3 The credit card net sales concern all small banks.
4 The bids for that leased land had a bank late fee.
5 Most men belt BASEBALLS.  Three bids came in late.
```

Locate the W Key

The W is keyed with the S finger. Place your fingers on the home keys and practice the reach to W.

```
sws sws sws sws
```

57 Review Editing Compositions

GOALS

- Build Language Arts Skills
- Improve Keying Skills
- Review Editing Compositions

Review

Key each line two times.

1 act runner rover getaway mission patronize juniper

2 yonder tangy oranges zesty ruthless hyper salesman

3 Will you please get 21,675 pieces of item #220978?

4 The future promises that computers will be available to all.

Build Language Arts Skills

An **antonym** is a word that means the opposite of another word. For example, an antonym of *hot* is *cold*. You do not need to key the underline.

Key each of the following sentences, replacing the underlined word with an antonym from the list.

Antonyms

resist	permanent	confident
accessible	novice	sporadic
easy	stringent	gratified
efficient		

1 Using impractical procedures when preparing input information will result in increased productivity.

2 Using a computer for word processing has made my job arduous.

3 Sheila put the desk in a transient location.

4 Jerilyn was apprehensive about the impact of her test results on the scholarship opportunity.

5 He was a masterful guitar player.

6 Linda was a habitual user of the computer network system.

Practice the W Key Reach

Key each line two times.

1 sws sws saw was cows how now we will with saw wads
2 who jaw well draw snow town down water elbow where
3 new now won workable know word flow wisdom awkward
4 web few west swim waken shown woman awkward follow
5 raw two walk swell window write hardware twin draw
6 weakness saw win law welfare warmer between follow
7 Will worked with Wat. Win wanted it to snow fast.
8 Walker wished we knew where that bank was located.
9 William wanted that snow to land on the west bank.
10 Mrs. Woodard wants the hardware to be well worked.

Keep your other fingers in home key position.

Locate the U Key

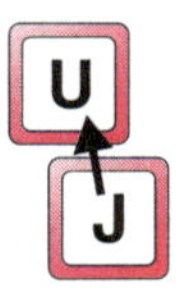

The U is keyed with the J finger. Place your fingers on the home keys and practice the reach to U.

juj juj juj juj

Learn to Use the Computer to Edit Compositions

When composing at the computer, you will find it helpful to follow the steps outlined in the previous lesson and below. By now you have the skill that enables you to key compositions directly on the computer. This process is a great time-saver.

Often it is helpful to have some time between when you write an article and when you edit or revise it. With a little "distance" between you and your original creativity, you may find ways to make your writing clearer, or you may catch errors in punctuation and grammar more easily.

1. Read the printed copy of the document LES54CM2 that you keyed in Lesson 54. Read it for content and meaning only. Do not make grammar, spelling, or punctuation changes at this time. Mark any needed content changes with proofreader's marks on the copy.
2. Retrieve the document and make the content changes. Print a copy.
3. Edit the printed copy for grammar, spelling, and punctuation. Mark needed changes on the copy with the proofreader's marks you have learned.
4. Make the final changes to the document and print a final copy.

End-of-Lesson Procedure

At the end of each lesson, you will have the following options:

1. To restart the same lesson, press the F1 function key.
2. To return to the Lessons Menu, press ESC. This action automatically will save the completed lesson.
3. To proceed to the next, or any other lesson, highlight your choice on the menu and press Enter.
4. To return to the Main Menu, press ESC again.
5. To print the lesson, select Print Activities.
6. To exit the program:
   a. Select the Exit option and press Enter.
   b. When the DOS prompt appears on the screen, remove your data disk.
   c. Turn off the monitor. (Your instructor also may ask you to turn off the computer and printer.)

PRACTICE THE U KEY REACH

Key each line two times.

```
1 juj juj jure just juts jute due ruts tuts muts use
2 out rub bulb hunt adult usual assure insure ensure
3 sun fun duel soul just rust nurse under module cut
4 mud turn fund uses fault build rumor fusion endure
5 but auto full fuel club sure junk true fourth shut
6 must truth audit usual manual musical rubbed about
7 refund actual just fault rub cut under build nurse
8 rush us brush sue due uses fused untie usual fruit
9 Our annual runs for fun should break that account.
10 The lures were a must to catch the four blue fish.
```

Practice keying while keeping your eyes on the copy.

LOCATE THE P KEY

The P is keyed with the ; finger. Place your fingers on the home keys and practice the reach to P.

;p; ;p; ;p; ;p;

Measure Progress

Minimum goal: 3-minute timing—38 wam with six or fewer errors; 5-minute timing—33 wam with ten or fewer errors

Take two 3- or 5-minute timings.

Work should be performed in an exciting and cheerful environment. People should feel rewarded for jobs and tasks completed. Often people dread going to work and have a negative attitude about their jobs. This is very disappointing because most people spend a third of their lives working.

People who have taken jobs they really do not like are asking for job dissatisfaction. Sometimes jobs are taken as a matter of convenience or circumstance rather than because the worker really wants the job. Often people apply for and are employed in jobs they really are not qualified to hold. They do not have the required training or experience to be successful in the position.

Other workers may settle for a job for which they are over qualified. This is sometimes necessary especially in poor economic times. With all of the problems, it is not unusual for many workers to feel inadequate and unhappy.

Practice the P Key Reach

Key each line two times.

1 ;p; ;p; ;p; pie pies pan pans piers pens maps pats
2 tap tape part price planet staple purpose percents
3 per plain hope happen person possible stop pail up
4 past people elapse napkin present special trip lap
5 appeal please support purpose price possible slain
6 hope part prices proper police past plain prim pad
7 These projects were not presented in proper plans.
8 Put pen on paper to write about personal problems.
9 Paul put staples on the tape per specific purpose.
10 The price of the pen part was too deep to present.

Use proper technique; check fingers and wrists.

Increase Keying Speed

Try to beat the computer. Key quickly.

1 All the banks can insure new credit card accounts.
2 A desk has four deep drawers for files and others.
3 Wallace told Sam and Kim to take the old teak pot.
4 Most banks like credit cards and that account fee.
5 The proper police accounts were filed on the disk.
6 The two black boats landed ten blues on that deck.
7 Joe lets annual land leases to banks for branches.
8 Williams wished we had known when the police came.
9 The woman walked the usual laps without a purpose.
10 Ms. White supported the special fuel price refund.

Keep your eyes on the copy—do not watch your hands.

Key the following sentences, selecting the correct number expression.

1 The meeting was set for (2 p.m., 2:00 p.m) on Monday.

2 Your appointments are scheduled for (11:30 a.m. and 3 p.m., 11:30 a.m. and 3:00 p.m.).

3 At your college, about 95 (percent, %) of the students use computers in their classes.

4 The new home required a 20 (percent, %) down payment.

5 The following grades were reported:

A 10 (percent, %)
B 25 (percent, %)
C 40 (percent, %)
D 20 (percent, %)
F 5 (percent, %)

Improve Keying Skills

Take two 1-minute timings on each paragraph. Set a speed or an accuracy goal. If you complete the paragraph before time runs out, start over.

Exercise 1

The worker with a good attitude and the willingness to learn new programs and systems is quite an asset to any organization. The ability to teach others and to set a good example for new personnel is also highly prized by office managers. The personality that resists change will not be very happy or successful in the word-processing field.

Exercise 2

A general rule when investing in stocks is to avoid new and untried companies. Although all stocks were untried at one point, the record of a company's past earnings is a good indicator of its future potential. Another consideration is the company's assets. The relation of assets to liabilities should be appropriate for the type of business.

Measure Progress

Take two 1-minute timings.

Minimum goal: 15 wam

Key quickly.

```
1 Net sales for that leased land told those men how.
2 This plain clock had two old warped, purple hands.
3 A man named Wilbur called to make her appointment.
```

End-of-Lesson Procedure

At the end of each lesson, you will have the following options:

1. To restart the same lesson, press the F1 function key.
2. To return to the Lessons Menu, press ESC. This action automatically will save the completed lesson.
3. To proceed to the next, or any other lesson, highlight your choice on the menu and press Enter.
4. To return to the Main Menu, press ESC again.
5. To print the lesson, select Print Activities.
6. To exit the program:
   a. Select the Exit option and press Enter.
   b. When the DOS prompt appears on the screen, remove your data disk.
   c. Turn off the monitor. (Your instructor also may ask you to turn off the computer and printer.)

56

Editing Compositions

GOALS

- Build Language Arts Skills
- Improve Keying Skills
- Learn to Edit Compositions

Review

Key each line two times.

1 or no an/it is at/if it is/of he at/to no by/oz or

2 A quaint quest for the queer cat was questionable.

3 Denny's call from 703-555-4327 was for 14 minutes.

4 An effective automated system required thorough preparation.

Build Language Arts Skills

Number Expression

Study the following rules.

- Numbers are used with a.m. and p.m. to express clock time. Use a colon between the hour and minutes. For even time, do not use the colon or any zeros.
- Percentages should be written in figures followed by the word percent. The percentage symbol (%) should only be used in statistical or technical tables or forms.

Key each line.

1 Please meet me at the Empire for dinner at 7 p.m.

2 Be sure to attend class promptly at 9:30 a.m., 2 p.m., and 4:30 p.m.

3 The state reported that about nine percent of its workers are unemployed.

4 Percent of Applicants Passing the Exams

CPS 55%
CPA 42%
CAM 89%
CLU 78%

9

X, Y, and G Keys

GOALS

- Reinforce Previous Learning
- Learn New Keys X, Y, and G
- Increase Keying Speed

Remember the "Get Ready" checklist.

Review

Key each line two times.

1 dcd dcd jmj jmj fbf fbf l.l l.l sws sws juj juj ;p
2 Wheel winner whether weather where pamphlet panic,
3 Parallel parent participate partition umbrella use
4 The winner decided not to keep the old blue pumps.
5 Warren and Carroll entered the annual run for fun.

Locate the X Key

The X is keyed with the S finger. Place your fingers on the home keys and practice the reach to X.

sxs sxs sxs sxs

Learning Activity 1

1. Choose one of the methods of brainstorming—automatic writing, linear outline, or a mind map. Develop your ideas for a report concerning "Solutions to Environmental Problems." This document is LES55CM1.
2. Using your brainstorming notes, prepare a draft of the report. This document will be LES55CM2. Use the standard report format. Be sure the report is double-spaced. Remember this is a draft. Key as quickly as you can. Just get your ideas down; do not be concerned about correctness at this point. If you can't think of the exact wording you want to express your ideas, just leave a blank or key xxxxx. Keep on writing. Don't get bogged down with searching for specific words.
3. Save the report. Print a copy and save it for use in a future lesson.

Sample Outline

```
         HOW TO CREATE AND EDIT A DATABASE

  I.   Define the Database Structure
       A.   Identify Records
       B.   Define and Name Fields
       C.   Determine Field Type
       D.   Determine Field Size
 II.   Create Database Entry Forms
       A.   Default Data Entry Screen
       B.   Fixed/Variable Length Fields
       C.   Customize the Input Screen
III.   Enter Data
 IV.   Save a Database File
  V.   Edit a Database File
       A.   Edit Fields
       B.   Add Records
       C.   Delete Records
```

End-of-Lesson Procedure

After completing the activity for this lesson, follow the appropriate end-of-lesson procedure.

Practice the X Key Reach

Key each line two times.

1 sxs sxs six fox fix axe ox six flex ax relax foxes
2 tax taxes next boxes complex exams Tex oxen ox wax
3 box next axle exhaust annex except excellent index
4 six excel text sixth export exact expedite mixture
5 extra extend express anxious maximum excellent box
6 expect exist deluxe excess excellent fix exact six
7 examine excels expedite approximate next axle text
8 Excellent expense report is as usual lax in taxes.
9 Six oxen flexed for Texas. Completed exams taxed.
10 Maxie examined the express text to expedite exams.
11 The approximate cost of the maximum expenses fell.

As you key the X, your A finger may lift slightly. Keep your other fingers in home key position.

Locate the Y Key

The Y is keyed with the J finger. Place your fingers on the home keys and practice the reach to Y.

jyj jyj jyj jyj

Measure Progress

Minimum goal: 3-minute timing—38 wam with six or fewer errors; 5-minute timing—33 wam with ten or fewer errors

Take two 3- or 5-minute timings.

Christopher Columbus discovered the Bahama Island chain during his search for the Far East. Columbus declared his discovery for Spain and called the new land San Salvador. The island was inhabited by the Arawak. These people referred to themselves as Lucayans or "island people." They were friendly and welcomed Columbus with a bounty of gifts, including parrots, handwoven hammocks, and a drinkable water supply. Over the next two years, Columbus explored the area and claimed additional islands of the Southern Bahamas for Spain.

In 1629, King Charles I of Great Britain laid claim to the Bahamas. At this time, many people were fleeing Great Britain for religious freedom. The Pilgrims set sail for Massachusetts, while others fled to Bermuda. Many later fled to Eleuthera, an island in the Bahamas. "Eleuthera" is the Greek word for freedom.

Learn to Organize Your Writing

Several types of brainstorming activities may be used to list your initial thoughts about a topic. In Lesson 54, you used the listing technique. Another technique that may be used is "automatic writing." With this method, you key everything that comes to mind about a subject without making any value judgments—just keep keying. Once all your thoughts are recorded, edit the copy for content changes, grouping, and moving ideas as needed.

Some people find it more helpful to use a formal linear outline. See the outline on the next page. Study the formatting notations. Because of the formality of the linear outline and the difficulty in keying it, you may not find it as useful in the brainstorming stage.

Mind-mapping is another technique often used. The writer uses a schematic drawing (diagram) to develop the report. The main idea is placed in a circle in the center of the drawing. Lines and circles branch out from the main idea as new ideas are added.

PRACTICE THE Y KEY REACH

Key each line two times.

1 jyj jyj yarn yet say plays lays pays types yet hay
2 pay copy type company money yellow yachts spy yawn
3 may obey yearly okay fully daily rhyme family they
4 policy system defy likely yield today study supply
5 fry easy maybe property company luxury rhyme daily
6 try styles study employees yields day easy yes may
7 All my new yearly net yields fluctuate like yoyos.
8 My yearly study of employees pay was not too easy.
9 Tony can type with rhythm and likely supply money.
10 Silly Stacey will defy the property systems daily.
11 The yield for the policy was forty or fifty daily.

Key quickly and use proper technique.

LOCATE THE G KEY

F→G

The G is keyed with the F finger. Place your fingers on the home keys and practice the reach to G.

fgf fgf fgf fgf

3 Computer programs use a binary system of (0s and 1s, zeros and ones).

4 Rodriquez covered his painting in specially lettered (18s, eighteens).

5 How many phone numbers in our area have (2s, twos)?

Improve Keying Skills

Take two 1-minute timings on each paragraph. Set a speed or an accuracy goal. If you complete the paragraph before time runs out, start over.

Exercise 1

Selecting a career in the word-processing field can be very challenging. There are many possible uses for word-processing skills. Some of the many jobs that require accurate keyboarding include medical records, legal records, and actuarial records. All of these types of records require absolute accuracy; and, of course, speed is also essential when entering large amounts of data.

Exercise 2

One of the most wasteful practices in education is the under-utilization of public school facilities. Many school buildings are closed after four o'clock in the afternoon and on weekends. Adult literacy education programs could make use of many of the public school facilities in the evenings and on weekends to teach adults. The summer period also is often wasted by the schools in terms of plant utilization.

Practice the G Key Reach

Key each line two times.

1 fgf fgf tugs go dog tog fog got gear good goat hag
2 page high again filing gentle flight college legal
3 sign glasses gadget pledge adjust refuge glad page
4 budget sprung urgent program oxygen angry again go
5 The dogs will not growl at the great green trucks.
6 My good agreement will not get a good arrangement.
7 Granted, great arrangement would get good golfing.
8 The college program took three gifted giant gains.
9 Gene will judge the urgency of the budget, George.
10 Gale was going to adjust and judge the oxygen gas.
11 Guy will adjust the pledge for all yearly exports.

Use proper technique.

Increase Keying Speed

Race to beat the computer and increase your speed.

Key each line two times.

1 In the future, people will use computers each day.
2 Most new business transactions might occur orally.
3 Net expenses for the past month are on the tables.
4 I wished that annual land leases were not illegal.
5 The Feds blocked the bid for all yields for taxes.
6 New employee styles are good and can yield yearly.
7 Big red fish can be tracked with future computers.
8 You need two business transactions for generosity.
9 Paula expedited the budget policy for the company.
10 The angry judge pledged to grant the urgent price.

55

Organizing Your Writing

GOALS

- Build Language Arts Skills
- Improve Keying Skills
- Learn to Organize Your Writing

Review

Key each line two times.

1 of it at/go to do/of an at/it is at/to no am/as it

2 A proper and pleasant pastime is planning parties.

3 The number 148,572 needed to be changed to 72,168.

4 My personal computer uses a hard disk for records.

Build Language Arts Skills

Number Expression

Study the following rules.

- To make a plural of a figure, add *s*.
- Express round amounts of money in millions, billions, and trillions of dollars in combined word and figure form.

Key each sentence.

1 The account number contained many 8s.

2 The 1990s will be remembered as a time of great change.

3 The cost of the new plant exceeded $50 million.

4 The state estimates that $3.5 billion will be needed in additional revenue from the bond issue.

Key the following sentences, selecting the appropriate form of number expression.

1 Life during the (1800s, eighteen hundreds) was quite different than the way we live now.

2 Each new plan will cost ($1.5 million, one and one/half million dollars).

Measure Progress

Minimum goal: 16 wam

Try to reach a new speed goal.

Take two 1-minute timings.

1 `My annual family days taken were not too exciting.`

2 `Public bids for federal lands are considered good.`

3 `Many corporate business transactions are exciting.`

End-of-Lesson Procedure

At the end of each lesson, you will have the following options:

1. To restart the same lesson, press the F1 function key.
2. To return to the Lessons Menu, press ESC. This action automatically will save the completed lesson.
3. To proceed to the next, or any other lesson, highlight your choice on the menu and press Enter.
4. To return to the Main Menu, press ESC again.
5. To print the lesson, select Print Activities.
6. To exit the program:
   a. Select the Exit option and press Enter.
   b. When the DOS prompt appears on the screen, remove your data disk.
   c. Turn off the monitor. (Your instructor also may ask you to turn off the computer and printer.)

3. Study your list to identify ideas that can be grouped together. Use the move features of your software to reorder the list, grouping ideas that can be placed together. To move ideas within your list, follow these steps:
   - Place the cursor on the first character of the words to be moved. Press the F9 key to start blocking the text.
   - Move the cursor to highlight the text you want to move. Be sure to also move any end punctuation and the Enter space in order to leave items on individual lines.
   - Select Alt-X to cut the text.
   - Move the cursor to the pace where you want to put the text. Press Alt-V and the text will be retrieved.
   - Repeat these steps until you have organized your entire list. Delete any repetition.
4. Decide on appropriate subheads for each section of the list. For example, the need for keyboarding skills could be grouped under "Keyboarding," and the need to be able to compose at the keyboard could be grouped under "Writing and Composition." Insert the subheadings at the appropriate places in the list. Save this revised list. You can replace the original document.
5. Now, using the revised "Ideas" list as a guide, start a new document to draft a copy of your article. This new document will be LES54CM2. Center the title in capital letters two inches from the top of the page. Double-space the copy. Key each subhead on a separate line and underline it. Remember that during this drafting stage you do not need to worry about correctness just key your thoughts. Do not edit at this time.
6. Print a copy. Save the document for future use.

End-of-Lesson Procedure

At the end of each lesson, you will have the following options:

1. To restart the same lesson, press the F1 function key.
2. To return to the Lessons Menu, press ESC. This action automatically will save the completed lesson.
3. To proceed to another lesson, highlight your choice on the menu and press Enter.
4. To return to the Main Menu, press ESC again.
5. To print the lesson, select Print Activities.
6. To exit the program:
   a. Select the Exit option and press Enter.
   b. When the DOS prompt appears on the screen, remove your data disk.
   c. Turn off the monitor. (Your instructor also may ask you to turn off the computer and printer.)

10

V, Z, Diagonal, and Question Mark Keys

GOALS

- Reinforce Previous Learning
- Learn New Keys V, Z, Diagonal, and Question Mark
- Increase Keying Speed

Remember the "Get Ready" checklist.

Review

1 sws sws juj juj ;p; ;p; sxs sxs jyj jyj fgf fgf gy
2 Xerox xray extra excellent excess expand next flax
3 Ugly physical weary physicians unduly photography,
4 The employee taxes yielded gross percentage yield.
5 Guy had excise taxes and good agreements for sale.

Locate the V Key

Use correct finger position.

The V is keyed with the F finger. Place your fingers on the home keys and practice the reach to V.

fvf fvf fvf fvf

Measure Progress

Minimum goal: 3-minute timing—37 wam with six or fewer errors; 5-minute timing—32 wam with ten or fewer errors

Take two 3- or 5-minute timings.

Motivation is a complex process. What motivates one person may or may not have an effect upon another person. Better work environment, higher job titles, more responsibility, and job satisfaction are all proven motivators. Money, of course, motivates many people because it is a means to an end. In other words, money allows people to obtain other things that motivate them--new cars, homes, clothes, and college educations.

Factors that motivate people are closely related to their value systems. Value systems govern goal setting. People's goals reflect their values. One person may value education more than a new car; another may value a new car more than buying a home. At any rate, people are motivated by the things they desire both internally and externally.

Learn to Brainstorm Writing Ideas

You now have the skills you need to compose reports and correspondence directly on the keyboard. In the next several lessons, you will be given guidelines that should prove helpful in perfecting your computer composition skills.

Learning Activity 1

1. You have been asked to develop a report, "How Computers Will Change the Future Education of Students." Using the word processor, create LES54CM1. Key, at the top of a page, the heading, "How Computers Will Change the Future Education of Students."
2. Use the technique of *brainstorming* to develop as many ideas as possible. Brainstorming is a technique in which you just let your mind go. You write down everything that comes to mind, not judging any of the thoughts, just letting your imagination take charge. For this brainstorming exercise, use the following prewriting method: Make an unarranged listing of everything that comes to mind about the subject. Do not eliminate any ideas at this time. Print a copy of your list.

PRACTICE THE V KEY REACH

Key each line two times.

1 fvf fvf very vain vacant vacations vaccine vex vat
2 via even travel advise review seven private versus
3 arrival adverse advertise understand view division
4 visitors vocational waiver vault convenience seven
5 available waiver advise advertise vocational vault
6 The average vote has value. I vied for vice jobs.
7 Vic and Victoria have a very vain view of victory.
8 It is not vain to get a vaccine before a vacation.
9 Please review the division advertisement for Vera.
10 The arrival of the vocational visitors was urgent.
11 Please understand the inconvenience of the waiver.

Keep your fingers curved.

LOCATE THE Z KEY

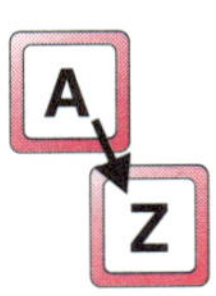

The Z is keyed with the A finger. Place your fingers on the home keys and practice the reach to Z.

aza aza aza aza

Key each line, selecting the correct number expression.

1 Only (nineteen, 19) people signed up for the trip.

2 All (seven, 7) team members were late for the game.

3 My new cordless microphone costs ($545, five hundred forty-five dollars).

4 We purchased a new roll of tape for (79 cents, $.79).

5 They asked for apples, pears, and peaches, which cost (89 cents, $1.25, and $2.98; $.89, $1.25, and $2.98).

Improve Keying Skills

Take two 1-minute timings on each paragraph. Set a speed or an accuracy goal. If you finish before time is up, start over.

Exercise 1

Worker satisfaction is a key to good morale. What satisfies one person may not satisfy another; and this, of course, relates to a person's value system and goals. New responsibilities or a new title may motivate and satisfy one employee whereas another might prefer more money or better working conditions. Managers must always be aware of what best motivates their employees.

Exercise 2

Office morale is directly related to production. Many studies have shown that when office morale is low, production and quality tend to decline. In other words, satisfied and happy workers are more productive. It also has been noted that when morale is low, absenteeism and job turnover rates increase. In today's competitive market, productivity concerns are of prime importance.

Practice the Z Key Reach

Key each line two times.

1 aza aza azalea azure Aztec buzz lizard zipper zoos
2 raze whiz citizen seize minimize recognize analyze
3 amaze hazard freeze bazaar zigzag organize itemize
4 lazy crazy hazy prize minimize zeal size raze whiz
5 Zebra zeal size jazz zip lazy freeze zero citizens
6 The fuzzy and zany lizard zipped by the zoo zones.
7 It was good to zealously zero in on frozen ozones.
8 Zelda analyzed the prizes from the citizen bazaar.
9 Itemize the dozen tax hazards for the whiz, Lizzy.
10 Buzz authorized a new text for the next tax class.
11 Those citizens voted to waive the division bazaar.

As you key the Z, your S finger may lift slightly.

Locate the ?/ Key

A diagonal or slash (/) is used between letters in some abbreviations, between the numbers in a fraction, and between certain interchangeable expressions, such as and/or. No space is left before or after a diagonal.

The / (diagonal) is keyed with the ; finger. Place your fingers on the home keys and practice the reach to /.

;/; ;/; ;/; ;/;

54 Brainstorming Writing Ideas

GOALS

- Build Language Arts Skills
- Improve Keying Skills
- Learn to Brainstorm Writing Ideas

REVIEW

Key each line two times.

1 lend bend tend extend append amend ascends friends
2 We awaited the voter's decision after an election.
3 Get Juanita 15 lbs. of #2 nails at $.45 per pound.
4 Stock market drops make me realize Jo needs better planning.

BUILD LANGUAGE ARTS SKILLS

NUMBER EXPRESSION

Study the following rules.

- Write out numbers from one through ten when used in general text.
- Use figures to express numbers above ten.
- Express even dollars with a dollar sign and no decimal point or zeros. (Example: $50)
- Express amounts less than a dollar in numbers followed by the word cents. (Example: 45 cents)
- If several amounts of money are used together in a sentence, they are all keyed in the same style. (Example: $.35, $5.39, and $9.75)
- Express units of measure in figures.

Key each line.

1 William included seven people to the theater.
2 The football team will have 16 members this year.
3 I will purchase a new computer for $1,245.
4 Please buy me a candy bar; it costs 52 cents.
5 The new dress costs $125.98, but it can be worn to several events.
6 The list of items included paper, tape, and folders, which cost $.79, $2.45, and $6.95 at Office Supply.

Remember: Do not space before or after the diagonal.

PRACTICE THE ?/ KEY REACH

Key each line two times.

```
1 ;/ ;/ ;/ either/or neither/nor or/for his/her a/an
2 yes/no high/low pass/fail right/wrong up/down a/an
3 My pass/fail rule was not his/her in/out decision.
```

LOCATE THE ?/ KEY

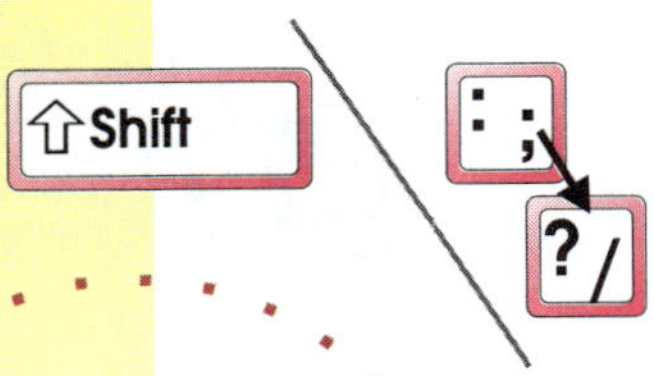

A question mark is used at the end of direct questions. Usee two spaces after the question mark.

The ? is the shift of the / and is keyed with the ; finger. Place your fingers on the home keys and practice the reach to ?.

```
;?; ;?; ;?; ;?;
```

PRACTICE THE ?/ KEY REACH

Key each line two times.

```
1 ;?; ;?; Did you buzz?  Who is it?  Whose vacation?
2 Where is our new pen?  Have you seen Tex?  Who me?
3 What is going on here?  Why do they work?  Pamela?
4 Will they come?  Has Kim called?  Where was Henry?
5 When will Vic get home?  Where was that prize bag?
6 Why did Lacy waive the decision?  Where is George?
7 What did the prize advertisement reveal to Walter?
8 How did Yvonne organize the items for convenience?
9 What were the pass/fail rates for the examination?
10 Will Irene become the new class computer whiz kid?
```

Space twice after a question mark at the end of a sentence.

UNIT 9

COMPOSITION

Increase Keying Speed

Try to reach a new speed goal.

Remember: Space twice after a question mark.

1 The vulture was a vulgar, vigorous big black bird.
2 It became evident when that vapor rose from a vat.
3 Our frozen and frizzy red dog walks like a zombie.
4 Vera and Vic have a very bad vain view of history.
5 Many business transactions occur at our new house.
6 Zelda, an irate citizen, organized a crazy bazaar.
7 The pass/fail rules were his/her yes/no decisions.
8 He/she decided one in/out motion was not a yes/no.
9 Where is the house? Is he in? What was it? Why?
10 Who took the letter? What did she say? Who said?

Measure Progress

Minimum goal: 17 wam

Try to exceed the minimum goal.

Take two 1-minute timings.

1 A chip technology allows less expensive computers.
2 The average vote has values. How did Jan find me?
3 Our exercise programs are needed for good muscles.

End-of-Lesson Procedure

At the end of each lesson, you will have the following options:

1. To restart the same lesson, press the F1 function key.
2. To return to the Lessons Menu, press ESC. This action automatically will save the completed lesson.
3. To proceed to the next, or any other lesson, highlight your choice on the menu and press Enter.
4. To return to the Main Menu, press ESC again.
5. To print the lesson, select Print Activities.
6. To exit the program:
   a. Select the Exit option and press Enter.
   b. When the DOS prompt appears on the screen, remove your data disk.
   c. Turn off the monitor. (Your instructor also may ask you to turn off the computer and printer.)

SILVERMAN & DEAN L.P.
STATEMENTS OF INCOME
(Unaudited, in thousands except per unit data)

Three Months Ended
March 31

	1997	1996
Revenues	$13,397	$13,354
Expenses	9,663	9,600
Income before taxes	3,734	3,754
Income taxes	31	72
Net income	3,703	3,682
Net income per unit	$ 0.37	$ 0.37
Average units outstanding	9,994	9,994

Twelve Months Ended
March 31

	1997	1996
Revenues	$54,210	$53,508
Expenses	39,489	38,326
Income before taxes	14,721	15,182
Income taxes	159	203
Net income	$14,562	$14,979
Net income per unit	$ 1.46	$ 1.50
Average units outstanding	9,994	9,997

Revenues and expenses for 1996 have been reclassified to reflect certain expenses previously offset against revenue in conformity with the current period's presentation.

11

Q, Hyphen, and Tab Keys

GOALS

- Reinforce Previous Learning
- Learn New Keys Q, Hyphen, and Tab
- Learn Word Wrap

Review

Key each line twice.

Use proper technique.

```
1 sxs sxs jyj jyj fgf fgf fvf fvf aza aza ;/; ;?; ;?
2 Was that public bid for the old federal land high?
3 That new pass/fail system was his/her new bid too.
4 Was it difficult to realize that ozone is not hot?
5 Janet indicated that something extra could happen.
```

Locate the Q Key

The Q is keyed with the A finger. Place your fingers on the home keys and practice the reach to Q.

```
aqa aqa aqa aqa
```

MEMORANDUM

TO: Arthur Warren, Public Relations Department

FROM: Naomi Smithson, Financial Services

DATE: April 6, 1997

SUBJECT: Contents of News Release for Silverman & Dean

As you requested, I am enclosing the following information to be used in the news release concerning the quarterly report of Silverman & Dean. Please call me if you need any further information.

NEWS RELEASE

FOR IMMEDIATE RELEASE
April 2, 1997

CONTACT: Robert J. Ellis
(415)555-3981

San Francisco, CA -- Silverman & Dean L.P. (NYS:SDP) today reported operating results for the quarter and twelve months ended March 31, 1997.

For the quarter ended March 31, 1997, revenues increased slightly to $13,397,000 from $13,354,000 in 1996. Net income was $3,703,000 or $0.37 per unit, up slightly from net income of $3,682,000 or $0.37 per unit in the same quarter of the prior year.

For the twelve months ended March 31, 1997, revenues of $54,210,000 were up 1.3% from last year's $53,508,000. Net income was $14,562,000 or $1.46 per unit, a decline of 2.8% from net income of $14,979,000 or $1.50 per unit in the same period of the prior year.

Silverman & Dean, Inc., general partner, stated that net operating results for the three-month period reflect an increase in the net income contribution of the mutual funds group compared with the comparable quarter of the prior year. This increase was largely offset by a decline in the earnings from marketing certificates of deposit due to a prolonged low interest rate environment. Low interest rates for CDs persisted throughout 1997 and resulted in a corresponding decline in the operating results of the Partnership's certificate of deposit business for the year. In addition, the overall net income contribution of the capital management division also declined in 1997 compared with the prior year, reflecting a decrease in assets under management. These declines, however, were largely offset during the year by an increase in the net income contribution of the mutual funds division attributable to increased asset levels and the introduction of new products.

Practice the Q Key Reach

Try to keep your wrist still as you key the Q.

Key each line two times.

```
1  aqa aqa aqua aquanaut aquariums aquatics equal aqa
2  quick quiet query quart delinquent adequate quorum
3  quota quality quire unique quantity request acquit
4  acquire inquire quotient antique quit quality quay
5  The question of the quiet quest was for the Queen.
6  Their quart is a quantity that must be questioned.
7  A question concerning the Queen was quietly posed.
8  The unique antique qualified as the quality quota.
9  Quint will acquire an adequate quantity of quilts.
10 Inquire about the delinquent quotas acquired Quan.
11 Did that quota require equal distribution of ages?
```

Locate the - Key

Hyphens are used to form compound adjectives, nouns, and verbs. Hyphens help readers understand that a combination of words has a single meaning, such as state-of-the-art software. Hyphens also show the division of syllables in a word, such as knowl-edge. The dash (--) is used in informal writing to introduce or summarize information. Dashes also may be used to set off information from the rest of the sentence. Dashes are constructed of two hyphens. Do not insert a space between the hyphen or dash and the characters that come before or after it.

The - (hyphen) is keyed with the ; finger. Place your fingers on the home keys and practice the reach to -.

```
;-; ;-; ;-; ;-;
```

Learning Activity 1

1. Start document LES53DC1 and key the memo on pages 338-339 using the standard memorandum style learned in Lesson 41. Single-space the body. Key only the memo and the news release body in this document.
2. Proofread the copy on the screen and use the editing keys to make any corrections. Reformat if necessary.
3. Have the computer check your document and print a copy. Note any uncorrected errors on the printout.

Learning Activity 2

1. Start document LES53DC2 and key the table on page 339. Single-space the table, pressing the Enter key to add the extra lines where needed. In the table, align the second and third columns on the right by using the right tab function. Set right tabs at 54 and 74. In order to extend the underline across the entire column, press the tab key to reach the column, turn on the underline, press the Space Bar the required number of times and then key the numerals. For those entries with more numerals, turn on the underline and key the numerals.
2. Proofread the copy on the screen and use the editing keys to make any corrections. Reformat if necessary.
3. Have the computer check your document and print a copy. Note any uncorrected errors on the printout.

End-of-Lesson Procedure

After completing the activities for this lesson, follow the appropriate end-of-lesson procedure.

1. To restart the same lesson, press the F1 function key.
2. To return to the Lessons Menu, press ESC. This action automatically will save the completed lesson.
3. To proceed to another lesson, highlight your choice on the menu and press Enter.
4. To return to the Main Menu, press ESC again.
5. To print the lesson, select Print Activities.
6. To exit the program:
   a. Select the Exit option and press Enter.
   b. When the DOS prompt appears on the screen, remove your data disk.
   c. Turn off the monitor. (Your instructor also may ask you to turn off the computer and printer.)

PRACTICE THE - KEY REACH

Key each line two times.

Remember: A dash is keyed as two hyphens.

```
1 ;-; ;-; ;-; self-concepts up-to-date part-time ;-;
2 His new mother-in-law gave him a part-time salary.
3 My part-time work requires up-to-date information.
4 Their resignation--not mine--begins tomorrow, Hal.
5 Newer negotiations--dated as of May--were resumed.
```

LEARN TO USE THE TAB KEY

When keying information, sometimes it is necessary to indent paragraphs or arrange text or data in columns. Tab settings allow you to move quickly to predetermined stops across the display screen and thus save time for many applications. Most microcomputer software packages have present tabs called **default tabs.** In this software program, one default tab is set at five spaces from the left margin. When the cursor is at the left margin, striking the Tab key will indent that line five spaces, the normal paragraph indentation. Other software programs may have different default settings.

Most word-processing programs also allow you to change default tabs or set new tab stops. You will learn how to change tab settings in this program in a later lesson. Until that lesson, you will use the Tab key only to indent the first line of a paragraph.

LOCATE THE TAB KEY

Strike Tab to indent a paragraph.

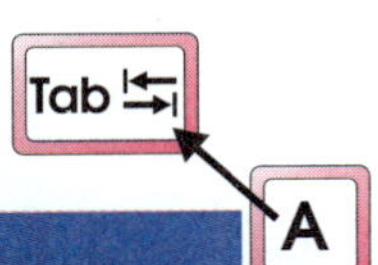

The Tab key is located to the left of the Q key and is struck with the A finger. The other fingers should remain in home key position. Place your fingers on the home keys. Practice striking the Tab key.

a ↑tab a ↑tab a ↑tab a ↑tab a ↑tab a ↑tab a ↑tab a ↵

MEASURE PROGRESS

Take two 3- or 5-minute timings.

Minimum goal: 3-minute timing—37 wam with six or fewer errors; 5-minute timing—32 wam with ten or fewer errors

Critical thinking is a skill. You use critical thinking to evaluate ideas and make a judgment before taking action. The ability to tell the difference between facts and opinions is necessary if you want to learn and make the best decisions for yourself. Determining what is fact and what is opinion is not always easy. If you cannot separate fact from opinion though, you may come to the wrong conclusion and, consequently, may take the wrong action.

A fact is a statement you can prove true. For example, it is a fact that the U.S. is a democracy. An opinion is a statement that has yet to be proved if it is right or wrong. For example, people have opinions about how good a job Congress is doing.

When reading or doing research, think critically about what you are reading. Watch for words that express feelings or values because they usually mean the statement is an opinion. To think critically, organize your thoughts, learn about your options, weigh the choices, and evaluate your actions.

Learn Automatic Word Wrap

Most word processing and microcomputer programs include an automatic "word wrap" feature. When a word is too long to fit within the established right margin, word wrap automatically will carry that word down to begin a new line at the left margin. With this feature, the operator needs to strike Enter only at the end of short lines and at the end of a paragraph. Word wrap is an efficient, time-saving feature for the operator.

In this program, word wrap will be on for any paragraph drill and for all composition and formatting exercises. Continue to strike Enter at the end of one-line drills only.

Practice the Tab Key Reach and Word Wrap

Strike Enter to end a paragraph.

Using the default Tab setting of five spaces, strike the Tab key to indent the following paragraphs. Key each paragraph one time. Strike Enter only at the end of each paragraph.

```
     Your order for a copy of the software program was received today.  The order will be shipped Monday.
     Please notify us as soon as you receive the shipment.  An invoice will be included.
     For additional information and service, please contact us.  We appreciate your business.
```

Practice Tabs in Paragraph Copy

Key each paragraph two times. Read the copy from the book and key the lines on the computer. Strike Enter only at the end of each paragraph.

```
     An exercise/fitness program is essential for your muscle tone.  The in-service training will be effective if the proper techniques/methods are used. Part-time application will not work.  Are there any questions?  Do you wish to begin?
     Many students like the pass/fail system.  It is an up-to-date approach to grading.  Your decision about pass/fail courses needs to be made as enrollment--not payment--starts tomorrow.
```

Fourth-Finger Reaches

tap cab lad map fad dam spa pay ail cap sea paw fad apt sags
top buzz haze quay coax jazz lope pane trap panic azure trap
quit quake vapor query fizzle puzzle savor expand quiz aspen
The payee happened to spark an exact escape from the bazaar.
The angry queen unwrapped the paper from the spoiled squash.

Improve Keying Skills

Take two 1-minute timings on each paragraph. Set a speed or an accuracy goal. If you finish an exercise before time is up, start over.

Exercise 1

Leadership is an important management skill. Many managers have some good leadership skills; however, there are certain leadership practices that can be improved. Leadership is not easy to define, and there are many ideas as to what skills or characteristics comprise leadership. Some believe that leadership is a hereditary characteristic you are born with and that it cannot be learned. Others believe it is a cluster of skills anyone can develop.

Exercise 2

Many agree that if you are a leader you exhibit certain skills. One of these is the skill to motivate people. A leader must have followers, and motivating people to pursue common goals is an essential leadership skill. Another common leadership skill is the ability to communicate effectively. If you are going to lead a group of people, you must be able to explain and articulate where you are headed, how you will get there, and why you and the group should be going in that direction.

Measure Progress

Starting with this lesson, all Measure Progress paragraphs will begin with a standard five-space indentation. Press the Tab key to indent each paragraph. Word wrap will be turned on automatically so you should not strike Enter except to end the paragraph.

Also, each paragraph is rated according to its syllabic intensity (S.I.). Syllabic intensity is one measure of the difficulty of the copy. The higher the syllabic intensity, the more difficult the copy.

Minimum goal: 18 wam
1.4 S.I.

Take two 1-minute timings. Word wrap is active.

```
     A compound word is made from two or more words combined to form a new word.  A compound word may be written as one word, as two or more separate words, or as a hyphenated word.  Regardless of how it is formed, each newly formed word is considered one word.  In order to figure out the meaning, consider the separate meaning of each word and then combine them to arrive at a new definition.  The new definition will contain meaning from both of the combined words.
```

End-of-Lesson Procedure

At the end of each lesson, you will have the following options:

1. To restart the same lesson, press the F1 function key.
2. To return to the Lessons Menu, press ESC. This action automatically will save the completed lesson.
3. To proceed to the next, or any other lesson, highlight your choice on the menu and press Enter.
4. To return to the Main Menu, press ESC again.
5. To print the lesson, select Print Activities.
6. To exit the program:
   a. Select the Exit option and press Enter.
   b. When the DOS prompt appears on the screen, remove your data disk.
   c. Turn off the monitor. (Your instructor also may ask you to turn off the computer and printer.)

Key the following sentences, capitalizing as needed.

1 The meeting of the board of directors was scheduled for 1 p.m.

2 We enjoyed our trip to the empire state building when we visited new york city.

3 Her father, bob, was a cpa.

4 Was doctor hackler on duty monday?

Improve Keying Accuracy

Both speed and accuracy are analyzed and reported.

First-Finger Reaches

1 my hub bug tub hut run bun tug but mug hum mum mut hymn burn

2 buff thug turn hurt fury numb butt ruby tutu hand your muggy

3 myrrh thumb throb graph gamut tuber rhythm minimum gaunt bun

4 The tight mobs galloped at high rates until the two tripped.

5 The ringing alarms frightened the thugs entering the mounds.

Second-Finger Reaches

1 vie den cod eve keg ink lid lie elk ode did dad kid odd irks

2 hide kind nice side feel bide cite denim cried dice kick led

3 degree ticket deject tide adder pike hike bike keen keel die

4 The citizen did not like the offered price of the chief net.

5 The lower price on parking made it cheaper to drive the car.

Third-Finger Reaches

1 old ill sot ski bow how lot too sly now ski how sews zoo fox

2 glow howl scow pools sole woof would boss hello whose swoops

3 tallow bloom mellow poodle swain swooning swaps lox lobsters

4 All souls glow when the solar orb crosses the gloomy hollow.

5 Wax or tallow spilled on the wolf as he prowled the schools.

12

Skill Building

GOALS

- **Reinforce Previous Learning**
- **Increase Keying Speed**
- **Improve Keying Accuracy**
- **Learn Backspace-Key Correction Method**

Review

Key each line two times.

1 We saw seven very fat birds and photographed them.
2 The judges told the boys to fix the broken window.
3 The six zeros on my bad check were quietly erased.
4 Queens were not too excited about a voting frenzy.
5 Sometimes a good argument can obtain sure success.

Increase Keying Speed

Key and space quickly.

Key each line two times.

1 he in on so or of it at if be by ti do ha la it or
2 if it is or no an so in as at no up me en an of on
3 how cut big put hot ten lie was per its eve cab do
4 too for bag him did gas get out fly old bug cat as
5 was the/are you/and the/was all/can she/let go of/

Improve Keying Accuracy—Review All Keys Learned

The following drill serves three purposes. First, the drill lines review all alphabetic keys learned. Second, speed achievement for each line is analyzed and reported. Finally, accuracy of key strokes for each line is analyzed and reported.

53

Formatting a Memo with a Table

GOALS

- Build Language Arts Skills
- Improve Keying Skills
- Learn to Format a Memo with a Table

Review

Key each line two times.

1 vie for news hug yip yup jumpy yummy pretty hungry
2 The cashiers totaled receipts #457, #566, and #21.
3 The telephone call disrupted her keyboarding test.
4 The class plans to spend two weeks formatting reports.

Build Language Arts Skills

Capitalization

Study the following rules.

- Proper nouns (words that name a particular person, place or thing) are capitalized.
- Abbreviations are capitalized if the words they represent are capitalized.
- Professions, ranks, political offices, and family relationships are capitalized if they are used with names.

Key each line.

1 The train was scheduled to leave at 8 p.m.
2 The APA Style Manual was adopted for all papers.
3 Her degree was a B.S. from UNC.
4 When Father O'Malley arrives, bring him in.
5 Tell Senator Smith that he will receive my vote.
6 If Doctor Jenkins is speaking, I will attend.
7 The Duke of Kent was next in line for the honor.
8 The drive across the Chesapeake Bay Bridge Tunnel was exciting.
9 The Sears Tower is located in Chicago, Illinois.

For the following exercise, key each line. Strike Enter at the end of the line. Look at the screen. Your speed performance is reported as words a minute (wam). Your accuracy performance is reported as total errors in the line. Words that contain errors also are highlighted so you can find them easily. Note your performance on the first attempt. Then key the same line a second time. Compare the results of each attempt.

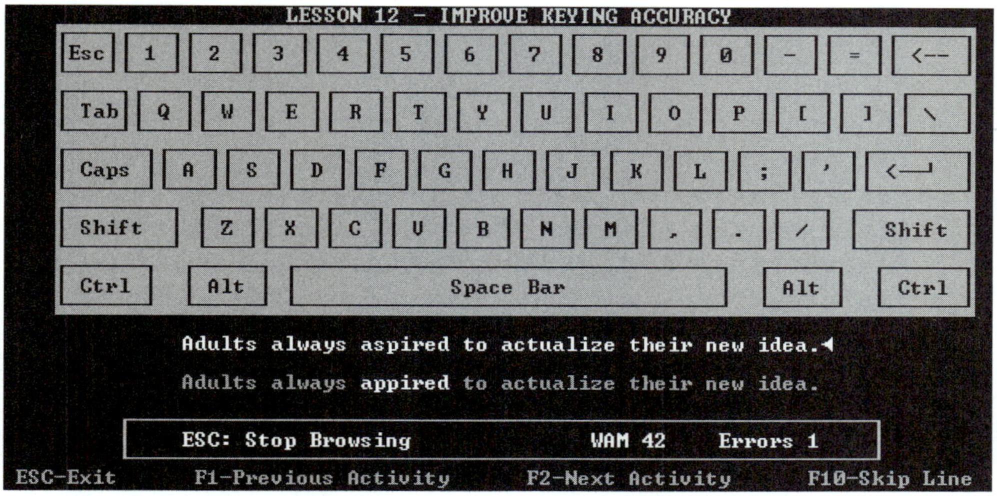

At this point, your goal is to key each line at an average speed of 18 wam with no more than two errors. If you are meeting the speed goal but have more than two errors, you may have to slow down slightly to gain accuracy. If you are not meeting the speed goal, you may want to repeat the Increase Keying Speed and Measure Progress drills in Lessons 6-11 before completing this lesson. Then return to this drill to reevaluate your progress.

After keying this exercise if you are meeting or exceeding both the speed and accuracy goals, proceed to the remaining activities in this lesson.

Minimum goal: 18 wam with no more than 2 errors per line

1 Adults always aspired to actualize their new idea.
2 Beware of bogus business battles that boost sales.
3 Careless careening cars caused a curious accident.
4 Did the untimely death of David Duncans deter her?
5 Ira easily sees that errors erase earnest efforts.
6 Family is the happy foundation of future fortunes.
7 Great Roger Greson generates good press greetings.
8 How will Hank Howel heat the homes for the hungry?
9 Will it be filled? Who will fill it? She did it.
10 Jack, Joe, and Julie jabbered and jumped jauntily.

In addition, please note the following procedures that we implemented. During the time the building remained closed, arrangements were made that allowed the people to enter the building so they could pack additional items located in their permanent offices. Two-hour blocks of time were set up to accommodate these groups.

Due to the electrical problems with the complex, there were no lights in the stairways. A priority during this period was the installation of a more sophisticated backup lighting system. This system ensures that it will not be necessary for people to leave the building in total darkness during any emergency in the future.

As always, it is the policy of the Security Chief not to allow individuals to enter the building while initial repairs are being made. Your adherence to this policy will be greatly appreciated.

End-of-Lesson Procedure

At the end of each lesson, you will have the following options:

1. To restart the same lesson, press the F1 function key.
2. To return to the Lessons Menu, press ESC. This action automatically will save the completed lesson.
3. To proceed to the next, or any other lesson, highlight your choice and press Enter.
4. To return to the Main Menu, press ESC again.
5. To print the lesson, select Print Activities.
6. To exit the program:
   a. Select the Exit option and press Enter.
   b. When the DOS prompt appears on the screen, remove your data disk.
   c. Turn off the monitor. (Your instructor also may ask you to turn off the computer and printer.)

11 Knowing how to knit crazy kits was good knowledge.
12 Free lands are like the lighting of liberty lamps.
13 A major machine can match the main and major mass.
14 Note the new number of major novels that are sold.
15 Oil spills in the ocean are offensive for oysters.
16 A pinch of pepper was put on top of the four pots.
17 Quality questions are quite quaint to Queen Betsy.
18 She was the real reason I refused to receive Raye.
19 Setting sail is serious business to salty sailors.
20 My tried technical technique was true to the text.
21 Use the unions to unite those usual loading units.
22 Vic valued the valves as the vapor rose from vats.
23 Where was that wall wanted when this war was over?
24 Excise taxes are taxing on the extra external tax.
25 If you look closely you will yearn for yummy yams.
26 A ZIP code may speed your dizzy letter to the zoo.

Practice correct techniques.

Try to exceed the minimum goals.

Learn Backspace-Key Correction Method

Often you will recognize misstrokes as you are keying. These can be corrected immediately using the Backspace key.

The Backspace key is located at the far right on the top row of the keyboard. It is keyed with the right little finger. When pressed, the Backspace key moves back one space and deletes the character in that space. If the cursor is at the left margin, pressing the Backspace key will move it to the line above.

software suppress the page number for page 1. Leave a 1-inch top margin on the second page.

6. Proofread your copy on the screen. Use the editing keys to make corrections.
7. Check the document and print a copy. Note any uncorrected errors.

SECURITY REPORT

As a result of the bomb in the World Trade Center in New York, it was necessary to obtain temporary quarters for businesses with offices in our complex. The following information is provided to you so that your records for the period are accurate. Please add these to your confidential database, keeping in mind the investigations that concern the safety of the building.

All these companies continue to maintain their office space in Building 1. This information can be provided to clients who may need to be informed of the temporary location that was provided for these psychologists.

DOCTOR	PERMANENT ADDRESS	TEMPORARY ADDRESS
Philip Rosenburg	Suite 505	14 N. Central Avenue, Suite 210
Anne Kozloski	Suite 410	4506 Elm Avenue, Suite 515
Marilyn Ching	Suite 9110	8416 Boston Circle, Suite 310
Robert Wells	Suite 4302	1410 Berkley Road, Suite 110
LeAnn Samuels	Suite 9901	110 Monticello Avenue, Suite 1400
Andrew Olegack	Suite 1410	8410 Huguenot Road, Suite 105

To practice using the Backspace key, complete the following:

1. Key the words `the program` but do not press Enter.
2. Using the semicolon finger, backspace four times. Notice that the characters `gram` are deleted.
3. Key `blem.` (Again, do not press Enter).
4. Notice that you have changed the *program* to the *problem*.

From now on, you can use the Backspace key during most composition and document formatting exercises. In addition, if your instructor wants the Backspace key to be available to you during a Measure Progress drill, you can activate it by selecting "Options" at the Main Menu. The following screen will appear:

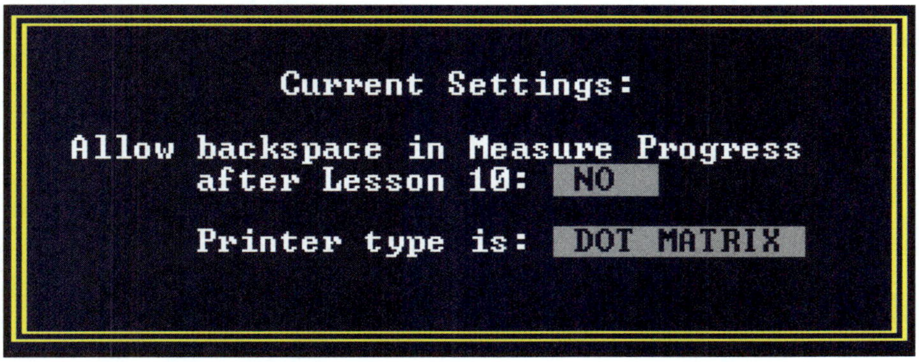

Remember: Turn on Backspace if instructed to do so.

When the program is first loaded, the Backspace setting defaults to "no." To activate Backspace, press the F6 function key. Look at the screen. Notice that "no" is replaced with "yes."

To change back to "no" again, press the F5 function key. The last option selected will remain as the default setting until changed. All Measure Progress drills completed with Backspace on will be marked so that you will know that this option was activated.

Note: The Backspace option is not available in Review, Practice, Increase Keying Speed, or Improve Keying Accuracy drills.

Measure Progress

Take two 3- or 5-minute timings.

Minimum goal: 3-minute timing—36 wam with six or fewer errors; 5-minute timing—31 wam with ten or fewer errors

The microcomputer is an excellent tool for individualizing instruction, whether or not it is presenting instruction as drill and practice, tutorials, or simulations. Computer instruction can be self-paced and use a variety of branches to accommodate the learner's needs. Microcomputers can maintain individual records and start or stop instruction at given points of time.

Basically, the microcomputer functions as an instructional medium in three ways. First, it can present content and planned sequences, units, or modules of information to students. In this function, it operates as a programmed teaching machine controlled by a program and student response.

In the second function, it manages the instructional process with diagnosis, instructional programming, competency testing, and recordkeeping. In the third function, it controls other media and literally branches the student to additional learning experiences.

Learning Activity 1

1. Start document LES52DC1. Format the two-page report on pages 331-332.
2. Double-space the body of a report and indent each paragraph five spaces.
3. Use 1-inch side margins.
4. Leave five spaces between the columns on the table. Keep in mind that the heading is the longest item in the second column. Key the headings for the columns in all capital letters. To key the top rule, turn on the underline, press the Tab key to move across the page, and then press the Space Bar until you reach the right margin. On the next line, key the column headings, pressing the Tab key as required. Press the Space Bar to add the rule to the right margin. Turn off the underline. Follow the same procedure for the rule at the bottom of the table.
5. Number the pages beginning with page 2, which means you must have the

MEASURE PROGRESS

Take two 1-minute timings.

Minimum goal: 19 wam with four or fewer errors 1.6 S.I.

Key quickly.

```
     Computers are very important and valuable in our lives today.  It is essential that we all become familiar with this wonderful tool.  If you want to become computer literate, you must have some knowledge about computers and their operation.  Also, you should have some experience using the computer.
```

END-OF-LESSON PROCEDURE

At the end of each lesson, you will have the following options:

1. To restart the same lesson, press the F1 function key.
2. To return to the Lessons Menu, press ESC. This action automatically will save the completed lesson.
3. To proceed to the next, or any other lesson, highlight your choice on the menu and press Enter.
4. To return to the Main Menu, press ESC again.
5. To print the lesson, select Print Activities.
6. To exit the program:
    a. Select the Exit option and press Enter.
    b. When the DOS prompt appears on the screen, remove your data disk.
    c. Turn off the monitor. (Your instructor also may ask you to turn off the computer and printer.)

Exercise 2

Simultaneous analysis utilized by today's computers is more realistic and more closely approximates the complex interactions that occur in everyday experience. All of this is done extremely fast, thus allowing a teacher to simulate, project, and accomplish vast amounts of data manipulation. Great advances have already been made for both educational and everyday purposes.

Increase Keying Speed

Spacing Drills

Concentrate on proper space bar techniques as you key these words and sentences.

```
to or as if so we me pa of in is by an un so or an in do ant
got ban did fat gad get hop hit ire jab jaw jet jar job laws
sap sit sot tad rap tip tie top tow van vat vip wan was wigs
bear dumb even gear hunt jump kelp lard numb open quit stops
vent what yawl zips bunt damp ends fast have jack knee loans
Did you get the new hat at the tie dye bar for the bold man?
```

Double Letter Drills

Even stroking will enable you to key double letters accurately.

Try to maintain an even rhythm as you key these double letter words.

```
accede eddy abyss tagged seer arrow array apple ballet moods
barrels terror cannon moon moose quizzed dazzle nuzzle dizzy
correct blood foot loot assist attention attic attach attune
attend attacks pillar pillow ballast bullion gallant gallery
acclaim torrent beggar bigger eggs arrive babble buddy seeds
The apparent aggressor was aggrieved at the offensive groom.
```

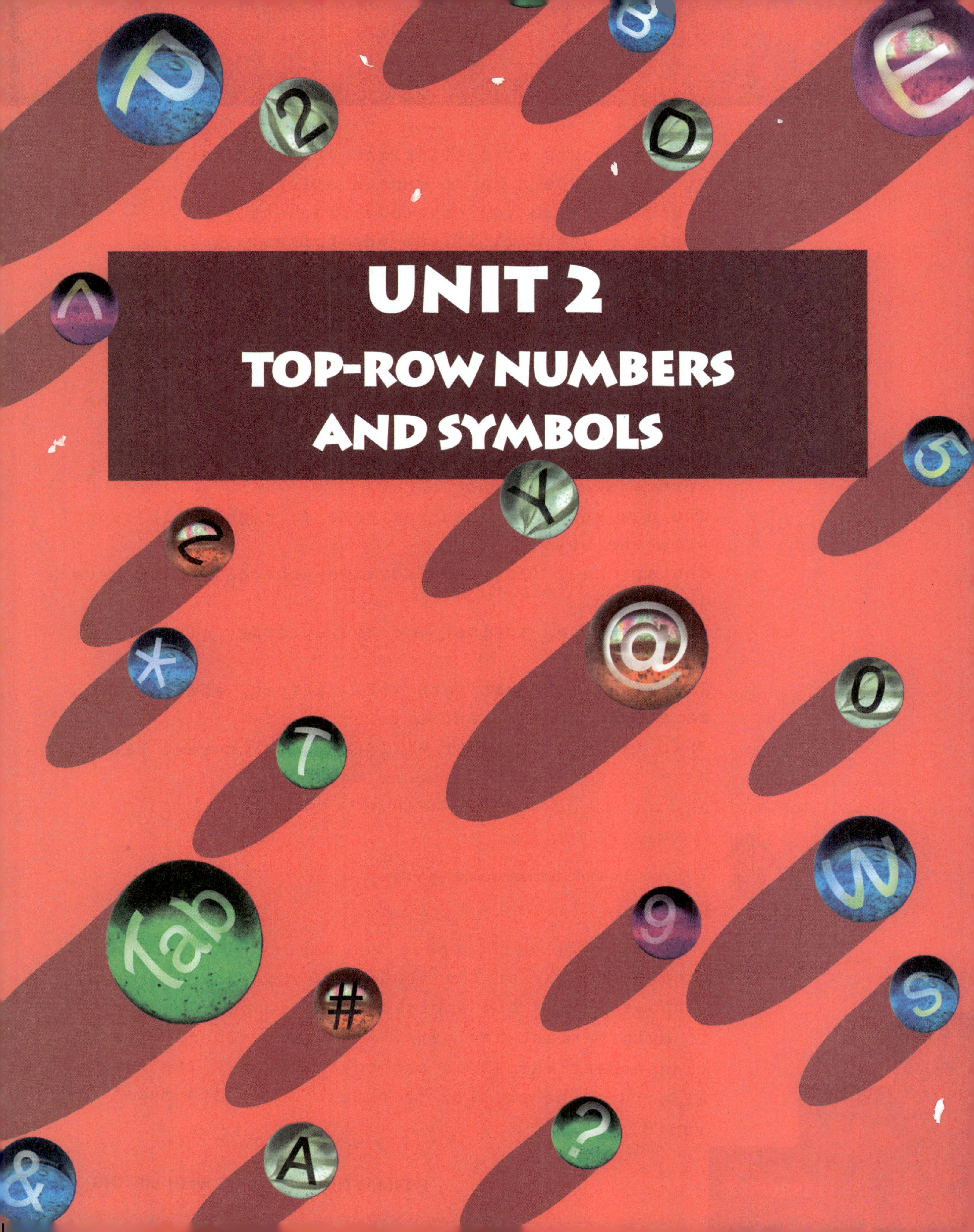

UNIT 2

TOP-ROW NUMBERS AND SYMBOLS

3 The new hours were all right with the managers.

4 My advice would be to remain silent.

5 I would advise you to study frequently.

6 Rising costs will affect our prices.

7 The computer's effect on production was positive.

8 The decrease in the stock market will effect lower interest rates.

Now key each of the following sentences, choosing the correct word.

1 The students were (all ready, already) to try the skiing course.

2 Have you (all ready, already) completed the keyboarding lessons?

3 The new office procedures were (alright, all right) with the staff.

4 The attorney (advised, adviced) the client to have a jury trial.

5 What (advice, advise) did the attorney give the judge?

6 The lower interest rate will (affect, effect) the rate paid on bank accounts.

7 What (affect, effect) will the new interest rates have on the certificate of deposits?

Improve Keying Skills

Take two 1-minute timings on each paragraph.

Set a speed or an accuracy goal.

Exercise 1

The computer's speed and memory place a powerful data processor at the student's command for research purposes. The old approach to science has given way to multivariant analysis. Numerous dependent and independent variables can be analyzed. The final effect is the ability to obtain more data more rapidly.

13

1, 5, and 0 Keys

GOALS

- Reinforce Previous Learning
- Learn New Keys 1, 5, and 0
- Learn Number-Reading Techniques
- Understand Speed vs. Accuracy Development

Remember the "Get Ready" checklist.

Review

Key each line two times.

```
1 Joe was excited about having a quiet meal with Oz.
2 He saw Tim fly.  Who was Rochell talking to today?
3 How many computers were ordered with green tables?
4 The survey is systematic and typical of Jo and me.
5 Their excited dogs bit the quiet small calico cat.
```

Locate the ! 1 Key

Keep your fingers in home key position so you don't lose your place.

The 1 is keyed with the A finger. Place your fingers on the home keys and practice the reach to 1.

```
aq1a aq1a aq1a aq1a
```

52 Formatting a Report with Listing

GOALS

- Build Language Arts Skills
- Improve Keying Skills
- Learn to Format a Report with Listing

Review

Key each line two times.

1 weather front telephone computer electronics wires
2 It is commonly believed that 12 + 56 = 68. Agree?
3 Hold onto your thought until I return from Tucson.
4 Using a word processor makes it easier to organize thoughts.

Build Language Arts Skills

Word Usage

Study the following rules.

All ready/Already
All ready collectively prepared
Already prior to or by a specific or implied past, present, or future time

All right/Alright
All right totally satisfactory; agreeable; unhurt; correct
Alright incorrect spelling of all right and should not be used in formal writing

Advice/Advise
Advise a recommendation; an opinion (noun form)
Advise recommend; counsel (verb form)

Affect/Effect
Affect influence (verb form)
Effect consequence or result (noun form when used in this way)
Effect make happen (verb form when used in this way)

Key each line.

1 We are all ready to learn keyboarding.
2 We have already learned keyboarding techniques.

PRACTICE THE !1 KEY REACH

Be sure to key the numeral 1 (one), not the letter l (el).

Key each line two times.

1 aq1a aq1a aq1a aq1a a1a a1a 11 ask 111 and 11 a1a1
2 11 at 111 ad 11 air 11.111 as 111,11 attire 1a1 at
3 His mailing address was 1 North Elmsquares Avenue.
4 The appointments were on 1/11, 1/1 and 11/1, Mark.
5 Please send me 111 orders of Number 1,111 pencils.

Keep your eyes on the copy.

LOCATE THE %5 KEY

The 5 is keyed with the F finger. Place your fingers on the home keys and practice the reach to 5.

fr5f fr5f fr5f fr5f

PRACTICE THE %5 KEY REACH

Key each line two times.

1 fr5f fr5f fr5f f5f f5f 5 55 555 555 5555 fast 5.5
2 555 fire 55,5 for 55 fan 55 far 5555 fast 5.55 of
3 Send 55 of the first 155 tickets you receive now.
4 The record indicated on 5/1/51 she was born here.
5 The 15 girls visited all 51 sites on February 15.

When keying the numeral 5, keep your other fingers in home key position.

Best Director Guidelines 19
Clint Eastwood 20
Neil Jordan 21
James Ivory 22
Martin Brest 23
Robert Altman 24

Best Actress Guidelines 25
Susan Sarandon 26
Catherine Deneuve 27
Mary McDonnell 28
Michelle Pfeiffer 29
Emma Thompson 30

Best Supporting Actress Guidelines 31
Judy Davis 32
Joan Plowright 33
Vanessa Redgrave 34
Miranda Richardson 35
Marisa Tomei 36

End-of-Lesson Procedure

At the end of each lesson, you will have the following options:

1. To restart the same lesson, press the F1 function key.
2. To return to the Lessons Menu, press ESC. This action automatically will save the completed lesson.
3. To proceed to the next, or any other lesson, highlight your choice on the menu and press Enter.
4. To return to the Main Menu, press ESC again.
5. To print the lesson, select Print Activities.
6. To exit the program:
   a. Select the Exit option and press Enter.
   b. When the DOS prompt appears on the screen, remove your data disk.
   c. Turn off the monitor. (Your instructor also may ask you to turn off the computer and printer.)

LOCATE THE)0 KEY

When keying the numeral 0, keep your J finger in home key position.

The 0 is keyed with the ; finger. Place your fingers on the home keys and practice the reach to 0.

```
;p0; ;p0; ;p0; ;p0;
```

PRACTICE THE)0 KEY REACH

Be sure to key the numeral 0 (zero), not the letter O (oh).

Key each line two times.

```
1 ;p0; ;p0; ;p0; ;0; ;0; ;0; 00 000 ;000; 00 ;or; 0;
2 00 was 000 and; 00.00 ;the; 00 for 0.00 or 00 old.
3 5 0 50 01 05 050 511 510 150 015 01.50 0.015 50 .5
4 af; 150; ;fa 051 fa; 510 a;f 105 ;af 015 5101; 500
5 Contact 501-5010 if you need 50 additional yachts.
```

LEARN NUMBER-READING TECHNIQUES

To key numbers more efficiently, practice the following number-reading techniques:

1. For one-digit numbers, say the number to yourself as you key it.
   Example: 5 Say five.
2. For two-digit numbers, say the number as a unit.
   Example: 55 Say fifty-five.
3. For three-digit numbers, say the first digit as a separate unit and the other two as a unit.
   Example: 511 Say five/eleven.
   Example: 555 Say five/fifty-five.

Learn to Format Table of Contents

Longer reports may include a table of contents to help the reader locate specific headings. A table of contents always includes the headings along with the page number where each one starts. Secondary headings may be included. Refer to your manual of style for the preference. The directions for keying the following table of contents are as follows:

1. Center the words Table of Contents, using the same margins as are used for the report. For this table of contents, there is a 1½-inch left margin and a 1-inch right margin. Key the title in all capital letters and double-space after it.
2. Key the headings at the left margin.
3. Use leaders (a series of dots) to connect the heading to the page number. Leave one space between the last character of the heading and the leader and between the last leader and first character of the longest page number. The page numbers are at the right margin. The leaders for each line should end at the same spot. (With some software packages, you can set a tab with leaders.)
4. Key the page number and press Enter. Single-space secondary headings of the table of contents.
5. Press the Tab key to indent the secondary heading listings.
6. Double-space between secondary headings and headings.

TABLE OF CONTENTS

Best Picture Award Guidelines 1
    A Few Good Men 2
    Unforgiven 3
    Scent of a Woman 4
    The Crying Game 5
    Howard's End 6

Best Actor Award Guidelines 7
    Clint Eastwood 8
    Al Pacino 9
    Stephen Rea 10
    Denzel Washington 11
    Robert Downey, Jr. 12

Best Supporting Actor Guidelines 13
    Jack Nicholson 14
    Jaye Davidson 15
    Gene Hackman 16
    Al Pacino 17
    David Paymer 18

4. For four-digit numbers, say the first two digits as a unit and then the last two as a unit.
   Example: 5511 Say fifty-five/eleven.
   Example: 5555 Say fifty-five/fifty-five.
5. For five-digit numbers, say the first two digits as a unit followed by a group of three.
   Example: 51155 Say fifty-one/one fifty-five.
   Example: 11555 Say eleven/five fifty-five.
6. If the numbers have other characters included in them, read the character as a separate unit and then continue with the pattern.
   Example: 1,111 Say one/comma/one eleven.
   Example: 238-58-9423 Say two thirty-eight/hyphen/fifty-eight/hyphen/ninety-four/twenty-three.

Do not become too concerned if you notice a speed drop in your performance when keying numbers and symbols. As you practice the upper-row reaches, speed performance will increase.

Understand Speed vs. Accuracy

Remember: Concentrate on speed or accuracy.

As you develop keyboarding skills, your progress is reported both in terms of speed (wam) and accuracy (number of errors). However, speed and accuracy should be practiced separately. When you are keying for speed, you should key as quickly as possible without concern for keying errors. To reach new speed goals, you probably will exceed suggested error limits. Once you reach a new speed goal, you can decrease your keying rate slightly to bring the number of errors you make back within the suggested error limits. The rule of thumb is: Increase your keying speed first; then control speed to improve your accuracy.

In this program, "Increase Keying Speed" drills emphasize speed development. "Improve Keying Accuracy" drills emphasize control or accuracy. If you do not reach the accuracy goal, repeat the line.

Always decide on only one goal—speed or accuracy. Do not attempt to accomplish both at the same time.

Exercise 2

In order to reinforce and ensure competency, the student completes a drill and practice session on the microcomputer. Many programs of this type are available to teach basic math skills, phonics, typing, spelling, vocabulary, reading, foreign languages, or almost any repetitive type of learning. The overall effect is usually quite satisfactory.

Measure Progress

Take two 3- or 5-minute timings.

Minimum goal: 3-minute timing—36 wam with six or fewer errors; 5-minute timing—31 wam with ten or fewer errors

It is well known that excellent teachers are hard to find. Computers can be programmed to present the instructional methods of the best teachers and to actually present on video the most outstanding teacher in a given subject area.

In addition, the computer never gets tired or bored. Therefore, repetition and endless practice can be provided. Various studies have concluded repeatedly that many skills can be learned only by repetition. It is all right when a human teacher repeats concepts for slower-paced learners, but the quicker learners may be negatively affected.

If properly used as a teaching tool, the new microcomputers are relatively inexpensive. Based on what the computer can accomplish, the cost of a medium-priced computer is less expensive than the cost of a teacher's aide over the same one-year period. It appears that as the demand for computers increases the cost will continue to decrease.

1 2 3 4 5 6 7 8 9 10

INCREASE KEYING SPEED

Only speed is analyzed and reported.

Key and space quickly.

```
of at or in an it if is to te ti do id di my fa go
an is he at me go bo as of it an am co to if at it
say day aim big way hat dim sit sin bet did war go
won all bar eat did cat ton saw tar vat was zip an
then sign half lake lens hand fish then than hands
```

IMPROVE KEYING ACCURACY

Both speed and accuracy are analyzed and reported.

Minimum goal: 17 wam

Try to exceed the minimum goal.

```
stall eggs hill tall flee need teen seed feed sell
kiss less heel knee hall fell add need skill shall
glee little indeed likeness allied settling assess
skiing lessen haggle feeling endless stiff gallant
egg install fiddle assist attend falling attendant
Edward came to work on 1/15/05 and left on 5/1/05.
51 015 050 1155 5500 15100 10015 5000 501550 5.055
My new ZIP code is 15100.  Janey lost 15.5 pounds.
Call me at 510-5501.  Is her number 510151-001550?
Please send our letters of 5/5/15 and 11/5/05 now.
```

MEASURE PROGRESS

Take two 1-minute timings.

Minimum goal: 20 wam with four or fewer errors 1.3 S.I.

Where are the new orders? We must fill them as soon as possible. The only way we can be competitive is to fill our orders faster than the other companies. If there is a problem, we must all pitch in and work overtime. Of course, you will be paid time-and-a-half for all overtime.

Left-Hand Words

sad dad fad see cad deer fear seer sear veer deed feed seeds
cease freed ad add fed dead dazed tweed secrets creases bear
decreases deceases breed cedar average extract distract west
retreat baste tastes abate after trade wage edge feast beast
We beat a quick retreat after a beast waged a fierce battle.

Both-Hands Words

endow aisle amend blame gland sight focus ivory panel rights
throw usual title dual form handy cycle quake then fight aid
section federal import mileage limited carefully even ounces
develop number hundred certain ready cartoon kindest destiny
Please let us endow the colleges with a careful pledge plan.

Improve Number Skills

Key each line two times. Use the top-row numbers.

9216 8724 2423 1622 9721 2047 3219 2118 8816 9317 7313 8314
2312 5911 5150 3709 2108 1903 7803 4307 1204 6793 5692 3841
3238 1493 9434 8033 8232 4932 2780 7130 1829 3927 5429 7350
4938 2348 3156 5183 9846 3403 7149 3845 7550 9429 7239 5803
2903 2094 1930 9834 9402 9067 1038 3028 7623 6854 0250 0192

Improve Keying Skills

Take two 1-minute timings on each paragraph. Set a speed or an accuracy goal. If you finish before the time is up, start again.

Exercise 1

In the drill and practice mode, the computer does not teach new material but reviews and reinforces already presented material. When a new math concept is presented by a teacher, computer, workbook, or film to a group or individual, the teacher must provide drill and practice material. The teacher may then offer advice about the parts of the program that will affect learning mastery.

END-OF-LESSON PROCEDURE

At the end of each lesson, you will have the following options:

1. To restart the same lesson, press the F1 function key.
2. To return to the Lessons Menu, press ESC. This action automatically will save the completed lesson.
3. To proceed to the next, or any other lesson, highlight your choice and press Enter.
4. To return to the Main Menu, press ESC again.
5. To print the lesson, select Print Activities.
6. To exit the program:
   a. Select the Exit option and press Enter.
   b. When the DOS prompt appears on the screen, remove your data disk.
   c. Turn off the monitor. (Your instructor also may ask you to turn off the computer and printer.)

3 The current reported rate of unemploy-
ment could not be tolerated.

4 Please list all of the known bene-
ficial effects of the drug.

5 He was not happy to learn that the deduc-
tion would not be allowed.

Now key each of the following sentences, correctly dividing the underlined word. Strike the hyphen key at the correct position and then press Enter to end the line.

1 A subdirectory is a division of the disk that
operates as an independent disk.

2 Communication is a two-way process in which
information is exchanged.

3 After a few weeks on the job, it became obvious to
everyone that Rosita was an excellent salesperson.

4 The interoffice memo can be stored electronically for
easy distribution and retrieval.

5 The appropriate information for each of our customers
should be keyed on the proper forms.

Improve Keying Accuracy

Both speed and accuracy are analyzed and reported.

Right-Hand Words

1 hip jip lip kip mile nil lop mop pup ho you join lumph poppy
2 phony mummy yummy oil poll poppy milk hook onion yippy nippy
3 minimum pupil jolly lolly noun minion loony moony holly pool
4 opinion million nylon polio poll oily phony plump hooky pill
5 The pupils put on a phony play for the million opinion poll.

14

3, 7, and 9 Keys

GOALS

- Reinforce Previous Learning
- Learn New Keys 3, 7, and 9
- Learn to Identify Errors
- Learn to Edit, Add, and Delete Copy

Remember the "Get Ready" checklist.

REVIEW

Key each line two times.

```
1 Zero is the winning prize number of quality gifts.
2 The two red tables ordered yesterday just arrived.
3 Texx purchased oil wells instead of topaz jewelry.
4 Al, 1 foot, 15 dogs, 10 nos.  My code is 5151; 50.
5 Volume 15, page 51 states that his age was not 51.
6 The order included:  15150 desks and 10151 chairs.
```

Practice reading numbers in units.

LOCATE THE #3 KEY

The 3 is keyed with the D finger. Place your fingers on the home keys and practice the reach to 3.

```
de3d de3d de3d de3d
```

51 Formatting a Table of Contents

GOALS

- Build Language Arts Skills
- Improve Keying Skills
- Learn to Format a Table of Contents

Review

Key each line two times.

1 junk moth hurry foghorn skiing where lackadaisical

2 Please give me the orders for #3496 & #865 & #012.

3 It's great that music is enjoyed around the world.

4 CD-ROM disks can store large amounts of data and graphics.

Build Language Arts Skills

Dividing Words

Most word-processing programs have automatic word wrap features and automatic dictionary hyphenation. Sometimes, however, word division at the end of a line cannot be avoided if you want the line lengths to appear uniform.

Study the following rules.

- Always divide words between syllables. Use an accepted dictionary to identify the correct syllables in a word.
- Avoid dividing words that are proper nouns.
- Do not divide the last word on a page and the last word in the last full line of a paragraph.
- Divide words after a prefix and before a suffix.

Study the divided words in the following sentences. Key each line. Press Enter to divide the words at the end of each line as indicated.

1 The rooms that were rented would not accom-
modate the entire group.

2 His trial was arranged on the specific pre-
condition that the D. A. required.

Practice the #3 Key Reach

When you key 33, say thirty-three.

Key each line two times.

1 de3d de3d de3d de3d d3d d3d 3 33 333 33 33 d3 d3d3
2 33 did 333 dare 33 debut 33 dorm 33 door 3333 dark
3 3 1 31 3 5 35 3 0 30 33 13 31 53 35 30 03 303 35.3
4 It is 3:33, so send number 3 to check the lid now.
5 The list included checks 13, 33, 35, 351, 153, 30.

Locate the &7 Key

The 7 is keyed with the J finger. Place your fingers on the home keys and practice the reach to 7.

ju7j ju7j ju7j ju7j

Practice the &7 Key Reach

Key each line two times.

1 ju7j ju7j ju7j ju7j j7j j7j j7j j7j 7 77 7j7j 77j7
2 77 jar 77 job 77 jacks 77 jam 77 jip 77 jeer 7 jaw
3 7 1 71 7 5 75 7 3 73 7 0 70 1/75 1/37 7/37 7/ 75.7
4 Your letter of 7/31/75 included 13 of the 75 here.
5 Order 77 was for 37, 73, 75, 70, 17, 707, and 757.

Learning Activity 2

Line 18→ USING MICROCOMPUTERS IN KEYBOARDING

Line 32→ Janice R. Saunders

DS

Department of Office Systems Technology

DS

Pacific Community College

Line 50→ March 11, 1996

END-OF-LESSON PROCEDURE

After completing the activities for this lesson, follow the appropriate end-of-lesson procedure.

LOCATE THE 9 KEY

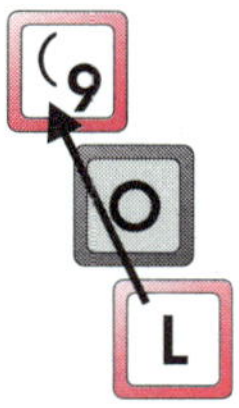

The 9 is keyed with the L finger. Place your fingers on the home keys and practice the reach to 9.

```
lo9l lo9l lo9l lo9l
```

PRACTICE THE 9 KEY REACH

Key each line two times.

Numeral 1, not letter l.

```
1 lo9l lo9l lo9l lo9l l9l l9l 9 9 9 99 9.99 9.9 99.9
2 99 lift 99 low 99 law 99 lure 99 lake 99 look 9999
3 9 1 91 9 7 97 9 3 93 9 5 95 9 0 90 1/99 9/9/9 9779
4 Jimmy sent 33, Sally 79, Kent 95, and Judith 3579.
5 The total invoice was:  99, 97, 93, 95, 90, and 9.
```

INCREASE KEYING SPEED

Only speed is analyzed and reported.

Note: Spaces are used with diagonals here only to emphasize the phrases.

```
1 if it /it is /as is /as it /if he /if in /in it
2 of it /do it /it is /as it /at us /of so /so he
3 art bug cat dud eat far fox had ill fog sap tow
4 non mud out son jar joy gad its but box toy pay
5 ant lake had the sign half disk lane tame eight
```

WORKS CITED

Bolin, D. E. (1982). Vocational Preparation of Persons with Handicaps. Columbus, OH: Charles Merrill, 1982.

Falvey, M. A. Community-based Curriculum: Instructional Strategies for Students with Handicaps. Baltimore: Paul H. Brookes Publishing, 1986.

Moon, S. M., K. J. Inge, P. Wehman, V. Brooke, and J. M. Barcus. Helping Persons with Severe Mental Retardation Get and Keep Employment. Baltimore: Paul H. Brookes Publishing, 1990.

Szymanski, E. M., and J. King. Contemporary Challenges to the Rehabilitation Counseling Profession. Baltimore: Paul H. Brookes Publishing, 1988.

Szymanski, E. M., J. King, R. M. Parker, and W. M. Jenkins. "The State-Federal Rehabilitation Program: Interface with Special Education." Exceptional Children, 56 (1989) 70-77.

Tooman, M. L., W. G. Revell, Jr., and R. P. Melia. "The Role of the Rehabilitation Counselor," Contemporary Challenges to the Rehabilitation Counseling Profession. Baltimore: Paul H. Brookes Publishing, 1988.

Wehman, P., M. S. Moon, J. M. Everson, W. Wood, and J. M. Barcus. Transition from School to Work: New Challenges for Youth with Severe Disabilities. Baltimore: Paul H. Brookes Publishing, 1988.

Wright, T. J., W. G. Emener, and J. M. Ashley. "Rehabilitation Counseling and Client Transition from School to Work." In S. E. Rubin and N. M. Rubin (eds), Contemporary Challenges to the Rehabilitation Counseling Profession. Baltimore: Paul H. Brookes Publishing, 1988.

Improve Keying Accuracy

Key with control—no more than one error per line. Repeat a line if necessary.

Both speed and accuracy are analyzed and reported.

```
The green cathode ray tube is used for displaying.
Down time is when the computer is not functioning.
Visible and vigorous exercise is viewed as worthy.
My last letter of 11/17/97 was mailed at 9:53 p.m.
That length of time was 39 minutes and 59 seconds.
Call 379-993-7937 and order 97 folders and 7 pens.
```

Learn to Identify Errors

Even though the software for this program will identify your keying errors in many exercises, it is an important skill to be able to proofread copy. In some activities, you will need to identify errors by marking them on the printout. In other activities, you will need to identify and correct errors on the screen.

Use this guideline when identifying errors in printed copy:

Count only one error per word. If errors occur in the punctuation and spacing that follow a word, count the word as one error.

Study the following paragraph to see how keying errors are counted. There are eight errors in the paragraph.

```
     Computers ate very imtorpant and valuable in out lives today. It is esssential that weall become familiar with this wonderful tool, If you want to become computer literate, you must have some knolwedge about computers and their operation. Also, you should have some experience using the computer. After identifying errors, the copy should be corrected. In some cases, all the material must be keyed again. With word-processing software, however, most corrections can be made within the copy already keyed.
```

2. Reference entries are single-spaced, with the first line beginning at the left margin and the second and additional lines indented five spaces under the first line. Double-space between each reference entry.
3. Pages of the works-cited list are numbered consecutively with the report. For example, if the last page of your report is 6, the first page of the works cited is assigned page number 7.

Learning Activity 1

1. Start document LES50DC1. Key the works-cited list line for line. If an underlined title covers more than one line, turn off the underline before pressing the Enter key, press the Tab key to indent the next line, and then turn on the underline again. Turn off the page numbering feature since this is not keyed consecutively with the report.
2. Proofread the copy on the screen, and use the editing keys to make corrections. Reformat if necessary.
3. Check the document and print a copy. Note any uncorrected errors on the printout. Save the document.

Learn to Format Cover Pages

Formal reports should include a cover page keyed on a separate sheet of paper. A cover page is not numbered. It contains the title of the report, the author's name and title, and the date of the report. Additional information, such as the school, business, or department name, should be included if needed. Center each line on the cover page between the margins that are used for the report.

The title begins on approximately line 18 and is keyed in all capital letters. The writer's name is keyed on approximately line 32. Any additional information, such as the course or school name, should be keyed a double space below the writer's name. Key the date on approximately line 50.

Learning Activity 2

1. Study the sample cover page on page 320 and key it using the margins and center point for a bound report. The line spacing between the parts may vary, depending on the amount of information included. Name the document LES50DC2.
2. Proofread the copy on the screen. Use the editing keys to make corrections. Reformat if necessary.
3. Have the computer check the document and print a copy. Note any marked errors on the printout.

Learn to Edit Copy

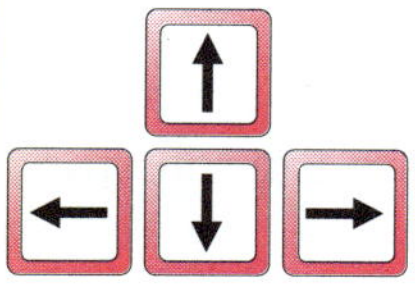

Once a document has been entered, it can be edited on-screen by using the Cursor Movement (Arrow) keys to move to the spot where a correction is needed. These keys are located either as a separate cluster of keys located between the alphabetic keyboard and the 10-key keypad or on the 10-key numeric keypad. Look at your keyboard to determine the location of the Cursor Movement keys.

When these keys are pressed, the cursor moves in the direction indicated by the arrow—left, right, up, or down.

Now do the following:

1. Key this paragraph.

    Selling is a skill and an art. You can learn the skills, but the unique application of those skills is an art form.

2. Practice using the Arrow keys by doing the following:

    Move the cursor under the r in art.

    Move the cursor to the right under the n in learn.

    Move the cursor down under the q in unique.

    Move the cursor to the left under the u in but.

Practice moving the cursor to other locations until you are comfortable with the procedure.

Before printing a document, you should proofread it on the screen. Use the Arrow keys to move to the beginning of a document. Then use the Down-Arrow key to scroll through the document as you proof it for errors.

Once you have printed a document, you should proof the printed copy for errors you may have missed.

When keying composition and application documents, you will be able to move the cursor to any location within the document. You will then be able to insert or delete text if you desire. You will not be able to use the Arrow keys during drills or Measure Progress activities.

Learn to Format Works-Cited List

At the end of a formal report in which you have keyed internal citations, you must provide a listing of all those citations. Cite each source by presenting the information in the following order:

1. Author(s), name inverted (last name first) for first listing; additional authors' names are not inverted
2. Title
3. Place of publication or presentation (books and speeches) Magazine title and volume or other work in which an article was published
4. Publisher
5. Date of publication or presentation
6. Pages (if part of a larger work)

Examples:

Book

Sherron, Jo Ann E. and Ronald H. Sherron. *EMC Keyboarding and Applications*. St. Paul, MN: EMC Publishing, 1993.

Speech

Venduzi, C. Keynote Address. Twenty-fifth Annual Meeting of Midwest Lawyers. Chicago, Dec. 19-21, 1994.

Article

Remakeo, L. "Computers in the Classroom." *American Journal of Educators* 11 (1995): 15-22.

The format for the works-cited list depends on the manual of style being used. The format presented in this lesson is consistent with the report in the previous lesson, but a manual of style always should be consulted to be sure the references are consistent with the report.

The citations are arranged in alphabetical order by author. The directions for keying the works-cited list shown in this lesson are as follows:

1. A 2-inch margin should be left at the top of the page. The title is centered between the margins being used and is keyed in all capital letters. Double-space after the title.

Learn to Add and Delete Copy

When you identify errors in copy that already has been keyed, you can correct the copy before printing. In some software programs, you can replace the incorrect characters by keying over them. In other software programs, you must first delete the incorrect character and then key the correct character. In this program, you can insert characters at the cursor position. If you are changing an incorrect character, it is best to delete the incorrect character first and then key the correct character.

Practice adding/inserting characters by doing the following:

1. Key `Micrcompiter Fornating` exactly as shown with the errors.
2. Identify the keying errors in the words.
3. Move the cursor under the second *c* in `Micrcompiter.`
4. Key `o`. Notice that the *o* is inserted in the proper place and the cursor moves under the *c*. To add omitted text, you move the cursor to the character to the right of the point where you wish to add text, and key the omitted character. It is then inserted.
5. Move the cursor under the *t* in `Fornating.`
6. Key `t`. The new character is inserted.

To delete or correct a character:

1. Move the cursor under the *i* in `compiter`. Before you can key the correct character, you must delete the *i*. With the cursor under the *i*, press the Delete key. Notice that the *i* is removed from the screen and the text automatically moves over to fill in the space. Now key u. Remember: If you have unwanted characters, you must delete them using the Delete key before keying the correct character.
2. Use the Delete key to delete the incorrect character in `Fornatting.` Then insert the proper character so that the word is correct.
3. Remember: You also can use the Backspace key to delete incorrect characters. Position your cursor at the end of the word `Formatting.` Backspace two times. Notice that a character is removed each time you backspace. Now key the correct characters again.
4. Practice adding, deleting, and backspacing until you are comfortable with these editing keys.

You will be able to use these editing keys only in the composition and word-processor activities.

Exercise 2

Those adverse to constant repetition of vowel sounds and syllables in reading skills, spelling, and vocabulary and the drill and practice required in mathematics may find it easier if the drills are handled by the computer. The computer, along with various software editions, is able to summarize learning and essential points as well as to review previously taught content.

Measure Progress

Minimum goal: 3-minute timing—35 wam with six or fewer errors; 5-minute timing—30 wam with ten or fewer errors

Take two 3- or 5-minute timings.

In the future, our society may see many changes. Companions and pets may be custom-designed. Aging may become obsolete as new parts are implanted or replaced for control by our brain. The ultimate may be a brain transplant into a never-aging humanoid body impervious to disease. Loneliness will be banished as a variety of specialized companions are made available to individuals. Labor and drudgery may be unknown as robots do all of our distasteful tasks. Manual labor, garbage collection, building maintenance, and most service and repair tasks will be completed by robots.

Social hierarchies may be based on knowledge and interpersonal skills. Self-actualization opportunities will be infinite as unlimited energy sources are provided. The future will indeed be rosy if we can rise above our selfishness. Perhaps our latest ally, the computer, will help us solve some of our problems and help us to reach our true potential.

MEASURE PROGRESS

Minimum goal: 21 wam with four or fewer errors 1.5 S.I.

Try to exceed the minimum goal.

Take two 1-minute timings.

In word processing, duplicating means to copy. In order to copy data from the monitor screen, you must follow the copy instructions in your computer manual or software program. Copy is a BASIC language command. If you want hard copy or print copy of your work, you will use the print instructions or print command.

There are times when the computer is not functioning properly. This time is called down time. Down time may hamper production schedules.

END-OF-LESSON PROCEDURE

At the end of each lesson, you will have the following options:

1. To restart the same lesson, press the F1 function key.
2. To return to the Lessons Menu, press ESC. This action automatically will save the completed lesson.
3. To proceed to the next, or any other lesson, highlight your choice on the menu and press Enter.
4. To return to the Main Menu, press ESC again.
5. To print the lesson, select Print Activities.
6. To exit the program:
   a. Select the Exit option and press Enter.
   b. When the DOS prompt appears on the screen, remove your data disk.
   c. Turn off the monitor. (Your instructor also may ask you to turn off the computer and printer.)

4 The secretary is not averse to learning the new computer procedures.

5 The statue of the late president was very impressive.

6 His seven-foot stature was most imposing.

7 The statute of limitations has expired on the felony charges.

Now key each of the following sentences, choosing the correct word.

1 The students in the class were especially skilled at (addition, edition).

2 The new (addition, edition) of the text was eagerly awaited.

3 All of the students were (adverse, averse) to the new school rules.

4 Did the new rules have an (adverse, averse) effect on the students?

5 The legislature was responsible for enacting the new (statues, statures, statutes).

6 The (statues, statures, statutes) on Monument Avenue were badly in need of repair.

7 The senator was a person of high (statue, stature, statute).

Improve Keying Skills

Take two 1-minute timings on each paragraph. Set a speed or an accuracy goal. If you complete the paragraph before time runs out, start over.

Exercise 1

The computer never tires and can present the same material over and over without flaw or error. It is reliable and consistent in its presentation of data. This makes the computer an excellent drill and practice machine. The computer is especially useful in teaching math or other skills that require drill and practice.

15 2, 4, 6, and 8 Keys

GOALS

- Reinforce Previous Learning
- Learn New Keys 2, 4, 6, and 8
- Learn to Name, Save, Print, and Retrieve a Document
- Practice Composition Skills

REVIEW

Remember the "Get Ready" checklist.

Key each line two times.

1 An author is an originator of the stored document.
2 Store my computer documents on the storage medium.
3 Raze the yellow building for luxury prize hazards.
4 Rob asked Sara to keyboard the letter by 7:39 p.m.
5 Were the 9730 items not delivered on 10/1 at 3:09?
6 Orders 79, 30, 91, 15, 59, 13, 157, 173 are ready.
7 Please send tickets 973, 591, 715, 309, 510, 5170.

When you key 7:39, say seven/colon/thirty-nine.

LOCATE THE @2 KEY

The 2 is keyed with the S finger.

sw2s sw2s sw2s sw2s

50

Formatting Works-Cited List and Cover Pages

GOALS

- Build Language Arts Skills
- Improve Keying Skills
- Learn to Format Works-Cited List
- Learn to Format Cover Pages

Review

Key each line two times.

```
1 in my/so it was/a no it is/do it at/and so it goes
2 The original outlay only outfitted your one group.
3 The receipts #984 and #5985 were received in June.
4 Document-processing programs revolutionized our
  office work.
```

Build Language Arts Skills

Word Usage

Understand the correct usage of the following words.

Addition/Edition
Addition results of adding; combine or join
Edition specific version of printed material

Adverse/Averse
Adverse acting against; opposed to
Averse feeling of distaste; reluctance

Statue/Stature/Statute
Statue a manufactured image of something
Stature height of something; rank or status
Statute a law enacted by a legislative body

Key each line.

```
1 The addition of another computer would reduce the
  workload.
2 Often the second edition of a book is better than the
  first edition.
3 An adverse vote was reported from the senate.
```

Practice the @2 Key Reach

Key each line two times.

Keep your fingers curved.

1 sw2s sw2s sw2s sw2s s2s s2s s2s s2s 2 22 saw 22.22

2 22 silly 22 shoe 22 skirt 22 sure 222 sat 22.2 set

3 2 1 21 2 0 20 2 5 25 22 23 2/35 5/22 1/22 21/25 22

4 Flight 72 left at 2:27 on 2/2/92. It is 2:32 a.m.

5 These missing items are 201, 129, 723, 91, and 20.

Locate the $4 Key

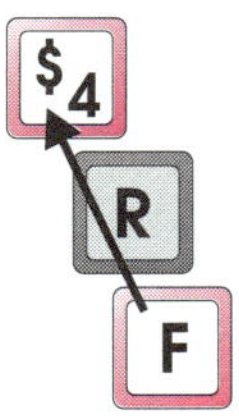

The 4 is keyed with the F finger.

fr4f fr4f fr4f fr4f

Practice the $4 Key Reach

Key each line two times.

When keying the numeral 4, keep the A finger in home key position.

1 fr4f fr4f fr4f fr4f f4f f4f f4f 44 four 44 far 444

2 44 fire 44 free 444 fore 44 file 444 fold 44.4 fig

3 4 1 41 4 2 42 4 5 45 4 0 40 1 44 14 1/44 4/41 4/40

4 My order arrived on 4/4/94. A gross is 144 items.

5 Please check these items: 40, 42, 24, 14, and 45.

a school district or a cooperative of districts (Szymanski & King, 1989); however, most counselors are employed by state vocational rehabilitation agencies and often have limited time and resources to devote to coordination of transition services.

Whether a counselor is school-based or state-agency-based, his or her activities may include career and psychosocial counseling; consultation with special education and vocational education teachers, school counselors, and other professionals; coordination with school, family and community efforts in career planning and implementation; job placement, analysis, modification, restructuring, and placement follow-up; coordination of job support services; referral to and coordination with adult services; planning and coordination with post secondary programs; and development of individual transition plans (Szymanski & King, 1989; Wright, Emener, & Ashely, 1988).

Adapted from "The Rehabilitation Counselor's Desk Top to Supported Employment," Virginia Commonwealth University

End-of-Lesson Procedure

At the end of each lesson, you will have the following options:

1. To restart the same lesson, press the F1 function key.
2. To return to the Lessons Menu, press ESC. This action automatically will save the completed lesson.
3. To proceed to another lesson, highlight your choice on the menu and press Enter.
4. To return to the Main Menu, press ESC again.
5. To print the lesson, select Print Activities.
6. To exit the program:
   a. Select the Exit option and press Enter.
   b. When the DOS prompt appears on the screen, remove your data disk.
   c. Turn off the monitor. (Your instructor also may ask you to turn off the computer and printer.)

Locate the ^6 Key

The 6 is keyed with the J finger.

ju6j ju6j ju6j ju6j

Practice the ^6 Key Reach

When keying the numeral 6, keep the ; finger in home key position.

Key each line two times.

1 ju6j ju6j ju6j ju6j j6j j6j j6j j6j 6 66 66.6 6/66

2 6 jar 66 juice 66 jury 66 janitor 66 judge 666 jam

3 6 66 6 1 61 6 5 65 6 4 64 6 3 63 56 0 60 466 76756

4 The computer compared 646 items with 626 criteria.

5 Ticket sales for 6, 65, 61, 16, 676 were reported.

Locate the *8 Key

The 8 is keyed with the K finger.

ki8k ki8k ki8k ki8k

TRANSITION FROM SCHOOL TO WORK

Students with Disabilities

Transition from school to work is a process that focuses on the movement of students with disabilities from school into the world of work. Facilitating a student's transition from a school program to the workplace requires movement through school instruction, planning for the transition process, and placement into meaningful community integrated employment (Wehman, Moon, Everson, Wood, & Barcus, 1988). Currently, special education and vocational rehabilitation programs are required by legislation to cooperatively plan for the transition of students with disabilities into the work environment.

Effective transition planning and implementation require the participation, cooperation, and coordination of all local school and adult service agencies that provide services and support to individuals with disabilities. A team effort increases the chances that all the necessary services and support are made available to a student so as to ensure a smooth transition into the labor force upon graduation. The rehabilitation counselor is a key player in the transition of students from school to work and must be an active participant in the transition team planning and implementation (Tooman, Revell, & Melia, 1988).

Counselor's Role

A rehabilitation counselor's role in transition programs varies according to the local needs and resources (Szymanski & King, 1989). In a few instances, rehabilitation counselors are school-based and employed by

Practice the *8 Key Reach

Key each line two times.

1 ki8k ki8k ki8k ki8k k8k k8k k8k k8k 8 88 8.88 .808

2 88 kite 88 kidney 88 kettle 888 kazoos 888.88 keys

3 8 88 884 886 883 388 588 288 881 2/82 28/850 14/85

4 It was 8:38 p.m. when my piece of luggage arrived.

5 Sales in 1987 increased by 86, 84, 80, 181, or 27.

Increase Keying Speed

Note: Spaces are used with the diagonals to emphasize the phrases.

Only speed is analyzed and reported.

1 to it /at up /to no /in my /do it so /on it /do a

2 by my /on it /is no /in so /so it is /as it /a to

3 must want true area quit rely room move dove love

4 sale must take here list hall want mark head take

5 In ancient times persons counted on their fingers.

6 Real speedy computers and calculators do formulas.

7 Does the military use a large number of computers?

8 The missile guidance system is computer-based now.

9 Most department stores use computers for checkout.

10 Robots controlled by a computer will do hard jobs.

11 At 8:26 p.m. the word-processing material was due.

12 Did Ed Smit install the new disk drive on 7/22/96?

Learn to Create Documents

A big advantage of computer software programs is the ability to "save" a document you have created. Once saved, the document can be recalled at a later time for editing corrections or other reference purposes. In order for the computer to find the correct document saved in "memory," you must assign a file name to the document.

Learn to Format Bound Reports With Internal Citations

1. Longer, more formal reports usually are placed in a cover or folder and are bound or stapled on the left side. Because extra space needs to be allowed on the left side for the binding, the left margin is moved to the right ½ inch.
2. For a bound report, use a 1½-inch left margin and a 1-inch right margin. With 10-pitch type, margins are at 15 and 75.
3. The center point should be centered between the margins; therefore, it is necessary to move the centering point of the paper to the right. For bound reports, use a center point of 46 for 10 pitch. Your software automatically will handle centering based on the margins you set.
4. Many times when writing a formal report, you borrow information from other written or spoken materials. You must give credit to the author or speaker if you are using his or her words or ideas in your written material. Even if you paraphrase the work (put it in your own words), you must indicate the source. These references are referred to as citations because you are citing or quoting someone else. Before formatting a formal report with quoted material, consult a style manual for the best way to acknowledge quoted material. In general, quoted material of less than four lines is keyed inside quotation marks. Quoted material of four or more lines is keyed single- or double-spaced, depending on the style manual used, and indented five spaces from the left and right margins. Quotation marks are not used with longer quotations that are indented.
5. One method used to indicate a source is to cite the author, year, and page number of the reference in the body of the report. The complete reference information is then listed in a bibliography, which is placed at the end of the report.

Learning Activity 1

1. Start document LES49DC1. Key the bound report with cited material on the following pages. Adjust the margins. Pay special attention to the format of the reference citations.
2. Proofread the copy on the screen and use the editing keys to make any corrections. Reformat if necessary.
3. Have the computer check your document and print a copy. Note any uncorrected errors on the printout.

Naming a Document

Various software programs have different rules for assigning file names. Most have restrictions on the number of characters that can be used (usually no more than eight). Some specify that no numbers, symbols, or spaces may be used in the name. Before assigning file names, consult the user's manual for the software program you are using.

The name you assign a document should be meaningful. It should help you find the document in the future. Because of character limitations, you will often abbreviate file names. Many operators use codes to identify the type of document such as "let" for letters or "mem" for memorandums.

When using the software that accompanies this textbook, the drills and Measure Progress exercises for each lesson automatically are named and saved when you exit the lesson. For example, the file name for Lesson 6 would be LESSON6.

For composition exercises and document formatting applications, which are completed using the word processor, you must assign the file name. Follow these steps:

1. When either a composition or document formatting activity is selected within a lesson, the program automatically branches to the word processor. A screen menu similar to the following will appear.

2. If you want to start a new document, select the first choice, "New Document." When prompted for the document name, follow these guidelines:

For a composition exercise:

- Key LES for "Lesson."
- Key two digits for the lesson number.
- Key CM for "Composition."
- Key another numeral for the composition in the lesson. (For example, use "1" for the first composition.)
- An example of a complete file name is LES15CM1.

Exercise 2

An organization that produces an inferior product may survive for a short period of time. Over the long run, companies that continue to produce a shoddy product will lose a significant portion of their market share. In essence, such companies waive their right to customer confidence. Who's really responsible for quality products? Whether or not this question can be answered is up for debate.

Measure Progress

Take two 3- or 5-minute timings.

Minimum goal: 3-minute timing—35 wam with six or fewer errors; 5-minute timing—30 wam with ten or fewer errors

Adult education is an old art but a young profession. We have very little valid research to guide our efforts. Educators have been an impossible but intriguing combination of administrator, teacher, accountant, psychiatrist, warden, and janitor. In this confusing role, a teacher attempts to be all things to all people.

Modern adult educators have access to a variety of professional resources to assist them in fulfilling their role. The professionals are the "image makers," media specialists, and communications experts. We need to organize a promotional team of adult educators, media personnel, and advertising experts to design a comprehensive promotional campaign that will make adult education as well known and accepted as soft drinks, toothpaste, and soup.

There are far too many under-educated adults in the country today. Both federal and state governments need to give more attention to this population.

For a document formatting application:

- Key LES for "Lesson."
- Key two digits for the lesson number.
- Key DC for "Document."
- Key another numeral for the document number within the lesson. (Example: use "1" for the first document; "2" for the second, etc.)

An example of a complete file name is LES22DC1.

Saving a Document

After completing a composition exercise or a document formatting application, press ESC to indicate that you are done. The following prompt will appear in the center of the screen:

Use the Up-Arrow or Down-Arrow keys to highlight your choice and press Enter.

Follow these guidelines for making a selection.

1. Select "Resume Editing" if you want to return to the document to do more work.
2. Select "Save" to save your work and return to the word-processing screen to make another choice or continue your work. This command will add the document to the "Existing Files" list.
3. Select "Exit/Save" if you want to save completed work and you want to exit from the word processor. This choice returns you to the "Existing Files" menu. Your new document should now be listed. At this point, you may select or create another file or press ESC to go to the Main Menu.
4. Select "Exit Without Saving" if you want to exit from the word processor without saving any completed work. **CAUTION:** When you select this choice, you will lose any work completed during that lesson. Be careful! Work not saved cannot be retrieved.
5. Select "Check (show errors)" if you are doing a production exercise that the computer will grade.

6 They will have to decide whether or not the profits will be shared.

7 Who's going to pick up the last delivery?

8 Whose idea was it to sell the property?

Now key each of the following sentences, choosing the correct word.

1 The (waives, waves) at the ocean were too rough for swimming.

2 The (tenants, tenets) (waived, waved) (there, their) rights to the property.

3 The (weather, whether) during the storm caused all the vacationers much concern.

4 We did not know (weather, whether) to leave or stay during the storm.

5 (Who's, whose) to make the evacuation decisions?

6 (Who's, whose) turn is it to clean the house?

Improve Keying Skills

Take two 1-minute timings on each paragraph. Set a speed or an accuracy goal.

Exercise 1

Rewards are more motivating than punishment and are certainly the preferable means if one has a choice. Often fear of failure motivates workers to exceed expectations. Research shows that companies that adequately reward their employees have a more loyal group of workers. Whether to use reward or punishment is often a decision based on the management style of the company.

PRINTING A DOCUMENT

All documents must be saved before they can be printed. To print a saved document, bring the Main Menu to the screen. Select "Print Activities." A Printing Menu similar to the following will appear.

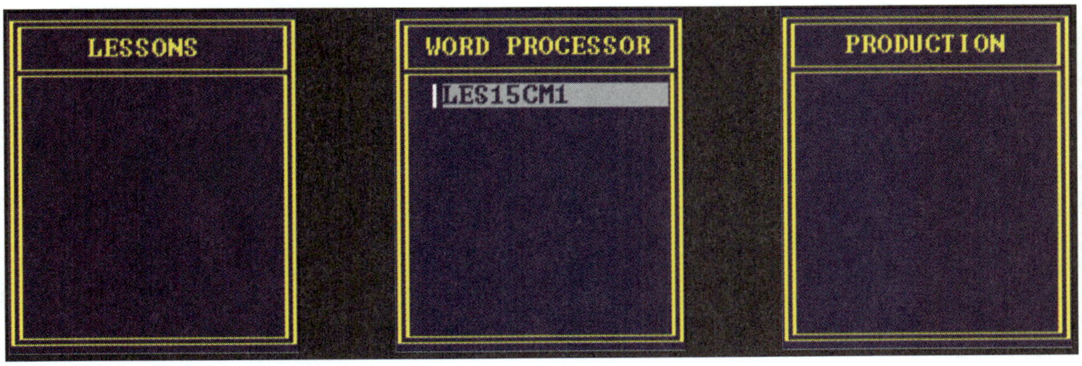

Lessons are listed by number under "Lessons." Composition exercises are listed by file names under the heading "Word Processor." Document formatting applications are listed by file names under the heading "Production." Use the Right-, Left-, Up-, and Down-Arrow keys to highlight the document you want to print and press Enter. The following prompt will appear in the center of the screen.

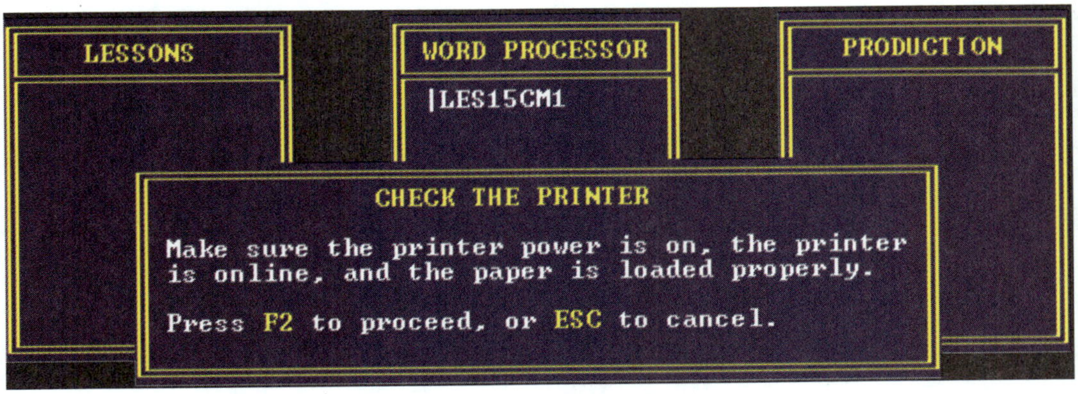

Your completed copy will include your name, the date that the document was printed, and the document file name. Retain the printout for your records or submit it to your instructor for evaluation.

It is a good idea to print your documents soon after completing them. If a document file name appears on the Printing Menu, it can be edited or printed as many times as you find necessary. Once it is removed from the menu, however, it cannot be retrieved. This software program saves only the last ten documents in each of the three categories.

49

Formatting Bound Reports and Internal Citations

GOALS

- Build Language Arts Skills
- Improve Keying Skills
- Learn to Format Bound Reports with Internal Citations

Review

Key each line two times.

```
1 go of in us are fin pet own bag you sat not banned
2 spot flag with gale call more tear rise next deeds
3 1 2 3 5 7 9 23 24 68 53 79 102 953 457 865 304 604
4 You are going on spring break with us in April of
  next year.
```

Build Language Arts Skills

Word Usage

Understand the correct usage of the following words.

Waive/Wave
Waive forgo
Wave hand signal; curl in hair; surge of water

Weather/Whether
Weather condition of atmosphere
Whether introduction of alternatives

Who's/Whose
Who's contraction of *who is*
Whose possessive form of *who*

Key each line.

```
1 The lawyer decided to waive that preliminary hearing.
2 Wave when you are ready to leave the meeting.
3 The wave in her hair fell over her left shoulder.
4 The large wave broke over the stern of the boat.
5 The weather grew steadily worse.
```

Retrieving a File

When a composition or document formatting activity is selected, any documents already created, named, and saved appear on a menu titled "Existing Files." Use the Up-Arrow or Down-Arrow keys to highlight the file you want to work with and press Enter. That document will then come to the screen.

Measure Progress

Minimum goal: 22 wam with four or fewer errors 1.6 S.I.

Try to exceed the minimum goal.

Take two 1-minute timings.

Word-processing programs are a very helpful tool in the modern office. They save a lot of time in producing final copy for correspondence and different kinds of manuscripts. Used with various types of graphics software, many very attractive report formats can be produced. There are a number of excellent word-processing programs available, but before purchasing one, be sure to try it out to see if it meets your needs.

Composition Exercise

Composition exercises included in this program give you an opportunity to create original documents while gaining practice using the word processor. For these exercises you will not key in material from the textbook or the screen. The contents of each document will be your own.

Your first composition document is LES15CM1.

Compose a draft sentence for each of the words listed below. Do not worry about errors for your first attempt. Try to key quickly; do not hesitate. Just get your thoughts down.

judgment difference quantity assume realize

Proofread the document on the screen. Use the editing keys to make any corrections. Save and print the exercise.

Proofread the printout and mark any errors you may have missed. Retrieve the document to the screen and make any more corrections that may be necessary. Save and print your corrected copy.

Conclusions

We should send a representative to this meeting each year, as it appears to be on the frontier of new keyboarding ideas and techniques. The idea of adopting a new style of keyboard for our office equipment is not feasible at this stage of development. At any rate, it is doubtful that the manufacturers will provide alternative keyboards.

We should explore the new laser disk technology for our training department. This technology has the capability to show one frame or image at a time or to show a series as a moving picture. Slow motion, fast action, and a number of other AV activities can be performed. Laser disk technology promises to be one of our most versatile tools.

END-OF-LESSON PROCEDURE

At the end of each lesson, you will have the following options:

1. To restart the same lesson, press the F1 function key.
2. To return to the Lessons Menu, press ESC. This action automatically will save the completed lesson.
3. To proceed to the next, or any other lesson, highlight your choice on the menu and press Enter.
4. To return to the Main Menu, press ESC again.
5. To print the lesson, select Print Activities.
6. To exit the program:
   a. Select the Exit option and press Enter.
   b. When the DOS prompt appears on the screen, remove your data disk.
   c. Turn off the monitor. (Your instructor also may ask you to turn off the computer and printer.)

REPORT OF A KEYBOARDING CONFERENCE

Location

The conference was held at the Plains Hotel in Omaha, Nebraska, on July 21, 1997. This conference was the annual conference of keyboarding researchers and practitioners.

Sessions Attended

Keyboarding theory. This session compared and contrasted the various approaches to teaching basic keyboarding. One of the theories discussed treated the problem of changing the standard keyboard to a simpler and more efficient keyboard design. The conclusion was that unless everyone made the change people would have to learn two or more keyboards. This change would result in much confusion and inefficiency.

New products. Several sessions dealt with new microcomputer word-processing software and electronic typewriters. One electronic typewriter that held considerable interest could check punctuation, spelling, and grammar. None of the electronic typewriters, however, performed as well as the microcomputers with word-processing software.

16 Skill Building

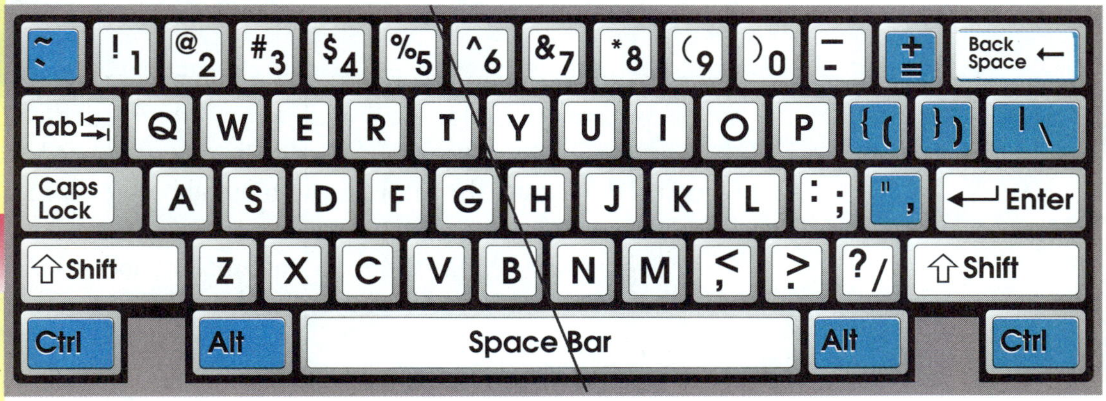

GOALS

- Reinforce Previous Learning
- Increase Keying Speed
- Improve Skill in Keying Top-row Numbers
- Practice Composition Skills

Remember the "Get Ready" checklist.

Review

Key each line two times.

```
1 Janice created 9,684 prizes for Tex and the queen.
2 Computers do dumb duties better than 1,000 people.
3 The number 99 is thought to be unlucky by the mob.
4 The series contained 1, 2, 3, 4, 5, 6, 7, and 189.
5 The tax yield qualified all budget annual reviews.
```

Develop Keying Skills with Numbers

Key across the columns.

Read four-digit numbers in groups of two: 2896 twenty-eight/ninety-six.

Key the exercise twice. Press the space bar twice between each group of numbers.

```
1 2896  3429  2338  2897  3510  2652
2 6247  2489  7898  0128  1987  3178
3 3629  1050  4264  7246  1440  4254
4 4289  2244  1312  6950  1610  1234
5 6215  6381  1510  1794  1763  0987
```

Learn to Format Unbound Reports with Secondary and Paragraph Headings

Reports often contain secondary and paragraph headings. These headings provide a logical presentation of the material and call the reader's attention to the main ideas of the report. The format of these headings may vary, depending on the manual of style being used. Consult the appropriate manual before formatting a report.

1. *Secondary headings* are the first major subdivision within a report. Secondary headings are keyed beginning at the left margin in upper- and lowercase letters and are underscored. Double-space before and after the heading.
2. *Paragraph headings* are subdivisions after the secondary heading. The paragraph heading begins at the paragraph indention. Only the first letter of the heading is capitalized. The paragraph heading is followed by a period and is underscored. Do not underscore the punctuation. The text begins on the same line as the heading, two spaces after the period.

Learning Activity 2

1. Key the report on the next two pages in correct format. This is document LES48DC2.
2. Proofread the copy on the screen and use the editing keys to make corrections. Reformat if necessary.
3. Have the computer check the document and print a copy. Note any marked errors on the printout.

End-of-Lesson Procedure

After completing the activities for this lesson, follow the appropriate end-of lesson procedure.

1. To restart the same lesson, press the F1 function key.
2. To return to the Lessons Menu, press ESC.
3. To proceed to another lesson, highlight your choice on the menu and press Enter.
4. To return to the Main Menu, press ESC again.
5. To print the lesson, select Print Activities.
6. To exit the program:
   a. Select the Exit option and press Enter.
   b. When the DOS prompt appears on the screen, remove your data disk.
   c. Turn off the monitor. (Your instructor also may ask you to turn off the computer and printer.)

Increase Keying Speed

Only speed is analyzed and reported.

Read and key in phrases.

1 do no /my by /go at /am it /to go /go to /in an end
2 go to by my /of it at /is it in /do in go /go at it
3 her day /put the /did not /you are /new car /so any
4 rain cook boys mind pear faze tear vote fades have
5 fork pair melt hair form soak down wisp pale gowns

Improve Keying Accuracy

Both speed and accuracy are analyzed and reported.

Try to maintain speed, but key with control—no more than one error per line.

1 John sold 46,734 sets of pens, and Sue sold 6,472.
2 Bring 282 envelopes, 71 cards, and 36 paper clips.
3 The combination is 6 right, 2 left, and back to 0.
4 The combinations of 100 and 500 equaled 1,572,689.
5 If I add 139,462 to 157,382 will it equal 996,884?
6 Take the 32.46 from Juan and give Bettie 4,650.50.
7 My number is 749-6843. Is your number 34231-5689?
8 If number 75689 rings, transfer it to extension 4.
9 What is the total of 981, 472, 301, 695, and 4031?
10 Bring me number 462, 793, 502, 103, 986, and 6381.

the "n," the Enter key, and the Space Bar. A minimum criterion performance level based on subject scores for one-minute timed writings was specified. A formative evaluation design was used in program tryout and revision. Sixty-six community college nontypists participated in three tryout cycles: initial developmental testing, Field Test A, and Field Test B. Two sources of background information were collected for each subject: demographic data and keyboarding aptitude data.

Diagnostic and revision data were analyzed from subjects' performance scores, time required to complete the program, researcher's technique ratings, subjects' interviews, and researcher's observations. Ninety percent of the subjects in Field Test A achieved the instructional objectives and reached the criterion level. Ninety percent of the subjects in Field Test B also reached criterion level.

The revisions made to the program during the formative evaluation process made the program more efficient as evidenced by the reduction in time required to complete the program. The decrease in the number of problems identified after each testing cycle also indicated that the program became more effective. Based on data analyzed from the study, the microcomputer is an effective medium for teaching initial keyboarding skills. The study recommends that teachers of typewriting or keyboarding consider microcomputer-based instruction as a teaching method.

Measure Progress

Exercise 1

Minimum goal: 23 wam with three or fewer errors 1.6 S.I.

Performance goals for the lesson are based on the 1-minute timings.

Take two 1-minute timings.

The ability to store basic paragraphs and form letters allows great variety and the ability to individualize correspondence. The added features of format changes, typestyle changes, and spelling checks are most attractive to various users. A variety of word-processing programs are available. Each brand has different features that you must learn. Some are easier to learn than others. DisplayWrite and WordPerfect are examples of two popular brands of word-processing software. Both are excellent word-processing programs.

Exercise 2

Minimum goal: 20 wam with six or fewer errors

Take two 2-minute timings on the preceding paragraph.

Composition Exercise

Using the word processor, name a document LES16CM1. Key your responses to the following questions on the screen. Do not worry about format or errors for now. Just try to get your thoughts down.

1. Where do you live? (Street, city, state, zip)
2. What are your parents' full names?
3. How long have you been learning to keyboard, and who is your instructor?
4. What do you like best about learning to keyboard?
5. What were three of the most difficult things for you to learn?
6. How will you use your new keyboarding skills?

Proofread the document on the screen. Use the editing keys to make corrections. Save and print the document.

Proofread the printout and mark any errors you may have missed. Make corrections if necessary. Save and print your corrected copy.

Follow the proper end-of-lesson procedure.

Learning Activity 1

1. Format the following two-page report. This is document LES48DC1.
2. Double-space the body of a report and indent each paragraph five spaces.
3. Begin keying the title on line 13 of page 1. Center the title and key it in all capital letters. Titles that are too long to fit attractively on one line should be broken into two or more lines and keyed in an inverted pyramid form. An inverted pyramid form means that the first line of a title is longer than the second, which in turn is longer than the third. Think of a pyramid that is turned upside down, an inverted pyramid, and you will be able to remember how to format a long title. Double-space between each line of the title. Double-space after the last line.
4. Number the pages beginning with page 2. The software automatically will number the pages. Leave a 1-inch top margin on the second page.
5. Leave 1-inch side margins. Leave at least a 1-inch bottom margin (6 blank lines). Do not key below line 60.
6. Leave at least two lines of a paragraph at the bottom of a page and carry at least two lines of a paragraph to the top of the next page. Do not have only one line from a paragraph appear either at the bottom or top of a page.
7. Proofread your copy on the screen. Use the editing keys to make corrections. Reformat if necessary.
8. Have the computer check the document and print a copy. Note any marked errors on the printout.

AN EMPIRICALLY VALIDATED MODEL PROGRAM FOR TEACHING

ALPHABETIC KEYBOARDING SKILLS VIA MICROCOMPUTER

The purpose of this study was the systematic development and formative evaluation of a research-based model program for teaching alphabetic keyboarding skills via microcomputer. A microcomputer instructional program was developed based on instructional strategies and psychological concepts that were considered appropriate during the early stages of teaching typewriting. These strategies and concepts were identified from a review of the literature and validated by subject-matter experts.

The model program was presented in two lessons and provided instruction on keyboarding the home row, the "e,"

17

Apostrophe, Quotation Mark, Exclamation Point, and Dollar Sign Keys

GOALS

- Reinforce Previous Learning
- Learn New Keys ', ", !, and $
- Increase Keying Speed

Review

Remember the "Get Ready" checklist.

Key each line two times.

```
1 Computer keyboarding is a skill that creates jobs.
2 Persons who can promptly access a computer are OK.
3 If it is in the red car, you may drive it to work.
4 Now is the time to learn to use keyboarding skill.
5 Can you add 1, 2, 3, 4, 5, 6, 7, 8, 9, 10, 20, 30?
```

Locate the Apostrophe " ' Key

The ' (apostrophe) is located to the right of the ; and is keyed with the ; finger. Key this line.

```
;'; ;'; ;'; ;';
```

Exercise 2

There are various opportunities to network that should always be taken. The informal communication and contacts made at conferences and social events can be very valuable to salespeople and managers. Many resources and opportunities are discovered through informal channels. One tenet should be remembered. Do not discuss anything at informal gatherings that you do not want communicated, as the informal network is very efficient.

Measure Progress

Minimum goal: 3-minute timing—34 wam with six or fewer errors; 5-minute timing—29 wam with ten or fewer errors

Take two 3- or 5-minute timings.

With proper application of computer technology, students may be more motivated than students in traditional classes. Software that incorporates motivational factors such as fantasy, curiosity, challenge, feedback, immediate knowledge of results, positive rewards, and student control should increase motivation and enhance the learning environment.

Students must be paced (forced to key at a faster rate) to help them develop proper stroking patterns that are essential for developing keying proficiency. Several methods of pacing have been used effectively. One is teacher-paced dictation. During early lessons, many teachers key with the students on selected drill material, calling aloud the keys to be keyed in a sharp, brisk voice. This forces students to attempt to keep up and force the rate. Although this method works well during the first few days of instruction, differences in students' performances develop rapidly, and other methods are more effective.

Practice the Apostrophe " ' Key Reach

Key each line two times.

Do not space before the apostrophe. Space after an apostrophe only if it is at the end of a word.

```
1 ;'; ;'; ;'; I'll try to find Tim's old blue coats.
2 Did you visit the children's new red brick school?
3 He bought the shirt for a week's pay.  Is it Al's?
4 We'll match the companies' earnings sometime soon.
5 Ask Mr. Jones' secretary for a copy of the report.
```

Locate the Quotation Mark " ' Key

The " (quotation mark) is the shift of the apostrophe. Use the Left Shift key and the ; finger.

Periods and commas are placed inside quotation marks. The question mark is placed inside the quotation mark when it is part of the quoted material. Place the question mark outside the quotation mark when the question is not part of the quoted material.

Practice the Quotation Mark " ' Key Reach

Note how the question mark is used with the quotation marks in line 3.

```
1 ;"; ;"; ;"; Joe said, "See the newly fallen snow."
2 "I am going skiing in the mountains," said LeAnne.
3 Did you read the article, "Word Processing Today"?
4 Quen said, "I'll bring Xiu's computer home today."
5 "I have completed my class report," said Jonathan.
```

Locate the Exclamation Point ! 1 Key

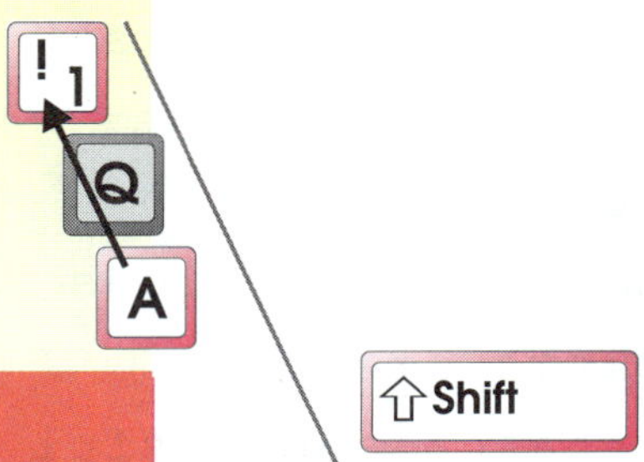

The ! (exclamation point) is the shift of the 1 and is keyed with the A finger.

a!a a!a a!a a!a

5 He was very vain about his wardrobe.

6 The vane pointed to the northwest.

7 The vein in her temple was pulsing rapidly.

8 The miner discovered a heavy vein of gold.

Now key each of the following sentences, choosing the correct word.

1 All (tenants, tenets) who rent the property should be treated equally.

2 Do you know what the (tenants, tenets) of his philosophy involved?

3 Why did the students bring (their, there) bicycles to school?

4 (Their, there) are a number of issues that need to be resolved before closure date.

5 The musician was extremely (vain, vane, vein).

6 The weather (vain, vane, vein) was blown away during the storm.

7 The tests were conducted on the major (vains, vanes, veins) in the body.

Improve Keying Skills

Take two 1-minute timings on each paragraph. Set a speed or an accuracy goal. If you complete the paragraph before time runs out, start over.

Exercise 1

Annual sales conferences can be very productive. A conference allows salespersons to share successes and to discuss their solutions to problems. The shared success stories can be very motivational to new sales personnel. Sharing problems and solutions helps everyone to see that many problems are experienced by all salespersons and that a successful solution can be implemented without using the trial-and-error method.

Space twice after an exclamation point at the end of a sentence.

The exclamation point is placed inside the quotation mark when it is part of the quoted material.

Practice the Exclamation Point ! 1 Key Reach

Key each line two times.

Key and space quickly.

1 He yelled, "Fire!" Wow! Our team won the trophy!
2 Study today! Earn tomorrow! Be a success always!
3 Stop! The car is still moving! Yes! Now! Stop!
4 I hate to study on Saturdays! Help! Here! Stop!
5 That school's new principal is a real "go-getter"!

Locate the Dollar Sign $ 4 Key

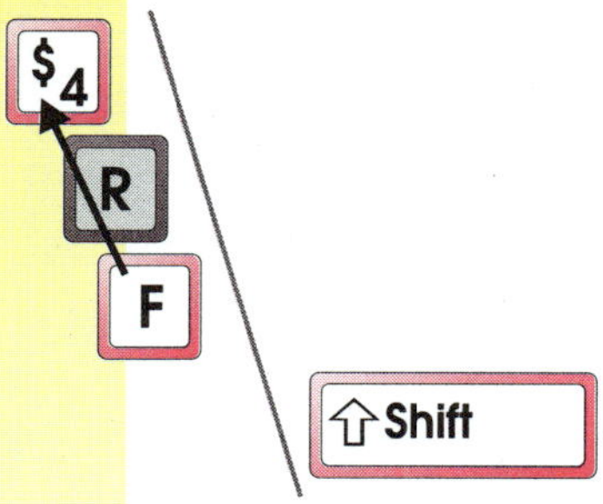

The $ (dollar sign) is the shift of the 4 and is keyed with the F finger.

f$f f$f f$f f$f

Practice the Dollar Sign $ 4 Key Reach

Key each line two times.

1 f$f $15 $380 $79 $36 $48 $4 $45.50 $374.89 $42 $89
2 Please send me $400. He owed me $12, $10, $15.50.
3 $1,234.50 The items cost $23.24, $54.28, and $300.
4 Do you have $15, $35.89, $46.21, $37.89, $4567.69?
5 The tickets were a real bargain at $20 and $50 ea.

48

Formatting Unbound Reports with Secondary Headings

GOALS

- Build Language Arts Skills
- Improve Keying Skills
- Learn to Format Unbound Reports with Secondary and Paragraph Headings

Review

Key each line two times.

```
1 who was it/was a boy/call the dog/all of it/who is
2 Virtuous view is voiced by my vested voter's veto.
3 The purchase order for model 438 is processed now.
4 Ease of use is an important aspect of computer
applications.
```

Build Language Arts Skills

Word Usage

Understand the correct usage of the following words.

Tenant/Tenet
Tenant one who rents
Tenet principle or belief

Their/There
Their possessive meaning belonging to
There at or in a place

Vain/Vane/Vein
Vain conceited
Vane device to indicate wind direction
Vein blood vessel; deposit of metal

Key each line.

```
1 The tenant moved without the required notice.
2 The major tenet of their philosophy was equality.
3 Their programs were all full of bugs.
4 There is the program I wanted you to buy.
```

Increase Keying Speed

Only speed is analyzed and recorded.

Try to beat the computer and increase your speed.

```
of it at up am me us an do of at us he if as no it
one way par run pad set new let vie gas has her it
hear trees make pain shut down hear card drab cars
as it is a/ at my by/ go to do/ to no by/ it is at
You may pay your dues when the reply form is sent.
A vote is the way to show what rules they desired.
The drills do not exercise the fingers adequately.
The sentences contain the letters on the keyboard.
Many programs are simple and others quite complex.
Programs that check spelling are helpful to learn.
```

Improve Keying Accuracy

Now key each line above for control; no more than one error. Try to maintain your previous speed.

Measure Progress

Exercise 1

Take two 1-minute timings.

Minimum goal: 24 wam with three or fewer errors 1.6 S.I.

Performance goals for the lesson are based on the 1-minute timings.

Computer literacy means having a basic understanding of how to access and use a computer system. This also implies that a person has a simple vocabulary of computer terminology. In the near future, persons who do not have basic computer literacy will be at a disadvantage in their home and work lives.

Computers in the home will keep budgets, checking accounts, menus, and schedules of future events. These functions will help people to become better organized and manage their resources more efficiently.

production of the merchandise. Regardless of the causes of the defective product, some action must be taken as soon as possible.

Training can be the solution to a quality-control problem if the employees assume ownership of the problem and agree it is a problem that can be solved through training. After the training has occurred, it will be necessary to observe employees on the job to see if the new skills are being used. If the problem still exists, then it may be an employee attitudinal problem. Just because people know what to do does not mean that they will do it.

Minimum goal: 21 wam with six or fewer errors

Exercise 2

Take two 2-minute timings on the preceding paragraphs.

End-of-Lesson Procedure

At the end of each lesson, you will have the following options:

1. To restart the same lesson, press the F1 function key.
2. To return to the Lessons Menu, press ESC. This action automatically will save the completed lesson.
3. To proceed to the next, or any other lesson, highlight your choice on the menu and press Enter.
4. To return to the Main Menu, press ESC again.
5. To print the lesson, select Print Activities.
6. To exit the program:
   a. Select the Exit option and press Enter.
   b. When the DOS prompt appears on the screen, remove your data disk.
   c. Turn off the monitor. (Your instructor also may ask you to turn off the computer and printer.)

QUALITY CONTROL

A quality-control program will prevent a lot of unnecessary trouble for a company. Irate customers can do more harm than promotional campaigns can correct. Quality control's first goal is to ensure that as few as possible defective products are released for public use. Many companies have been involved with defective merchandise and have suffered the frustration of recalls. If a company discovers that a defective product has been produced, every effort should be made to replace the product with no cost to the customer. The customer should be inconvenienced as little as possible. In fact, if the company gives the customers something extra for their inconvenience, the company may benefit from improved public relations.

An occasional mistake can be tolerated, but when a certain percentage of a company's products are routinely defective, the cause must be identified. The cause will be either in the process or in the personnel running the process.

Within the process, there are a number of possible causes of defects. One could be inferior materials that are used to produce the defective merchandise. Another problem could be worn or broken equipment used in the

18

Parentheses, Ampersand, and Percent Keys

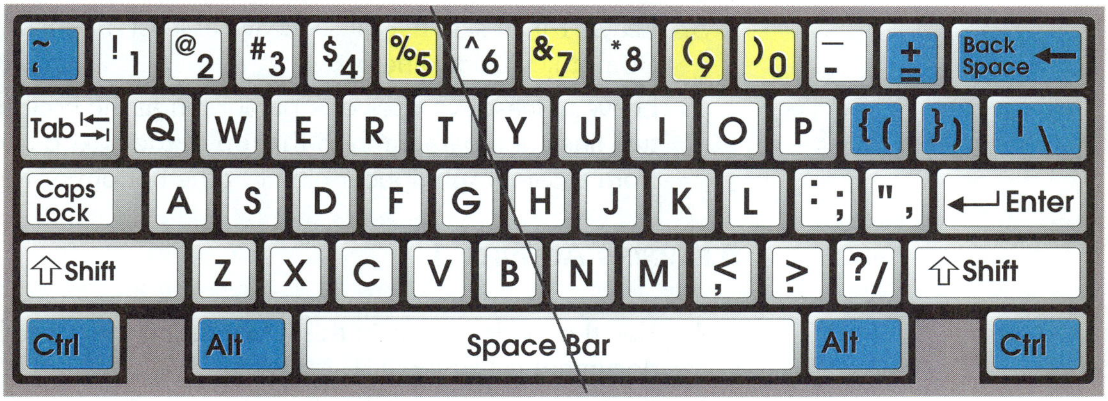

GOALS

- Reinforce Previous Learning
- Learn New Keys ( ), &, and %
- Increase Keying Speed

Remember the "Get Ready" checklist.

REVIEW

Key each line two times.

Remember the rules about punctuation and quotation marks.

1 Take the credenza back to Joe and let him keep it.
2 When Zoro comes home, tell him to wash the dishes.
3 The accounts are due and payable on the first day.
4 Jimmy's dad said, "Send $5.10 as soon as you can!"
5 Will said, "I'll need $4 before the trip is over!"
6 When the dog ran away, she yelled, "Stop the car!"

LOCATE THE LEFT PARENTHESIS (9 KEY

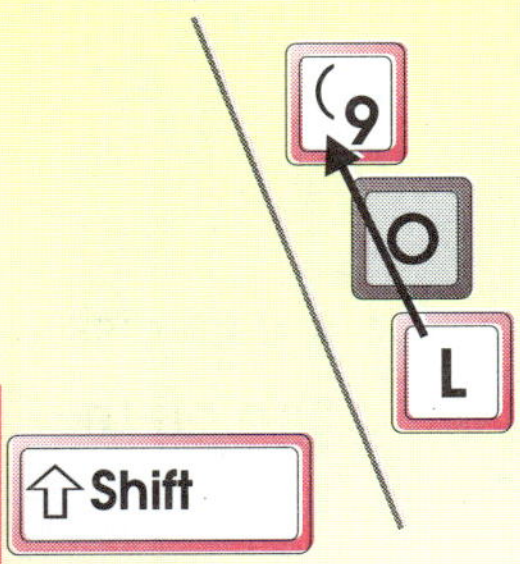

The ((left parenthesis) is the shift of the 9 and is keyed with the L finger.

l(l l(l l(l l(l

4. Pages are numbered beginning with page 2. The software automatically will number the pages. Leave a 1-inch top margin on the second page.
5. Leave 1-inch side margins. Leave at least a 1-inch bottom margin (6 blank lines). Do not key below line 60.
6. Leave at least two lines of a paragraph at the bottom of a page and carry at least two lines of a paragraph to the top of the next page. Do not have only one line from a paragraph appear either at the bottom or top of a page.

Learning Activity 1

1. Key the model report in this lesson using the preceding layout directions. The document is LES47DC1.
2. Set the page numbering feature in the software so that page 1 is not numbered. Page 2 should be numbered. Set the page number feature accordingly. Note: If you are using word-processing software with automatic word wrap, you may have to key the page number a few spaces from the right margin to prevent the number from automatically being moved to the next line.
3. Proofread your copy on the screen. Use the editing keys to make corrections. Reformat if necessary.
4. Press ESC to have the computer check the document and print a copy. Note any uncorrected errors on the printout.

End-of-Lesson Procedure

At the end of each lesson, you will have the following options:

1. To restart the same lesson, press the F1 function key.
2. To return to the Lessons Menu, press ESC. This action automatically will save the completed lesson.
3. To proceed to the next, or any other lesson, highlight your choice on the menu and press Enter.
4. To return to the Main Menu, press ESC again.
5. To print the lesson, select Print Activities.
6. To exit the program:
   a. Select the Exit option and press Enter.
   b. When the DOS prompt appears on the screen, remove your data disk.
   c. Turn off the monitor. (Your instructor also may ask you to turn off the computer and printer.)

Practice the Left Parenthesis (9 Key Reach

Key each line two times.

```
1(1 1(1 1(9 1(9 1(91 (40 (50 (191 (92 (10 (345
```

Locate the Right Parenthesis)0 Key

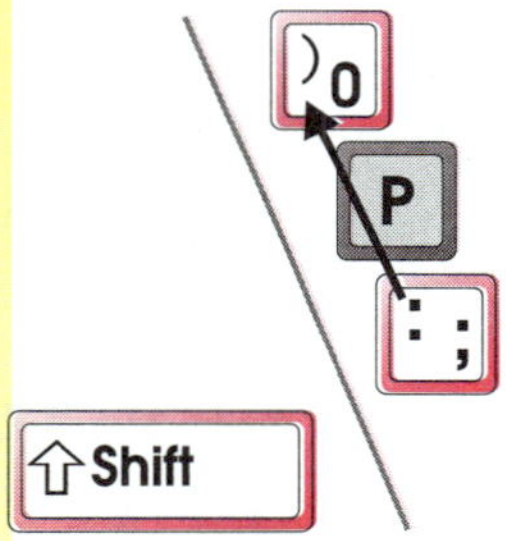

The) (right parenthesis) is the shift of the 0 and is keyed with the ; finger.

```
;); ;); ;); ;);
```

Practice the Right Parenthesis)0 Key Reach

Key each line two times.

```
;); ;); ;)0 ;)0 0) 00) 90) 10) 11) 49) 50) 21) 27)
```

Practice the Left and Right Parenthesis (9)0 Key Reaches

```
1 Route these:  (1) letter, (2) card, and (3) lists.
2 We will determine (a) what, (b) why, and (c) when.
3 Kenneth may (1) telephone, (2) meet, and (3) test.
```

Two spaces after :
No space after (
One space after)

Measure Progress

Minimum goal: 3-minute timing—34 wam with six or fewer errors; 5-minute timing—29 wam with ten or fewer errors

Take two 3- or 5-minute timings.

The microcomputer can be used to accomplish a variety of personal tasks using either commercial software or user-produced programs. Using the computer for these types of tasks, though not primarily designed to be educational, is in fact very educational. As people program the computer or learn to use commercial software packages to accomplish various tasks, they learn a great amount about the computer and the process being used.

A number of magazines include regular features on programs that can be run on a variety of microcomputers. The bookstore abounds with books full of programs to accomplish personal tasks, from balancing the checkbook to menu planning, as well as every type of game you possibly could want to play.

Future software programs will be designed to adapt to the abilities of the user. In other words, the software will have a limited intelligence allowing modification and adaptation of certain functions.

Review Unbound Reports

Layout for Unbound Reports

Study the model report in this lesson and read the following information:

1. Double-space the body of a report. (Some reports may be single-spaced according to a company's style.)
2. Indent each paragraph five spaces.
3. Center the title and key it in all capital letters. Double-space after the title. Leave a 2-inch top margin and begin keying the title on line 13 of page 1. With this software, press the Enter key to reach line 13. Do not reset the top margin when creating multiple-page documents.

Locate the Ampersand &7 Key

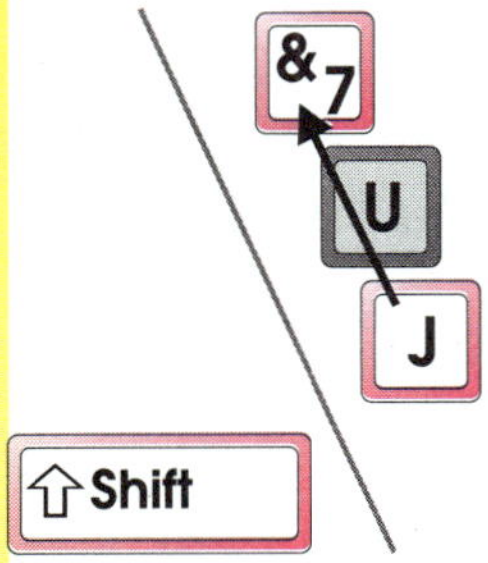

The & (ampersand) is the shift of the 7 and is keyed with the J finger.

```
j&j j&j j&j j&j
```

Practice the Ampersand &7 Key Reach

Key each line two times.

The ampersand is not used in formal writing.

```
1 j&j J7j j& John & Bill; Pam & Paul; Sherry & Andy.
2 George & Juao & Gail & Hua played tennis & soccer.
3 Harris & Henley & Jackson will buy all that stock.
4 Joyner & Lowenstein will merge with Chez & Varner.
5 Chan & Son and Su & Ling will move to 12 N. 82 St.
```

Now key each of the following sentences, choosing the correct word.

1 Georgio was quite (adapt, adept, adopt) at gymnastics.

2 We need to (adapt, adept, adopt) the software for the new computers.

3 The committee (adapted, adepted, adopted) the new guidelines for the campaign.

4 Did you (choose, chose) new (stationary, stationery) for all your (correspondence, correspondents)?

5 The rock was so heavy that it remained (stationary, stationery) during the hurricane.

Improve Keying Skills

Take two 1-minute timings on each paragraph. Set a speed or an accuracy goal. If you complete the paragraph before time runs out, start over.

Exercise 1

The action plan should be agreed upon by all concerned parties. A good action plan will include the following: resources available, schedule of activities with dates, persons responsible, and criteria for judging the success of the plan. Various departments should have the power to adopt a plan in total or adapt parts of it for specific purposes.

Exercise 2

Smoking in the workplace has become an important employee issue. With numerous studies that indicate the hazard of exposure to smoke, nonsmokers are demanding a smoke-free work environment. Building managers must be adept at planning an environment that will not offend nonsmokers.

Locate the Percent Sign %5 Key

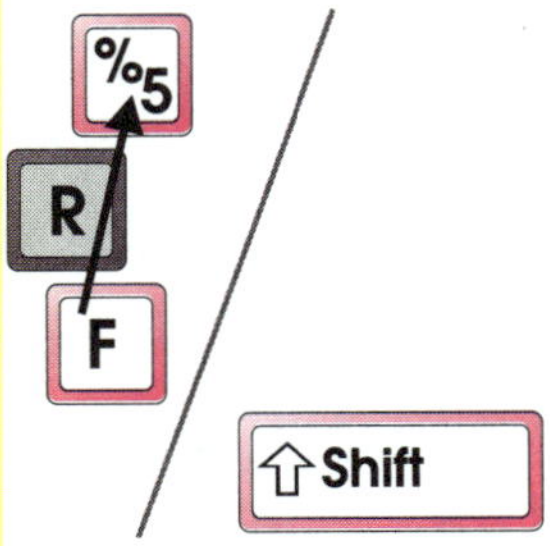

The % (percent sign) is the shift of the 5 and is keyed with the F finger.

```
f%f f%f f%f f%f
```

Practice the Percent Sign %5 Key Reach

Key each line two times.

```
1 f%f f%f % Please add these items:  6%, 15%, & 30%.
2 All terms are 10% discount or 15% (within 5 days).
3 Their percentage rate was 18% (we paid 15% & 12%).
4 The loan rates were 8% & 10% & 11% & 12% & 6-3/4%.
5 Discounts of 5%, 10%, 15%, 20%, and 25% are given.
```

Increase Keying Speed

Work to increase your speed goal.

Key each line two times for speed.

```
1 in go hi co to me ex he if at id or in he at in up
2 day elf may can fan did end let two sad but jar if
3 cool brat open buzz dude list mark plea good lines
4 The sale was fair; the cost was not over the mark.
5 or it at /go to do an /of an at /it is a /to no am
6 Keep your fingers on correct keys for quick speed.
7 Laser printers are fast and have printing options.
8 Many expensive laser printers make fancy graphics.
9 Desktop publishing involves multifaceted software.
10 Thermal transfer printers are economical but slow.
```

47 Formatting Unbound Reports

GOALS

- Build Language Arts Skills
- Improve Keying Skills
- Review Unbound Reports

Review

Key each line two times.

1 go to by/of it at/is it in/do in go/by at it/if it
2 Moisture surely will make a mainframe miss orders.
3 The new alpha formula was 2(5x-2y) + 7(4a + 3b).
4 Communication skills are still most important for successful business executives.

Build Language Arts Skills

Word Usage

Understand the correct usage of the following words.

Adapt/Adept/Adopt

Adapt adjust or modify; make fit
Adept highly skilled; expert
Adopt choose; take; follow as one's own

Stationary/Stationery

Stationary still; not moving
Stationery writing paper

Key each line.

1 The margins have been changed to adapt to the new printing requirements.
2 An adept keyboarder doesn't look at the keys.
3 Did the company adopt the last proposal?
4 The building remained stationary during the earthquake.
5 Your stationery was most appropriate for the occasion.

Improve Keying Accuracy

Now key each line on the preceding page for control. Try to maintain your speed while keying no more than one error per line. Repeat a line if you have more than one error.

Measure Progress

Exercise 1

Minimum goal: 25 wam with three or fewer errors 1.6 S.I.

Try to exceed the minimum goal.

Take two 1-minute timings.

```
     An exercise program is often used as a treatment
for muscle strain.  Proper muscle tone can improve
posture and help prevent the risk of muscle strain.
It is essential that you consult with your physician
prior to attempting any strenuous exercises.
     Exercise regularly throughout your life, and you
will feel better and stay in shape longer.  Those
persons with a regular exercise program tend to be
healthier.  Research studies have shown that people
can continue to exercise their entire lives.  They
should find an appropriate exercise for their current
physical condition.
```

Exercise 2

Minimum goal: 22 wam with five or fewer errors

Take two 2-minute timings on the same paragraphs.

End-of-Lesson Procedure

At the end of each lesson, you will have the following options:

1. To restart the same lesson, press the F1 function key.
2. To return to the Lessons Menu, press ESC.
3. To proceed to the next, or any other lesson, highlight your choice on the menu.
4. To return to the Main Menu, press ESC again.
5. To print the lesson, select Print Activities.
6. To exit the program, select the Exit option and press Enter. Remove your data disk and turn off the monitor. (Your instructor also may ask you to turn off the computer and printer.)

UNIT 8

REPORTS

19

Pound/Number, Equal, Plus, Asterisk, and At Symbols

GOALS

- Reinforce Previous Learning
- Learn New Keys #, =, +, *, and @
- Increase Keying Speed
- Improve Keying Accuracy

Remember the "Get Ready" checklist.

Review

Key each line two times.

1 The usual (20% & 10%) profit margins will be used.
2 Katie said, "The discount rate is 10% on $125.50."
3 Over 58% (234) of the class voted the 4-year plan.
4 The 9-3/4% note ($13,248.25) was paid February 21.
5 ZIP codes speed the mail to everyone for February.
6 An excited red dog bit the small quiet calico cat.
7 Tex created six quaint prizes for Janice and Bill.

Locate the Number or Pound Sign #3 Key

Remember to use proper technique.

Learning Activity 3

1. Start document LES46DC3. Key the following edited table using double-spacing. Make the indicated corrections to the copy. Leave eight spaces between the columns.
2. Check the document and print a copy. Mark any uncorrected errors.
3. Save and print a corrected copy.

REGIONAL DATA RETURNS

(Includes returns mailed, returned, and percent)

North	1,568	987	62%
South	997	~~356~~ 298	~~35%~~ 29.9%
East	3,426	1,527	44%
West	5,381	2,846	52%
Totals	11,3~~90~~72	~~5,716~~ 5,658	~~50%~~ 49.7%

(997 and 3,426 are circled together with a transposition mark.)

End-of-Lesson Procedure

At the end of each lesson, you will have the following options:

1. To restart the same lesson, press the F1 function key.
2. To return to the Lessons Menu, press ESC. This action automatically will save the completed lesson.
3. To proceed to the next, or any other lesson, highlight your choice on the menu and press Enter.
4. To return to the Main Menu, press ESC again.
5. To print the lesson, select Print Activities.
6. To exit the program:
   a. Select the Exit option and press Enter.
   b. When the DOS prompt appears on the screen, remove your data disk.
   c. Turn off the monitor. (Your instructor also may ask you to turn off the computer and printer.)

The # (number or pound sign) is the shift of the 3 and is keyed with the D finger. When it is keyed in front of a number, it stands for number. When it is keyed after a number, it stands for pounds.

`d#d d#d d#d d#d`

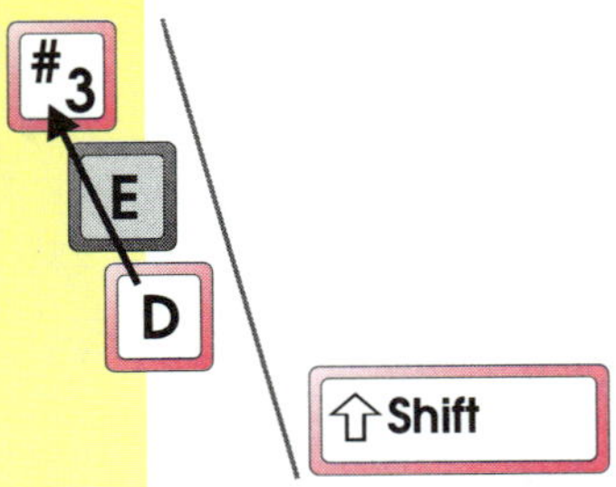

Practice the Number or Pound Sign #3 Key Reach

Key each line two times.

```
1 d#d d#d d#d 33# #29 21# #4 Will needs a #3 pencil.
2 The order calls for #4, #402, #56, #4765, & #4678.
3 Please send me items #223, #4625, #3570, & #89654.
4 Do the machines weigh 34#, 478#, 89#, 76# or 856#?
5 Orders #1459, #2370, #1498, & #1621 were for 978#.
```

Locate the Equal Sign += Key

The = (equal sign) is located to the right of the - and is keyed with the ; finger.

`;=; ;=; ;=; ;=;`

Practice the Equal Sign += Key Reach

Key this line two times.

`;=; ;=; ;=; ;=; A=B G=AB 1=f 100=a 44=BC ;=;`

YEARLY MILEAGE REPORT

(Reimbursement @ $.20 per mile)

Banks, J.	12,487	$ 2,497.40
Cameron, B.	22,569	4,513.80
Dameron, L.	7,842	1,568.40
Eisenbury, J.	15,598	3,119.60
Farmer, A.	42,367	8,473.40
Fuller, T.	58,421	11,684.20
Green, P.	12,345	2,469.00
House, B.	67,890	13,578.00

Learning Activity 2

1. Start document LES46DC2. Key the following handwritten table in an acceptable format using single-spacing. Leave 8 spaces between columns. Change to double-spacing before keying the totals.
2. Proofread the document and print a copy. Mark any uncorrected errors.
3. Make any corrections. Press ESC to have the computer check the document.

STUDENTS CREDIT COSTS

Allen, J.	*32*	*$576*
Brown, L.	*17*	*306*
Cameron, J.	*06*	*108*
Dowing, B.	*42*	*756*
Etheridge, K.	*75*	*1,350*
Fowler, D.	*15*	*270*
Green, F.	*03*	*54*
Rodriquez, L.	*15*	*270*
Williams, P.	*62*	*1,116*
Young, A.	*18*	*324*
Zarda, B.	*49*	*882*
Totals	*334*	*$6,012*

Locate the Plus Sign + Key

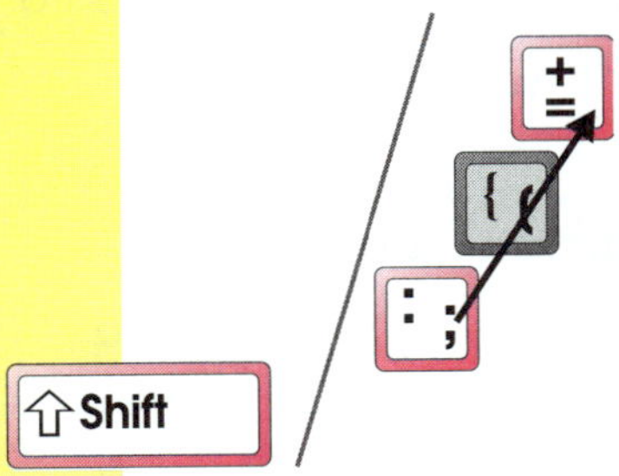

The + (plus sign) is the shift of the = and is keyed with the ; finger.

;+; ;+; ;+; ;+;

Practice the Plus Sign + Key Reach

Key each line two times.

1 ;+; ;+; ;+; A + B + C + D = K + J 1 + 4 + 3 + 2 = 10

2 L + J + T + A = R 6 + 8 + 14 + 12 = 40 1 + 2 + 3 = 6

Locate the Asterisk * 8 Key

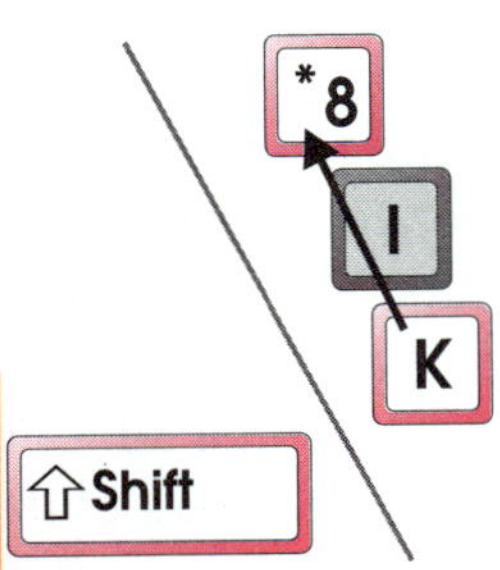

The * (asterisk) is the shift of the 8 and is keyed with the K finger.

k*k k*k k*k k*k

Measure Progress

Take two 3- or 5-minute timings.

Minimum goal: 3-minute timing—33 wam with six or fewer errors; 5-minute timing—28 wam with ten or fewer errors

The expanded use of computers and microcomputers in homes, offices, and schools has increased the need for effective keyboarding skills. Keyboarding skills are now considered essential by many persons who did not find it feasible to enroll in traditional typewriting classes.

Included among this group of nontraditional keyboarding students are various professionals and persons whose work did not previously demand keyboarding skills. The search for alternative methods of learning to keyboard recently has focused attention on the need for the development of software designed for teaching keyboarding with a microcomputer.

If current trends continue, the person who knows nothing about computers may be as disadvantaged as a person who cannot read or write. The growth in the use of small computers has led many educators to stress computer literacy for all graduates.

Learn to Format Tables From Unarranged, Handwritten, and Edited Copy

Learning Activity 1

1. Start document LES46DC1. Key the unarranged table on the next page in an acceptable format using double-spacing. Leave 8 spaces between columns. use a left tab for the first column, a right tab for the numbers in the second column, and a decimal tab for the third column. To set a decimal tab, key and center the key line. Place the cursor on the ruler line and press d to place a decimal tab at the correct position. The numbers in that column will align at the decimal point.
2. Proofread the document and print a copy. Mark any errors.
3. Make corrections then press ESC to have the computer check your document.

Practice the Asterisk *8 Key Reach

Key each line two times.

Keep your eyes on the copy.

1 k*k k*k k*k Please see the quotation* noted below.
2 Zavier and Alexander* called for #150, #80, & #96.
3 Fill the order* with 1,287#, 345#, 789# & 27,520#.
4 Please identify the following: 16*, 18*, and 29*.
5 What is this balance* 17 + 49 + 38 = 38 + 49 + 17?

Locate the At Sign @2 Key

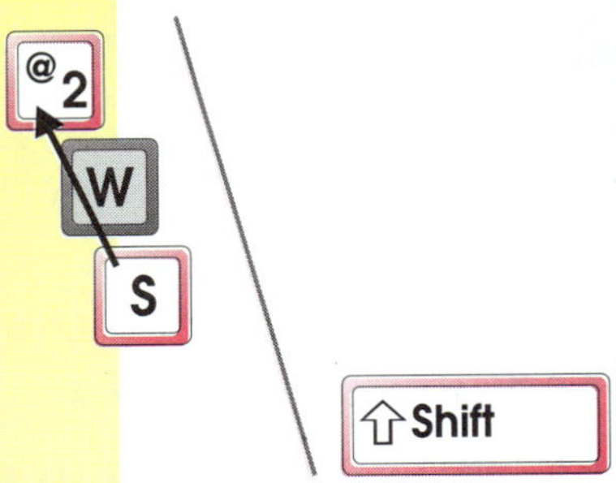

The @ (at sign) is the shift of the 2 and is keyed with the S finger.

s@s s@s s@s s@s

Practice the At Sign @2 Key Reach

Key each line two times.

1 We bought #10's @ $85, #25's @ $40, & #30's @ $49.
2 The order* was for 6# @ $79, 30# @ $5, & 4# @ 20#.
3 The quotation* was 24 @ $69, 32 @ $17 & 45 @ $356.
4 The stock purchase was 10 @ $6, 20 @ $9, 35 @ $78.
5 Order 100 shares @ 59 1/8 and 200 shares @ 15 3/4.

First to Third Row Reach

nat zap eat ran vat hay bad cam even vary vast balk zany zip
baby call hand exam bald cafes banjo scarfs pizza many cargo

Third to Home Row Reach

wax era tab old ill rid was nil rat bed pool yoke okra plods
trod wasp rasp trap rose web zoned wart yard pared cool peel

First to Third Row Reach

mug ant not zen cry bee bin men nip vet mop milk brat zenith
mast moons bent veer cramp milk bilk venom cramp brag vixens

Third to First Row Reach

web reb win pin bum rim mom tin web tex pox pock rock robots
dine time decal funny text bomb rent plumb thumb lymph micro

Improve Keying Skills

Take two 1-minute timings on each paragraph. Set a speed or an accuracy goal. If you complete a paragraph before time runs out, start over.

Exercise 1

Employee evaluation can be a very productive activity. Many people feel threatened when they are being evaluated. This, however, does not need to be anxiety-producing at all. Evaluations can be a time when employees set goals and are rewarded for good performance or are counseled about areas that need improvement.

Exercise 2

A key activity in performance evaluation is to get the person being evaluated to accept the feedback and to set mutually agreeable goals for future performance. Once the goals are set, it is necessary and very important to develop an action plan. There is no single recipe for success, but the basic principles of goal-setting always apply.

Increase Keying Speed

Key each of the following lines two times for speed.

1 your very sent daze lead pave lose weed days time
2 near fade plea foot case took both walk hand girl
3 past due/home town/rain falls/star gaze/what then
4 Voice-input computers are being researched today.
5 In the future, voice input may replace keyboards.
6 Experts want a computer to accept various voices.
7 Tone and pitch differences make the task complex.
8 Automatic speech recognition is very complicated.
9 Acoustical ambiguity of speech may be understood.
10 For now, we must accept the faults of the system.

Try to reach a new speed goal. Beat the computer.

Improve Keying Accuracy

Both speed and accuracy are analyzed and reported.

1 Eliza purchased topaz jewelry from the quiet lady.
2 Zoe was having a quiet meal with Joyce and Bettie.
3 Jody hid the blue topaz in the vault in zone four.
4 That jigsaw puzzle caused great anxiety to Fawzia.
5 Those ballet dancers were quite nimble and lively.

Try to maintain speed, but key for control—no more than one error per line. Repeat any line with more than one error.

4 The principle of individual differences accounts for varied performance.

5 Do you have your receipt for the dress?

6 Your recipe for chili was chosen as the best in the state.

7 Set the monitor on top of the computer.

8 You may sit in any chair that is not occupied.

Now key each of following sentences choosing the correct word.

1 Have you paid the (principal, principle) on the loan?

2 The new (principal, principle) at the school makes many changes.

3 It is important to keep your (principals, principles) in all situations.

4 You should keep your (receipt, recipe) for the charge purchase until the bill is received.

5 Many people now keep their (receipt, recipe) files in a computer software program.

6 The new chair was very comfortable for (sitting, setting).

7 Please (sit, set) the new furniture in the room.

Improve Keying Accuracy

Key each line with no more than one error. If accuracy goal is not met, repeat the line.

Home to Third Row Reach

log hop fly jug sea hog how lip awe hip fret inky awed sways
kiln rode away gift kitty verse libel lawns swims hose await

Home to First Row Reach

jam ban dab nab axe sax alm jam lab can scan scar taxi lambs
jamb waxy axes actor avid aces tree flab cam dream scald lan

Measure Progress

Exercise 1

Minimum goal: 25 wam with three or fewer errors 1.8 S.I.

Try to exceed the minimum goal.

Take two 1-minute timings.

Many times software designed for one brand of computer will not run on another brand of computer. If two different brands of computers will run the same software, they are considered compatible. Incompatible computers will not run the same software programs due to differences in the disk operating systems and other internal operating systems.

Many programs are written in BASIC programming language and others use machine language. Different computers interpret the commands and languages in different ways, thus producing incompatibility.

Exercise 2

Minimum goal: 23 wam with five or fewer errors.

Take two 2-minute timings on the preceding paragraphs.

End-of-Lesson Procedure

At the end of each lesson, you will have the following options:

1. To restart the same lesson, press the F1 function key.
2. To return to the Lessons Menu, press ESC. This action automatically will save the completed lesson.
3. To proceed to the next, or any other lesson, highlight your choice on the menu and press Enter.
4. To return to the Main Menu, press ESC again.
5. To print the lesson, select Print Activities.
6. To exit the program:
   a. Select the Exit option and press Enter.
   b. When the DOS prompt appears on the screen, remove your data disk.
   c. Turn off the monitor. (Your instructor also may ask you to turn off the computer and printer.)

46

Problem Solving: Tables

GOALS

- Build Language Arts Skills
- Improve Keying Accuracy
- Improve Keying Skills
- Learn to Format Tables from Unarranged, Handwritten, and Edited Copy

Review

Key each line two times.

1 but for/for him/was them/was she/the man/saw those

2 The last liens can be lifted when you are lenient.

3 Models #142, #9176, and #288 will not be produced.

4 Ergonomics is the science of work environment production.

Build Language Arts Skills

Word Usage

Understand the correct usage of the following words.

Principal/Principle

Principal school official; capital sum of money
Principle a basic truth or belief

Receipt/Recipe

Receipt record of receiving money or goods
Recipe directions for food preparation; formula for a desired end

Set/Sit

Set place an object
Sit be seated

Key each line.

1 The principal closed the school early.

2 Your loan payment will be split between the principal and the interest owed.

3 A principle of good accounting is accuracy.

20

Remaining Symbols

GOALS

- Reinforce Previous Learning
- Learn Other Symbols
- Learn to Center and Underline Text

Remember the "Get Ready" checklist.

Review

Key each line two times.

```
1 Two #3 or four #6 pencils @ $.50 ea. will = $9.00!
2 Invoice #4876 was paid by checks #248, #763, #215.
3 The formula for the spreadsheet is (A7 + B3 = C8).
4 The quote* was for 150 @ $14, 275 @ $63, 86 @ $94.
5 The prize elm was cut down by five angry citizens.
6 A quaint bronze box held four green emerald rings.
7 You can learn to keyboard easily with zero errors.
```

Learn Other Symbols

The locations of certain symbols will vary on different microcomputer keyboards. Study the keyboard on your machine to determine the location of any additional symbols.

LEARNING ACTIVITY 4

1. Start document LES45DC4. Center the following table, double-space it. Leave 6 spaces between columns. Use right tabs for the number columns.
2. Check the document and print a copy. Mark any uncorrected errors on the printout. Check the horizontal and vertical centering. Align columns of figures on the right side using the right tab function.
3. Press ESC to have the computer check the document.

APTITUDE TEST RESULTS

by Test Area

Betty Hamilton	587	497	1084
Ron Basil	1142	1050	2192
Joyna Forseo	699	789	1488
Gina Matino	876	942	1818
Kou Tong	932	780	1712
Sun Li Tan	1240	1060	2300
Michael Andrews	1165	937	2102
Dora Williams	895	479	1374

END-OF-LESSON PROCEDURE

After completing the activities for this lesson, follow the appropriate end-of-lesson procedure.

Practice Other Symbols

Practice keying these lines two times each. Omit the lines containing any symbols not on your keyboard.

1 This ^ sign means 4^4 or four to the fourth power.
2 Is A > B or J > L or K > M or Q < P or Y < Z or X?
3 Is [AA - BB] = [KK - LL] or [MM + ZZ] = [JJ + RR]?
4 You can load the WordPerfect program with WP51\WP.

Increase Keying Speed

Try to set a new speed goal.

Key each of the following two times for speed.

1 Both mail norm hand shot half gain loss bare dues
2 zone bone home star tear each when bull over then
3 for it /for a /and the /but all /had she /and all
4 all of the /for you /you are /she was /I will see
5 Voice output from a computer is fairly primitive.
6 Linking a phone and computer enhances capability.
7 Video conferencing reduces business travel costs.
8 Communications can be made better with computers.
9 Many computer voices sound very mechanical to us.
10 Soon letters will be replaced by electronic mail.

Improve Keying Accuracy

Try to maintain speed, but key with control—no more than one error per line. Repeat any line with more than one error.

Both speed and accuracy are analyzed and reported.

1 Roma's letter indicated that he could type 50 wam.
2 Jo said, "Call the operator--the tape has broken!"
3 Create a new subdirectory for \memos for the file.
4 Johnson, Smith & Co.* mailed the order on 12/6/97.
5 The desk is 6' wide and 42" high--a bargain @ $98.
6 The invoice she typed was for 6 #2 loads @ $10 ea.
7 We will need 48 @ $145.98 to place the next order.
8 Order 12 #2 pens & 36 #6 (hard) pencils @ $.20 ea.
9 Sarah knew that (1/2 + 1/4) - (2-1/4 - 1-1/2) = 0.
10 Profits were 110% last quarter and for last month.

Learning Activity 3

1. Start document LES45DC3. Use the automatic centering feature to center the following table.
2. Key the table double-spaced. Leave 4 spaces between columns. Align column 3 on the right side by setting a right tab.
3. Check the document and print a copy. Mark any uncorrected errors on the printout. Check the horizontal and vertical centering.
4. Press ESC to have the computer check the document.

Use the right tab feature to align numbers on the right in Activity 3.

CALENDAR OF EVENTS

July 1 - January 15

July 1	Groundbreaking Ceremony	8:00 a.m.
	Meet the Press	9:00 a.m.
August 15	Parent's Luncheon	12:00 noon
September 23	Assembly Meeting	2:30 p.m.
October 15	Annual Conference	9:00 a.m.
November 24	Thanksgiving Holiday	12:00 noon
December 14	Holiday Party	3:00 p.m.
	Bank Reception	7:00 p.m.
January 12	Conduct Inventory	9:00 a.m.
	Order Deadline	11:00 a.m.
January 15	Report Due	2:30 p.m.

Learn Automatic Horizontal Centering

Most microcomputer word-processing software programs have an automatic centering feature. This feature is activated by entering an automatic centering command when keying the line to be centered. Some programs use one of the function (F) keys to enter this command; others use the CTRL plus an alphabetic key, such as CTRL+C or CTRL+X. In this program, the F6 key is a toggle switch that controls centering. Follow these steps to activate the automatic centering feature:

1. Centering can be done only on a word-processing screen.
2. Press the F6 key. Centering is now activated.
3. Key the text you would like to have centered. If you want more the one line of text centered, you can press Enter and then key the next line.
4. Press the F6 key to turn off the centering feature.

Practice Centering

Reminder: F6 is the automatic centering key.

Using the word processor, name a document LES20DC1. Center the following lines using the automatic centering feature. Remember: The F6 key is a toggle switch, which means that you only need to turn it on once to center all of these lines. Press Enter at the end of each line.

```
MICROCOMPUTER FORMATTING
Automatic Centering
Word-Processing Programs
Keyboarding with Technique and Skill
```

Print the document. Study the printout to see if each line is centered properly. Proofread and mark any errors you may have missed. Make corrections if necessary. Save and print your corrected copy. When satisfied with your work, have the computer check your document. Press ESC and select the check option.

Learn to Underline

Reminder: F8 is the key to underline copy.

Underlining on a microcomputer usually requires a special command. When using other software, consult the software manual to determine the procedures for that particular software. In this software, the F8 key is the toggle switch that controls underlining. Follow these steps to underline copy.

1. Underlining can be done only on a word-processing screen.
2. Before keying the text to be underlined, press the F8 key to start the underline. Notice that the word "Underline" appears on the prompt line.
3. Key the text. The text to be underlined appears highlighted on the screen.
4. Do not space at the end of the copy to be underlined. Press the F8 key to end underlining.

Learning Activity 2

1. Start document LES45DC2. Use the automatic centering feature to horizontally center the following table.
2. Key the table with the body single-spaced, but double-space between each pair of lines. Press the Enter key to create the double-spacing. Leave 10 spaces between columns.
3. Check the document and print a copy. Mark any uncorrected errors on the printout. Check the horizontal and vertical centering.
4. Press ESC to have the computer check the document.

WORDS FREQUENTLY MISUSED

(In Alphabetic Order)

access (n)	approach; use
assess (v)	to set a value
bare (adj)	without covering
bear (v)	to carry; take on
carat (n)	unit of weight
caret (n)	punctuation mark
deferential (adj)	very respectful
differential (adj)	making a difference
elusive (adj)	hard to grasp
illusive (adj)	unreal
patience (n)	endurance; persevering
patients (n)	persons receiving care
stationary (adj)	fixed; not moving
stationery (n)	writing paper

Practice Underlining

Name a document LES20DC2. Practice these sentences. Use the F8 key to begin and end underlining.

1 Not all software uses the same procedures to underline.

2 Consult the software manual to determine the procedures for underlining.

3 Her book, Introduction to Office Automation, was well received.

4 Have you read the book The Stock Market Report?

5 John's book, A Beginner's Guide to Wise Decision Making, was a best-seller.

Print the document. Proofread and mark any errors you may have missed. Make corrections if necessary. Save and print your corrected copy. When satisfied with your work, have the computer check your document. Press ESC and select the check option.

Measure Progress

Exercise 1

Minimum goal: 25 wam with two or fewer errors 1.6 S.I.

Try to exceed the minimum goal.

Take two 1-minute timings.

Soon people will be able to talk to their computers. These new computers will allow all types of creative work. Think of interacting with a talking word-processing program as you prepare a letter or report. People who use these computers will require a new type of thinking skill. They will have to learn to arrange their thoughts in a logical order.

LEARN TO FORMAT TABLES WITH SECONDARY HEADINGS

Some tables require secondary headings for clarity or to add information. If a secondary heading is needed in a table, key it a double-space below the main heading. Double-space between the secondary heading and the body of the table. For secondary headings, capitalize only the first letter of each word. (Note: In the following table, DOS is always capitalized.) Study the following model table.

INTERNAL DOS COMMANDS

From DOS User's Manual

CLS	clears the display from the screen
COPY	copies a file or files from one disk to another
DEL	deletes a file or files from a disk
DIR	lists the directory of files on a specified disk
ERASE	erases a file or files from a disk
PROMPT	changes the appearance of the prompt
RENAME	changes the name of a file
TYPE	displays the contents of a file
VER	displays the current version of DOS

LEARNING ACTIVITY 1

1. Start document LES45DC1. Use the automatic centering feature to determine the horizontal center of the above table.
2. Key the table double-spaced. Leave 4 spaces between columns.
3. Compute the vertical center and key the main heading and secondary heading. Double-space before and after the secondary heading. Capitalize only the first letter of each word in the secondary heading.
4. Check the document and print a copy. Mark any uncorrected errors on the printout. Check the horizontal and vertical centering.
5. Press ESC to have the computer check the document.

Minimum goal: 23 wam with four or fewer errors 1.4 S.I.

EXERCISE 2

Take two 2-minute timings.

A compound word is made from two or more words combined to form a new word. A compound word may be written as one word, as two or more separate words, or as a hyphenated word. Regardless of how it is formed, each newly formed word is considered one word. In order to figure out the meaning, consider the separate meaning of each word and then combine them to arrive at a new definition. The new definition will contain meaning from both of the combined words.

COMPOSITION EXERCISE

Using the word processor, name a document LES20CM1. Briefly think about a job you have had, currently have, or would like to have in the future.

1. Make a list of the words that describe the characteristics of the job. Center each word using the F6 key.
2. Write four or five sentences using these words to describe the position. Using the F8 key, underline the words in your sentences that come from your original list.
3. Do not worry about errors on your first attempt. When finished, proofread the document on the screen. Use the editing keys to make any corrections.
4. Save and print the document. Proofread the hard copy and mark any errors you may have missed. Retrieve the document and make corrections as necessary. Save and print your corrected copy.

END-OF-LESSON PROCEDURE

At the end of each lesson, you will have the following options:

1. To restart the same lesson, press the F1 function key.
2. To return to the Lessons Menu, press ESC.
3. To proceed to another lesson, highlight your choice and press Enter.
4. To return to the Main Menu, press ESC again.
5. To print the lesson, select Print Activities.
6. To exit the program, select Exit option.

Measure Progress

Minimum goal: 3-minute timing—33 wam with six or fewer errors; 5-minute timing—28 wam with ten or fewer errors

Take two 3- or 5-minute timings.

With robotics and the expansion of language systems, androids may become feasible. The studies of artificial intelligence combined with exciting new discoveries that allow specialized cell growth all point to specifically designed human-like robots, androids, or cyborgs.

A glimpse into the home of the future includes a master computer which, under your command, would control all household functions and processes. Some of these functions would be food preparation, trip arrangement, wardrobe design, appliance repair, cleaning, entertainment, health, and exercise. Each activity or process would be performed by a specialized robot.

These robots will have to be serviced and repaired by someone. In one scenario, the robots will be able to service and repair themselves; or one of the robots will be a robot repair person. Other robots will be designed to cook, clean house, babysit, and perform tasks that you want them to accomplish.

21

Skill Building

GOALS

- Reinforce Previous Learning
- Increase Keying Speed
- Improve Keying Skills

Remember the "Get Ready" checklist.

Review

Key each line two times.

1 Zelda earned extra pay for a violin she gave Quin.
2 Jeff asked Kim to explain the zoo project to Jack.
3 All you need do is practice to refine your skills.
4 Key as quickly as you can, and you will be expert!
5 Ken said, "I'll meet you at the park at 4:30 p.m."
6 The stock market quote* was for 100 shares @ $975.

Increase Keying Speed

Only speed is analyzed and reported.

1 who was it/was the boy/call the man/all of it/will he/ask me
2 for hers/the men/one of them/was the/are you/and the/was all
3 can she/let the/tore past fast/they play hard/they must lead
4 both half shot/mark zone lines/turn each over/must mark down
5 send cash now/sale must take/here list hall/want marked sale
6 Personal computers have lost popularity because of software.
7 All workers should field-test software before use in office.
8 Sharing terminals has expanded the use of computer networks.
9 Lengthy keyboarding projects are best done by trained staff.
10 Several word-processing software packages are on the market.

Now key each of the following sentences, choosing the correct word.

1 Sometimes we spend too much time dwelling on the (passed, past).

2 We (passed, past) the road before we realized that it was upon us.

3 All (personal, personnel) must report to work on time.

4 Many (personal, personnel) decisions are very private matters.

5 Please (precede, proceed) with the plans for construction of the new library.

6 The drawing of the plans should (precede, proceed) the construction.

Improve Keying Skills

Take two 1-minute timings on each paragraph. Set a speed or an accuracy goal. If you complete a paragraph before time runs out, start over.

Exercise 1

Career studies estimate that people will have seven different jobs in their working life. During a career, a top or middle management person may change positions several times. Many have passed up good opportunities, though, for personal reasons.

Exercise 2

Staff recruitment is an essential activity of any organization. Many organizations have full-time recruiters who visit the major universities that produce the types of personnel needed. Staff recruitment also is related to the organization's image and how they are perceived by the public. Recruiters must proceed with a solid understanding of the image they hope to convey.

11 Consider how long it takes to learn a program before buying.
12 Unfortunately, many programs do not deliver what's promised.
13 Notebook computers help people do work away from the office.
14 Managers use computers to prepare reports while on the road.

Improve Keying Accuracy

Both accuracy and speed are analyzed and reported.

1 An average annual income for an adult is actually amortized.
2 Behold the bonus buys brought back the best bountiful books.
3 Catch the crazy cat quickly! Carry the calf to that corral.
4 Deep diving does drive dumb ducks daffy. Diets deny donuts.
5 Easy earnings earn early debts. Easy exit earns in the end.
6 Five fervent firefighters find funds in foundation benefits.
7 Great Golden Gate grant got good publicity for the governor.
8 Hair is hard to have. Harvey heaved that herring head high.
9 Igor intends to initiate the initial initiative immediately.
10 Jill just junked Joe's jalopy. Jana jabbed the juicy jewel.
11 Kim knew the kettle was a keepsake. Know how to knit kites.
12 Labor is like leisure if you laugh at your load. Let loose.
13 Mega machines mean the maximum mastery of major measurement.
14 Neither Nels nor Nate neglected to negate Ned's nominations.
15 Oxen obstruct the only overpass. You owe the order the oil.
16 Provoke payees to pay promptly. Partial payments permitted.
17 Quan equipped the quartz quarry with quietly quality quotas.
18 Rest and relaxation render diverse rewards for the recruits.
19 Sam's seven system symbols are sequenced in successive sets.
20 Theory throws time travel to tomorrow. Tentative trial set.
21 Ursula was unsure about your uproar. Usurp universal unity.
22 Vain VIPs value victory. Value of a good valve was evident.
23 Workers wish Winona would waste less wild water in workouts.

45 Formatting Tables with Secondary Headings

GOALS

- Build Language Arts Skills
- Improve Keying Skills
- Learn to Format Tables with Secondary Headings

Review

Key each line two times.

1 thank you/thank you for/thank you very much/thanks
2 Let us enjoy the opportunities of education today.
3 We are going on our summer break this warm August.
4 Dear Sir or Madam: Ladies and Gentlemen: Sincerely

Build Language Arts Skills

Word Usage

Understand the correct usage of the following words.

Passed/Past
Passed go by
Past gone by or ended

Personal/Personnel
Personal private
Personnel employees; workers

Precede/Proceed
Precede go before
Proceed start; continue

Key each line.

1 They passed the final examination.
2 Their bills were all past due.
3 A personal secretary is a real help to an executive.
4 All personnel received the recent pay bonus.
5 Your good performance must precede your promotion.
6 The corporation cannot proceed toward its goals without your commitment.

24 Xenophobics exhibit extreme anxiety of Xingu's xenolith sea.
25 Yearly yields for young yams yoyo in the Yucatan and Yanzee.
26 Zigzagged zoning mazes crazed zany, zingy, zippy zoologists.

MEASURE PROGRESS

EXERCISE 1

Minimum goal: 25 wam with two or fewer errors 1.4 S.I.

Take two 1-minute timings.

The model 1150 printer is very fast and produces letter-quality print. The 5015 dot matrix printer produces excellent graphics.

Turnaround time is the amount of time from the keying of data to the printing out of the results. The turnaround time on the last job was about 15 minutes.

EXERCISE 2

Minimum goal: 23 wam with four or fewer errors 1.7 S.I.
Try to maintain speed, but key with control.

Take two 2-minute timings.

Sometime in the future you may need to make a decision to stay with a company or move on to new challenges. This type of decision causes a great amount of stress. When you are under stress, you usually do not make good decisions.

A career change requires a thorough study of the alternatives and the effects of each. Making important decisions takes time; therefore, one should not make career decisions on a crisis basis. Consider the alternatives and weigh the pros and cons of each. Reach important decisions in a rational way, and you will be pleased with the decision.

Learning Activity 3

1. Key the following table centered vertically and horizontally. Use the automatic centering method. Key the table double-spaced leaving 10 spaces between columns.
2. In order to have the second column align on the right, move the cursor to the last position in the key line.

   `Neptune    2,821,686,000`

   The last zero is at position 57.
3. Press the F7 key to go to the tab and margin setting screen. Clear all existing tabs. Set a left tab at position 28. Set a right tab at position 57. To set the right tab, key a greater than symbol (>) at the correct position. Press Enter to return to the lesson.
4. Press F5 to double-space the table. Key the title centered. Press Tab to start keying the first column. Press Tab to key the second column. Note how keyed characteres move to the left from the second tab.
5. Check the table and print a copy. Make certain the numbers are aligned at the right.
6. Press ESC to have the computer check your work.

PLANETS AND MAXIMUM MILES FROM THE SUN

Mercury	43,403,000
Venus	67,726,000
Earth	94,555,000
Mars	154,936,000
Jupiter	507,046,000
Saturn	937,541,000
Uranus	1,859,748,000
Neptune	2,821,686,000
Pluto	4,551,386,000

End-of-Lesson Procedure

After completing the activities for this lesson, follow the appropriate end-of-lesson procedure.

Exercise 3

Take two 3-minute timings.

Minimum goal: 20 wam with six or fewer errors 1.5 S.I.

Entering data into a computer system can be accomplished in a number of ways. You can input data from a soft or hard disk. The keyboard can be used to type in alphabetic and numeric data. Light pens can be used to touch or draw on the computer screen.

Graphics also can be entered using a graphics tablet directly attached to the central processing unit. In the future, many computers will have voice input, which will allow the user to have conversations with the computer and merely tell the computer what to do.

Advanced computer designs are creating computers that can learn and do their own problem solving. You will be able to teach the computer unique things that you want done a certain way, and then the computer will solve a given program using the data you have entered with the method you have taught it.

Composition Exercise

Name a document LES21CM1 in the word processor. Compose a short paragraph (four or five sentences) describing how you would respond to the following problem.

Problem: You are assigned to a team to complete a project. Two people on the team are not doing their share of the work. This affects what you and the other team members are responsible for doing. What steps you can take to solve the problem?

When finished, proofread the document on the screen. Use the editing keys to make any corrections. Save and print the document.

Proofread the printout and mark any errors you may have missed. Retrieve the document and make corrections as necessary. Save and print your corrected copy.

Follow the appropriate end-of-lesson procedure.

Learning Activity 2

Automatic Horizontal Centering

You can use the automatic features of your software to simplify the horizontal centering of a table. Follow these step-by-step directions to key the following table using the automatic features. This is the document LES44DC2.

1. Complete steps 1 and 2a from Learning Activity 1 for the manual centering method. The procedures for vertical centering and keying main headings do not change.
2. Key the key line. `Beth Williams (8 spaces) B`
3. Press the F6 key to center the line.
4. Note the position where the first column, Beth Williams, starts. It should be at column 32. Note the position where the second column, B, starts. It should be at column 53.
5. Press the F7 key to go to the tab and margin setting screen. Clear all existing tabs. Set a tab for column 1 at position 32 and a tab at column 2 at position 53. Press Enter to return to the lesson.
6. Delete the key line. Key the title centered on line 27. Press F6 to remove the center command you placed for the key line.
7. Press the F5 key to change to double-spacing. Key the rest of the table. Key across the columns. Press the Tab key to start keying the first column. Press the Tab key again to key items in the second column. Press Enter at the end of each line.
8. Check the table and print a copy. Compare it with the model. If the table is not properly centered vertically and horizontally, key it again.
9. Press ESC and have the computer check your work.

CLASS GRADES

Laura Jones	A
Bill Smith	B
William Sykes	F
Jane Bowling	C
Oscar Zonks	A
Beth Williams	B

UNIT 3
NUMERIC KEYPAD

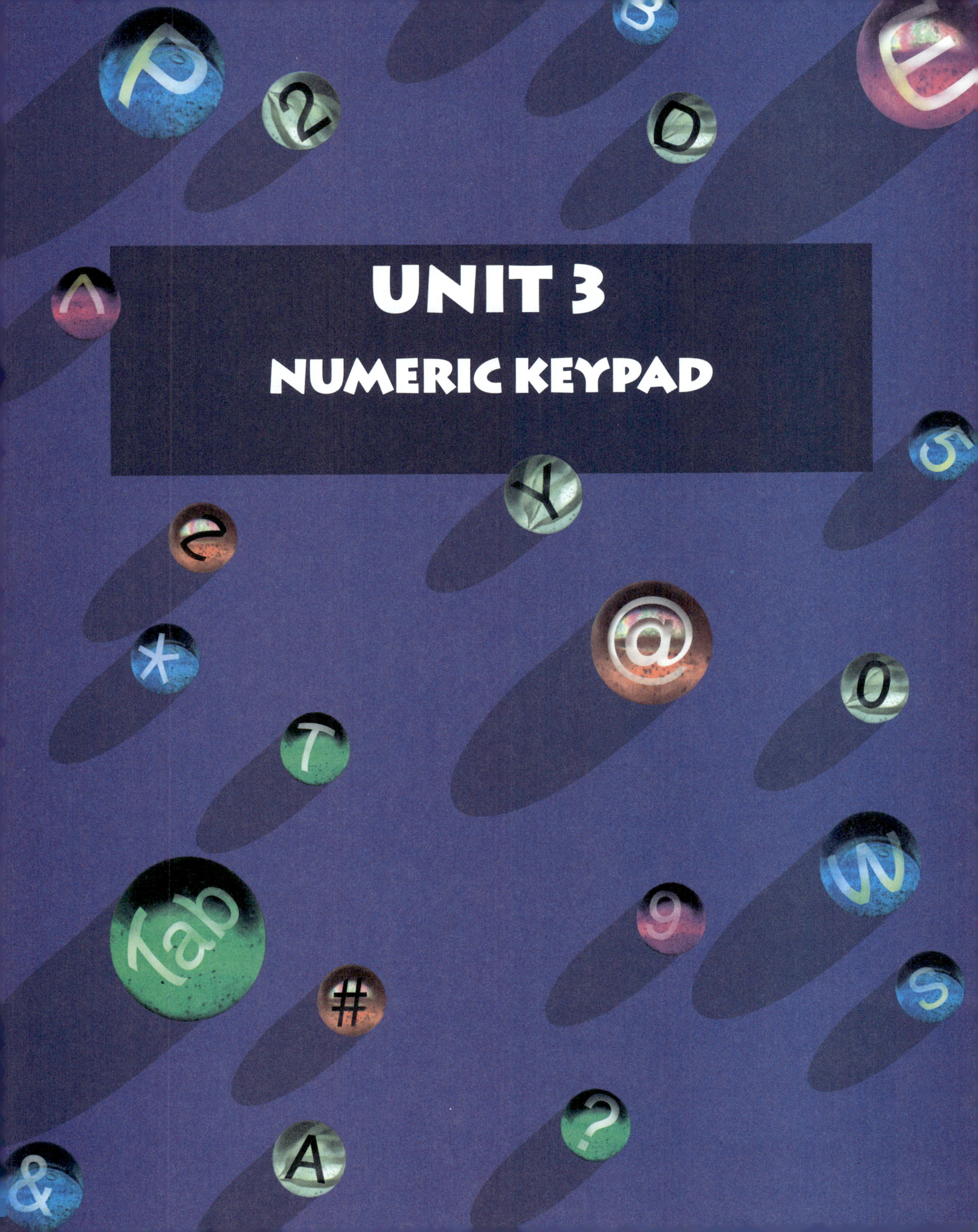

d. Backspace once for each 2 spaces between columns (8 2 = 4): so backspace 4 times for the space between columns. If you backspaced properly, you should be at column 23 in 10 pitch (using 43 for center). If you did not backspace properly, try it again.

e. Note this setting for the tab for the first column. Do not key anything at this time.

f. Space forward from the first column setting for each letter or space in *Vice President* plus the 8 spaces between the columns. You should be at column 45. If not, try again. Note this setting for the tab for the second column. Do not key anything at this time.

3. Press the F7 key to go to the tab and margin setting screen. Clear all existing tabs. Set a left tab at position 23 for the first column and at position 45 for the second column. Press Enter to return to the lesson.
4. Key the main heading centered in all capital letters on line 26. Use F6 to center the heading. Press the F5 key to change the line spacing to double-spacing.
5. Key the body of the table. Press tab to key the first column. Key across the columns. Press Enter at the end of each line. Check the document and print a copy. Compare it with the model. If it is not properly centered vertically and horizontally, key it again.
6. Press ESC and have the computer check your document.

Note: The computer checks all tables for exact spacing. If you are off by even one space, errors will be indicated. Check with your instructor before rekeying.

Line 26 → OFFICERS OF THE GOVERNANCE COUNCIL

President	Marina Schneidt
Vice President	Diep Trinh
Secretary	Mikel Salamonov
Treasurer	Ann Lewis Wiltshire
Director	Maria DeSilva
Director	Keiko Tsuboi
Director	Andrew Belangia

8 spaces

Tab Tab

22

Learn the Numeric Keypad 4, 5, 6, 7, 8, and 9

GOALS

- Reinforce Previous Learning
- Learn 4, 5, 6, 7, 8, and 9 Using Numeric Keypad
- Learn to Enter Numbers in Column Format

Remember the "Get Ready" checklist.

REVIEW

Key each line two times.

1 Sometimes a fine argument can obtain good success.

2 Roz was excited about eating a quiet meal with Bo.

3 The winning number for a quaint gift was fourteen.

4 How many computers were ordered with topaz chairs?

5 The police officer yelled, "Stop that yellow car!"

6 Please call me at 748-6972 (extension 15) at 8:30.

LEARN THE NUMERIC TEN-KEY KEYPAD

Most microcomputers have a numeric keypad that is used for material containing intensive numeric applications. Numeric data can be entered faster with the ten-key keypad than with the top-row number keys.

On the IBM PC, the numeric keypad is located to the right of the alphabetic keyboard. This location may differ on other microcomputers, but the arrangement of the numeric keys is basically the same. The ten-key keypad arrangement is the same as on electronic calculators.

To activate the numeric keypad, press the Num Lock key. On some keyboards, this key is located above the numeric keypad. On other keyboards, it is located below the numeric keypad. After the data has been entered, press the Num Lock key again to resume regular keyboarding functions. This key is a toggle switch.

1. Center tables horizontally and vertically on the page. (If a table is to be incorporated into another document such as a letter or report, center the table horizontally and leave two blank lines above and below the table.)
2. Center the main heading and key it in all capital letters. Double-space after it.
3. Format the body of the table in columns. The body may be single- or double-spaced, depending on the desired layout.
4. Center the columns horizontally, leaving the same amount of space between each column. This space usually ranges from 4 to 8 spaces. It is easier to work with even spacing between the columns.
5. Align word columns on the left and numerical columns on the right or at the decimal point. For example:

Words	**Numbers**
Betty Hamilton	497
Ron Basil	2
Horace Abernathy	1050

Learning Activity 1

Manual Horizontal Centering

Follow these step-by-step directions to key the model table on the following page using the manual method of horizontal centering. This is document LES44DC1.

1. Compute the vertical center. Allow for a double-space after the title and double-space the body. If you compute the vertical center properly, the title should start on line 26. If your answer was not line 26, refigure the vertical center. Do not key anything at this time.
2. Compute the horizontal center and set tabs for the columns. To compute the horizontal center:
   a. Begin by determining the key line. The key line includes the longest line in each column and the number of spaces between columns. For this table, leave 8 spaces between columns. Therefore, the key line for this table is:
      `Vice President (8 spaces) Ann Lewis Wiltshire`
   b. Space to the center of the line (43 for 10 pitch in this software).
   c. Backspace once for each 2 spaces required by the key line. Ignore a single leftover character. The longest line in column 1 is *Vice President*. The longest line in column 2 is *Ann Lewis Wiltshire*. Backspace once for each 2 letters and spaces as follows:

      `Vi/ce/spaceP/re/si/de/nt/An/nspace/Le/wi/sspace/Wi/`
      `lt/sh/ir/e` ←Drop the *e*.

The Principles of Reading Numbers

The same principles of reading numbers that apply to top-row numbers also apply to the numeric keypad. Review Lesson 13 before beginning the next section.

Locate the 4, 5, and 6 Keys

Use proper technique.

The home keys on the numeric keypad are the 4, 5, and 6. Place the J K L fingers on the 4, 5, 6 keys.

Assume Correct Finger Position

When operating the numeric keypad, use the correct finger position:

1. Rest your fingers lightly over the home keys.
2. Keep your fingers curved and upright.
3. Use quick, snappy strokes.

The ten-key keypad is most often used to key numbers or amounts that appear in columns. To keep the numbers in column format, strike Enter after keying each line of the column. On most microcomputers, the Enter key is located to the right of the 3 key. Use the little finger of the right hand (the ; finger) to quickly strike Enter after keying a group of numbers. On some microcomputers, the Enter key is located to the left of the 4 key In this case, use the 4 finger to strike the Enter key.

Measure Progress

Take two 3- or 5-minute timings.

Minimum goal: 3-minute timing—32 wam with six or fewer errors; 5-minute timing—27 wam with ten or fewer errors

Communication is a vital factor in the paperless office. Files and processes must be shared with the various offices and departments within and outside the organization. This is often accomplished through networking.

Most networking is through the telephone lines and other direct link cables. The flow of communication is directly related to the quality of the service available.

Often this service is poorly planned or maintained, and that leads to breakdowns in the data-sharing process. This could result in losing an important letter or file.

Maintenance of equipment is very important. Many offices do not think of maintenance until a piece of equipment breaks down. There may be long delays while waiting for service. A well-run office has a regular maintenance schedule for all its equipment.

As offices become more automated, more persons will be needed who can service and maintain technical equipment. People who are already employed also may wish to retrain.

Review Simple Tables

Review the directions for simple tables from Lesson 26. Then follow the steps below to key the model table on page 277.

Table Formatting Guidelines

Study the two-column table on the following page, and review these general guidelines for formatting it.

Practice the 4 ←, 5, and 6 → Key Reaches

Look at your fingers as you make the initial reaches. Then practice keying these drills until you can key them by touch. Key down each column.

You do not need to total these columns.

1	44	55	44	444	444	444	444	555
2	44	54	55	555	555	555	555	444
3	44	44	66	666	666	666	666	655
4	55	45	64	646	654	456	654	654
5	55	44	65	654	456	654	546	545
6	55	55	46	456	466	455	655	645
7	66	66	56	566	544	644	544	546
8	66	65	64	456	456	456	465	546
9	66	56	65	654	654	645	654	556
10	55	65	45	546	466	545	655	544

Locate the 7 Home, 8 ↑, and 9 Pg Up Keys

The 7, 8, and 9 keys are located in the row above the 4, 5, and 6 keys. Keep your fingers resting on the 4, 5, and 6 keys and practice the reach to the 7, 8, and 9 keys.

Now key each of the following sentences, choosing the correct word.

1 The woman was very skilled in the (marital, martial) arts.

2 The couple took their (marital, martial) vows very seriously.

3 It is important to keep the (moral, morale) of the employees at a positive level.

4 Many issues are cause for (moral, morale) dilemmas for today's youth.

Improve Keying Skills

Take two 1-minute timings on each paragraph. Set a speed or an accuracy goal. If you complete the paragraph before time runs out, start over.

Exercise 1

Management is basically the task of getting people to work toward common goals. Good management requires a variety of interpersonal skills, including communicating and motivating. Those managers who involve employees in goal setting usually have more motivated workers. Motivated workers, in turn, seldom suffer from low morale.

Exercise 2

Often employees do not understand the basic goals and objectives of their employer. This prevents them from seeing the connection between their job and the company's success. Companies that communicate the goals and objectives of the company to the employees in a nonmartial manner will have better informed workers. These companies can be characterized as having open communication.

Practice the [7 Home], [8 ↑], and [9 Pg Up] Key Reaches

Look at your fingers as you make the initial reaches. Then practice keying these drills until you can key them by touch. Key down each column.

1	4 4	4 4 4	5 5	5 5 5	6 6	6 6 6
2	4 7	7 7 7	5 8	8 8 8	6 9	9 9 9
3	7 7	7 7 6	8 8	8 5 7	9 9	6 9 5
4	4 4	4 7 5	5 5	8 4 6	6 6	5 9 9
5	7 7	5 7 7	8 8	6 4 8	9 6	4 9 8
6	7 4	7 4 5	8 5	5 4 8	6 9	8 9 7
7	4 7	5 4 7	5 8	4 8 8	9 9	5 7 9
8	7 7	6 4 7	8 8	7 4 8	6 6	7 8 9
9	4 4	7 4 7	5 5	8 5 7	9 6	8 7 8
10	4 7	5 7 4	5 8	7 8 4	6 9	9 4 5

Keep your fingers curved and strike each key quickly.

Practice All Numeric Keypad Key Reaches

Practice keying these drills until you can key them by touch. Key down each column.

1	9 4 6	4 9 5	9 8 7	9 7 6	4 7 8	8 7 8	4 7 9 8
2	8 5 7	6 9 9	4 5 8	6 7 5	7 9 4	6 9 9	6 4 5 7
3	7 4 8	9 7 8	8 6 4	5 9 8	5 5 6	5 5 6	8 5 9 6
4	9 5 6	8 4 6	7 5 8	4 6 7	6 7 8	7 8 7	7 8 4 5
5	4 6 5	7 5 9	8 4 6	7 4 5	8 7 5	6 4 5	5 9 6 8
6	5 4 6	4 6 9	9 8 7	6 9 8	9 8 9	5 7 5	7 5 4 6
7	7 5 9	5 4 6	7 4 6	7 4 8	6 7 7	8 4 9	8 4 9 5
8	8 6 4	6 4 8	8 4 7	6 5 9	9 8 5	6 5 8	5 6 7 8

44

Review Formatting Simple Tables

GOALS

- Build Language Arts Skills
- Improve Keying Skills
- Review Simple Tables

REVIEW

Key each line two times.

1 ask her/buy car/had not/one way/get him/too big/it

2 Initial the interest instead of investing incomes.

3 The extra billing cycles were to begin on 7/11/95.

4 Regardless of how automated the office becomes, communication skills will be essential.

BUILD LANGUAGE ARTS SKILLS

WORD USAGE

Understand the correct usage of the following words.

Marital/Martial

Marital relating to marriage
Martial relating to military

Moral/Morale

Moral ethical
Morale mental attitude

Key each line.

1 Marital happiness is desired by all married couples.

2 The captain acts in a martial manner.

3 The office climate was very moral.

4 Treat everyone in a moral manner.

5 The morale of the workers was very positive.

Measure Progress

Exercise 1

Minimum goal: 25 wam with two or fewer errors 1.3 S.I.

Try to exceed the minimum goal.

Take two 1-minute timings.

Software quality is often not as good as we would prefer. Many programs have flaws or bugs in them. Your best bet is to try out the software before buying it or be sure the company has a return policy. If software is to be used in a classroom setting, it should be tried out by students before it is purchased. Classroom software needs to be dependable.

Exercise 2

Minimum goal: 23 wan with four or fewer errors 1.7 S.I.

Take two 2-minute timings.

Debugging a program means to remove the flaws to get the program to perform properly. The term "debug" comes from the past when computers had a large number of electromagnetic relays. The heat generated by the relays attracted bugs and lint, so debugging actually meant removing the bugs from the relays.

Computers are becoming smaller and smaller as advances in chip technology are made. The ability to build very small and compact computers will allow great advances in robotics and artificial intelligence.

Learning Activity 5

1. Center the following table in proper format. Double-space after the title and double-space the body. Use the default margins.
2. Proofread the copy on the screen and make corrections. Save and print a copy.
3. Check to see if the table is centered vertically and if each line is centered horizontally. If the table is not centered properly, repeat the exercise.
4. Press ESC to have the computer check your work.

ATLANTIC COAST CONFERENCE

Clemson University

Duke University

Florida State University

Georgia Tech

North Carolina State University

University of Maryland

University of North Carolina

University of Virginia

Wake Forest University

End-of-Lesson Procedure

At the end of each lesson, you will have the following options:

1. To restart the same lesson, press the F1 function key.
2. To return to the Lessons Menu, press ESC. This action automatically will save the completed lesson.
3. To proceed to the next, or any other lesson, highlight your choice on the menu and press Enter.
4. To return to the Main Menu, press ESC again.
5. To print the lesson, select Print Activities.
6. To exit the program:
   a. Select the Exit option and press Enter.
   b. When the DOS prompt appears on the screen, remove your data disk.
   c. Turn off the monitor. (Your instructor also may ask you to turn off the computer and printer.)

EXERCISE 3

Minimum goal: 20 wam with six or fewer errors 1.6 S.I.

Try to exceed the minimum goal.

Take two 3-minute timings.

```
     Artificial intelligence implies that the computer will be able to learn and change its behavior based on new information.  The computer's behavior will become adaptive.  The user or owner of a robot will be able to teach it special or required behavior designed to accomplish a given task.
     Imagine being able to teach your personal robot to cook, clean house, tend the garden, or be a security guard at night.  How about teaching it to take care of your pet?  In reality, the possibilities are limited only by the imagination of the owner.
     The possibilities for the use of artificial intelligence in business are unlimited also.  Programmers of these expert systems may be called knowledge engineers.  The careers available in this field are very exciting.
```

COMPOSITION EXERCISE

Using the word processor, name a document LES22CMP. Compose a short paragraph (four or five sentences) describing how you would respond to the following problem. Do not worry about errors on your first attempt.

Problem: A new student at your school asks how to apply for admission and register for a course. List, in order, the steps that the student should follow.

When finished, proofread the document on the screen. Use the editing keys to make any corrections. Save and print the document. Proofread the hard copy and mark any errors you may have missed. Retrieve the document and make corrections as necessary. Save and print your corrected copy.

Follow the appropriate end-of-lesson procedure.

3. Check the printout to see if the quotes are centered vertically and horizontally. If they are not centered properly, repeat the exercise before beginning Learning Activity 4.
4. Press ESC to have the computer check your work.

"Who are a free people? Those who live under a government so constitutionally checked and controlled that proper provision is made against its being otherwise executed." John Milton

"Those who reap the blessings of freedom must undergo the fatigue of supporting it." Thomas Paine

"If a nation expects to be ignorant and free, in a state of civilization, it expects what never was and never will be." Thomas Jefferson

"We should all be concerned about the future because we will have to spend the rest of our lives there." Charles F. Kettering

Learning Activity 4

When a heading is needed for a listing, it is keyed in all capital letters and centered over the listing. Double-space after the heading before beginning the first line of the listing.

1. Start a new document, LES43DC4. Key the following table. Center it vertically and center each line horizontally. Use the default margins.
2. Center the heading of the table over the listing in all capital letters. Double-space before beginning the first line of the listing. Single-space between the entries. Press Enter at the end of each line. Press F6 to horizontally center each line.
3. Proofread the copy on the screen. Use the editing keys to make corrections. Save and print a copy.
4. Press ESC to have the computer check your work.

Remember to double-space after the heading.

TEAMS IN THE LEAGUE
DS
Braves
Colts
Broncos
Redbirds
Blue Jays
Mud Hens
Cougars
Jaguars
Bisons
Bears

23

Learn the Numeric Keypad 1, 2, 3, 0, and Decimal Point

GOALS

- Reinforce Previous Learning
- Learn 1, 2, 3, 0, and . Using the Numeric Keypad

Remember the "Get Ready" checklist.

REVIEW

Key each line two times.

```
1 Good skills are crucial in information processing.
2 Queries to the computer prompted a quick response.
3 Some people are initially afraid to use computers.
4 Programs that do not operate properly are not fun.
5 The measurement for the living room was 12' x 26'.
6 Call 1-800-893-4952 for information about records.
```

LOCATE THE 1 End, 2 ↓, AND 3 Pg Dn KEYS

The 1, 2, and 3 keys are located in the row below the 4, 5, and 6 keys. With your fingers resting on the 4, 5, and 6 keys, practice the drills until you can key them by touch.

3. Check to see if the announcement is centered vertically and if each line is centered horizontally. If the announcement is not centered properly, repeat the exercise before beginning Learning Activity 2.
4. Press ESC to have the computer check your work.

Remember to accurately count all lines—both text and spaces.

Learning Activity 2

1. Start document LES43DC2. Center the following table vertically and each line horizontally. Single-space it. Use the default margins.
2. Proofread the copy on the screen. Use the editing keys to make corrections. Save and print a copy.
3. Check to see if the table is centered vertically and if each line is centered horizontally. If the table is not centered properly, repeat the exercise before beginning Learning Activity 3.
4. Press ESC to have the computer check your work.

```
         Durango, Colorado
         Aurora, Illinois
    Fort Lauderdale, Florida
         Sioux City, Iowa
        Paducah, Kentucky
   Worcester, Massachusetts
       Bemidji, Minnesota
      Natchez, Mississippi
          Havre, Montana
       Muskogee, Oklahoma
     Altoona, Pennsylvania
      Sheboygan, Wisconsin
```

Learning Activity 3

The F6 command will center horizontally a block of text. To center a block strike F6, key in the paragraph or block of text, and press F6 again. Pressing F6 the second time stops the centering command since F6 is a toggle key.

1. Start a new document, LES43DC3. Center the following quotes vertically. Single-space the quotes. Double-space between each one. Use the default margins. Center each quote horizontally by pressing F6. Remember: Do not press F6 again until you want to end the centering command.
2. Proofread the copy on the screen. Use the editing keys to make corrections. Save and print a copy.

Practice the 1 End, 2 ↓, and 3 Pg Dn Key Reaches

Key down the columns.

1	44	444	55	555	66	631
2	11	111	22	222	33	321
3	41	144	52	257	63	723
4	14	511	25	722	36	123
5	44	614	55	521	66	443
6	11	751	22	124	33	322
7	41	681	25	219	63	113
8	14	171	52	812	36	324
9	11	145	22	176	33	321
10	14	164	25	152	63	362

Remember to read the numbers in groups.

Practice All Numeric Keypad Key Reaches

Key down the columns.

1	111	456	324	478	641	721	4251
2	222	123	586	581	986	423	6382
3	333	789	732	692	321	647	4793
4	453	983	346	736	158	313	6821
5	936	458	329	137	326	892	5147
6	123	312	831	462	215	476	9284
7	322	241	762	151	163	298	2673
8	243	156	363	231	224	214	3461
9	641	752	143	591	642	519	2572

Double-Spacing

```
Office Automation Association

cordially invites you to

the fifth annual

Business Machines Exposition

The World Trade Center

Boston, Massachusetts

February 28, 1998
```

3. Subtract the lines to be keyed from the total lines available on the page.

	Single-Spacing	**Double-Spacing**
	Full Sheet	Full Sheet
Available	66	66
Used	-7	-13
Unused	59	53

4. Divide the unused lines by 2 to determine the number of blank lines to leave for the top and bottom margins. Disregard any fraction.

	Full Sheet
Single-Spacing	$59 \div 2 = 29\frac{1}{2} = 29$
Double-Spacing	$53 \div 2 = 26\frac{1}{2} = 26$

5. To leave the correct amount of space in the top margin, add 1 line to the number of lines calculated, and then begin keying on this line.

	Full Sheet
Single-Spacing	$29 + 1 = 30$
Double-Spacing	$26 + 1 = 27$

6. Some microcomputer software leaves a set amount of space at the top before printing begins. Check the software you are using and include those lines as a part of your count from the top. **Remember:** This software automatically leaves 6 blank lines in the top margin.

Learning Activity 1

1. Start a new document named LES43DC1. Key the announcement on the preceding page. Center the announcement vertically. Center each line horizontally by pressing F6. Single-space the copy. Use the default margins.
2. Proofread the copy on the screen. Use the editing keys to make corrections. Save and print a copy.

LOCATE THE 0 Ins AND . Del KEYS

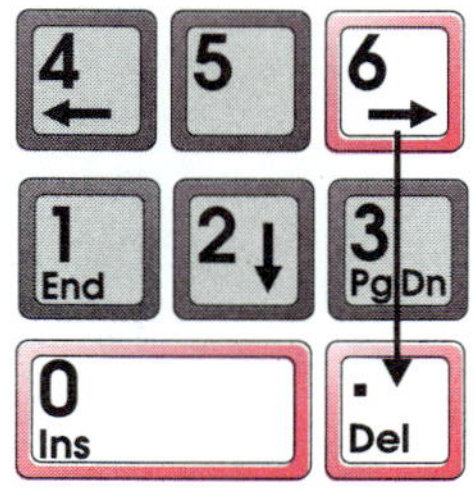

The location of these keys may vary on different keyboards. Use the appropriate finger for the location of the keys on your keyboard.

PRACTICE THE 0 Ins AND . Del KEY REACHES

The 0 is keyed with the thumb (on most machines). The . (decimal) is keyed with the 6 finger (on most machines). Practice keying these drills until you can key them by touch. Key down the columns.

The decimal points do not need to align in this exercise.

1	44	410	666	4.50	45.90
2	11	203	.66	0.5	6.150
3	00	120	6.6	.01	72.49
4	40	010	44.3	.60	6.381
5	10	050	2.01	5.0	00.01
6	04	400	3.56	60.	49.04
7	40	700	45.3	.01	63.01
8	01	303	65.9	.05	78.02
9	00	101	98.7	.11	63.73
10	07	809	41.5	6.80	89.40

Review Vertical Centering

Before printing a document, decisions must be made about the page layout. The page layout determines the placement of a document on a page. Some documents need to be centered vertically as well as horizontally on a page. To center text vertically on a page, you must determine how many blank lines to leave at the top of the page before you begin to key. Follow these procedures, which were introduced in Lesson 26, to center text vertically:

1. Determine the number of vertical lines available on the paper on which you will be printing. Standard $8\frac{1}{2}$ by 11-inch paper has 66 vertical lines (11 inches x 6 lines per inch).
2. Determine the number of printed and blank lines in the copy to be keyed. Assume you wish to horizontally and vertically center the following:

```
        Office Automation Association

          cordially invites you to

             the fifth annual

       Business Machines Exposition

          The World Trade Center

          Boston, Massachusetts

            February 28, 1998
```

Based on your spacing selection, count the number of lines to be keyed.

Single-Spacing

```
1 Office Automation Association
2 cordially invites you to
3 the fifth annual
4 Business Machines Exposition
5 The World Trade Center
6 Boston, Massachusetts
7 February 28, 1998
```

Practice All Numeric-Keypad Key Reaches

Practice keying these drills until you can key them by touch. Remember to apply the number-reading principles to these drills. Key down the columns.

1	.005	54.12	231.1	7801	1234	10987
2	6.05	20123	45.12	6420	5678	21098
3	.212	1.001	11.33	6947	9009	32109
4	22.6	.0005	104.0	4279	8765	43210
5	2.14	1.789	20.10	8346	4321	54321
6	1.03	.6112	100.1	1059	0246	65432
7	.001	761.2	20.10	2001	8135	76543
8	70.0	40.03	233.9	3042	7901	87654
9	61.1	987.1	87.06	4110	3690	10987
10	34.5	492.6	05.01	6710	4905	23947

Measure Progress

Exercise 1

Minimum goal: 25 wam with one or fewer errors 1.7 S.I.

Try to exceed the minimum goal.

Take two 1-minute timings.

Legal secretaries, medical records secretaries, and general office secretaries must learn keyboarding skills. A good typist only needs to learn the special computer keys to make the transition from typist to computer keyboarder. It is not difficult to become proficient on a computer keyboard if you are a good typist. The arrangement of the keys is essentially the same.

Exercise 2

Some companies look for individuals who have excelled in sports, especially team sports. Successful participation in team sports usually indicates a degree of competitiveness and teamwork, both of which can be helpful in a business environment. A business without teamwork may risk losing its competitive advantage.

Measure Progress

Minimum goal: 3-minute timing—32 wam with six or fewer errors; 5-minute timing—27 wam with ten or fewer errors

Take two 3- or 5-minute timings.

In a world of rapid change, one must develop some strategies for coping with the stress that change can incur. One strategy is to fully accept the change and learn all that you can about how the change will affect your life. The change might offer you a number of new opportunities for growth and improvement.

If you resist the change, it can be a source of worry and stress. If you truly feel that the change is bad or will not be beneficial in the long run, then you may take positive actions to prevent or modify the change. You may suggest that the change be tested and evaluated on a trial basis before being implemented on a wholesale basis. You could request further study and discussion of the important issues that concern you.

One thing is certain about the world that we live in today: it will be filled with change. Those who learn to cope will live a happier and more stress-free life.

EXERCISE 2

Take two 2-minute timings.

Minimum goal: 23 wam with three or fewer errors 1.6 S.I.

File cabinets may become totally obsolete when the paperless office is fully implemented. All records will be electronically stored on various media. Think of the trees that will be saved.

When voice recognition is perfected, keyboarding also may become obsolete. All one will have to do is give a verbal command, and the computer will respond. Using this computer will require a new skill of talking composition.

EXERCISE 3

Take two 3-minute timings.

Minimum goal: 20 wam with five or fewer errors 1.6 S.I.

Try to exceed the minimum goal.

The main purpose in keyboarding skill is to efficiently enter data for the computer to process. If the data is entered incorrectly, then the output will contain errors. This idea is expressed by the phrase "Garbage in, garbage out." Keyboarding speed is essential; however, accuracy is also important. Usually one works on speed and then concentrates on correctness. In the final result, both speed and accuracy are essential.

At this point in your keyboarding program, you should be proficient in keying alpha and numeric information. You should be able to use correct techniques and to key by touch. Your speed should be increasing, and you should be improving your accuracy also.

7 A loose cable caused the monitor to blink on and off.

8 Please do not lose my office keys.

9 You may lose the contest, but give it your best effort.

Now key each of the following sentences, choosing the correct word.

1 The reclining chair was so comfortable that Nadia wanted to (lay, lie) in it all day.

2 When you have finished the puzzle, (lay, lie) it on the table.

3 The attorney placed a (lean, lien) on the property.

4 Do not (lean, lien) on the fence; it does not have proper support.

5 The collar needs to be (loose, lose) around the dog's neck so that it will not choke him.

6 Did you (loose, lose) the new necklace that Franco gave you?

Improve Keying Skills

Take two 1-minute timings on each paragraph. Set a speed or an accuracy goal. If you complete the paragraph before time runs out, start over.

Exercise 1

This company has many opportunities for advancement. The salaries are above average, and the fringe benefits package is one of the best offered by companies of this type. We lean toward only the top graduates from school and look for evidence of leadership activities from both inside and outside the classroom.

Composition Exercise

Using the word processor, name the document LES23CM1. Suppose that you are very good at keyboarding, and your supervisor at work decides that you can answer some of the company correspondence. Using the word processor, compose a short paragraph (four or five sentences) describing how you would respond to the following problem. Do not worry about errors on your first attempt.

Problem: An irate customer has written a letter complaining about a repair person who made an appointment but never showed up.

When finished, proofread the document on the screen. Use the editing keys to make any corrections. Save and print the document.

Proofread the printout and mark any errors you may have missed. Retrieve the document and make corrections as necessary. Save and print your corrected copy.

End-of-Lesson Procedure

At the end of each lesson, you will have the following options:

1. To restart the same lesson, press the F1 function key.
2. To return to the Lessons Menu, press ESC. This action automatically will save the completed lesson.
3. To proceed to the next, or any other lesson, highlight your choice on the menu and press Enter.
4. To return to the Main Menu, press ESC again.
5. To print the lesson, select Print Activities.
6. To exit the program:
   a. Select the Exit option and press Enter.
   b. When the DOS prompt appears on the screen, remove your data disk.
   c. Turn off the monitor. (Your instructor also may ask you to turn off the computer and printer.)

43

Vertical Centering and Centering Headings

GOALS

- Build Language Arts Skills
- Improve Keying Skills
- Learn Vertical Centering
- Learn to Center Headings

Review

Key each line two times.

```
1 even more/even the/even though/end of/end of those
2 die rip reed maybe spend white where range grasses
3 I cannot pay for a new car without getting a loan.
4 13205 Maple Red Drive, 254 Pony Tail Road, 16 Faxe
```

Build Language Arts Skills

Word Usage

Understand the correct usage of the following words.

Lay/Lie
Lay put or place
Lie recline

Lean/Lien
Lean rest against; incline toward; opposite of fat
Lien legal right or claim

Loose/Lose
Loose not tight
Lose to misplace; opposite of win

Key each line.

```
1 Lay the finished manuscript in the out box.
2 The giraffe decided to lie down on the grass.
3 Lean the book against the shelves.
4 The report appeared to lean toward conservation.
5 She is a lean, muscular person.
6 A lien was placed on his salary.
```

UNIT 4

SKILL BUILDING AND FORMATTING

Measure Progress

Minimum goal: 31 wam with six or fewer errors

Take two 3-minute timings.

Often new inventions take years to be disseminated to the general population. It was years before the automobile was used universally. On the other hand, computers have spread among various groups at a very fast pace. Computers will be used universally much sooner than the auto, electric lights, and numerous other inventions ever were.

The reason for this lag in the adoption of new inventions is that people fear and resist change. If people perceive a new invention to be a threat to their employment or way of life, the invention will be resisted.

One way to overcome resistance is to involve people in the decision to make the change. Another way is to provide adequate training to alleviate any fears the change may foster. Usually it is the unknown features of a pending change that create anxiety in people.

Composition Exercise

Using the word processor compose a short report describing how you would respond to the following situation. This is document LES42CMP.

Situation: Your supervisor has given you a project that is due tomorrow. When you review it, you realize that there is more than one day's work.

When finished, proofread the document on the screen. Use the editing keys to make any corrections. Save and print the document. Proofread the printout and mark any errors you may have missed. Retrieve the document and make corrections as necessary. Save and print your corrected copy.

End-of-Lesson Procedure

After completing the exercises, follow the appropriate end-of-lesson procedure.

24 Skill Building and Formatting Reports

GOALS

- Reinforce Previous Learning
- Increase Keying Speed
- Improve Keying Accuracy
- Learn to Double-Space
- Learn to Format Unbound Reports

Remember the "Get Ready" checklist.

REVIEW

Key each line two times.

```
1 The zoo contained a number of very quaint animals.
2 Compare words a minute (wam) scores to gain speed.
3 Warm up fast!  Use all fingers!  Relax the muscle!
4 Their overhead for the first quarter will be >10%.
5 Jane said, "Stop the tape!  We produced 10% @ $1."
6 My number is 804-763-1529; Jack's is 203-723-7651.
```

INCREASE KEYING SPEED

Key each line two times.

```
1 her day/put the/did not/you are/new car/any one/take the car
2 make the mail list/turn left here/roll past the mark/call it
3 must want true area quit rely room move dove love sale minds
4 sale must take here list hall want mark head take note fifth
5 town star send sale fees fast cold half gain must tell reply
6 Everyone needs to know keyboarding within the next ten years.
7 Spreadsheets are used to prepare account ledgers and budgets.
8 Many software packages have tutorials and on-line assistance.
9 Paperless offices and modems initiate new cottage industries.
10 People working at home will eliminate many city traffic jams.
11 Menu-driven software lists accessible options for procedures.
12 A spreadsheet program lets me easily execute math operations.
13 Computers facilitate basing decisions on the up-to-date data.
14 A license agreement states how software programs can be used.
```

Improve Keying Skills

Take two 1-minute timings on each paragraph. Set a speed or an accuracy goal. If you complete a paragraph before time runs out, start over.

Exercise 1

War and threats of hostilities among nations and trade partners always affect domestic and foreign markets. A business that depends on trade with foreign companies must have strategic plans that allow for probable changes. The foreign balance of payments also can affect the profits that can be made with international trade partners.

Exercise 2

Career studies have indicated that the job itself is a motivator and that employees are motivated by responsibility and recognition. On the other hand, employees may take pride in the quality of their work whether anyone notices or not. This is an example of internal self-motivation. The intent of both types of motivation is to increase productivity.

Improve Keying Accuracy

Key each of the following sentences concentrating on accuracy—no more than one error per sentence. If you do not reach the accuracy goal, repeat the sentence. Try to maintain your already achieved speed.

1 The tight mobs galloped at high rates until the two tripped.
2 The lower price on parking made it cheaper to drive the car.
3 Wax or tallow spilled on the wolf as he prowled the schools.
4 A zebra sped past the zany chap napping under the palm tree.
5 A lawyer verified that a violent explosion caused the quake.
6 A van was acquired to give extra transportation to the lazy.
7 It is crazy to spend vast amounts to visit the exotic lands.
8 The plumber had to quickly fix a leak to calm our anxieties.
9 Robots were used to quell the acid flow from that explosion.
10 Daily planning allows Tim to fix goals and make quick moves.

Measure Progress

Exercise 1

Minimum goal: 25 wam with one or fewer errors 2.0 S.I.

Try to exceed the minimum goal.

Take two 1-minute timings.

Databases are collections of facts and figures that a person or organization needs to perform certain operations. Examples of databases could include names and addresses, telephone numbers, bank balances, various accounting ledgers, paragraphs for letter construction, and other specific data needed by an organization.

Now key each of the following sentences, choosing the correct word.

1 It was (a/an) old theater ticket.

2 Did you buy (a/an) horse?

3 She is (a/an) honest person.

4 The meeting will last (a/an) hour.

5 She needed to (hew/hue) the logs in six-foot lengths.

6 A blue (hew/hue) was cast over the entire sunset.

7 Her acceptance speech was very (intense/intents).

8 We were not sure of the (intense/intents) of the ambassador.

9 The discussion will be completed (a, an) hour before the meeting.

10 Did you buy (a, an) house with the extra money?

11 Was (a, an) unit needed to complete the force?

12 He called (a, an) instant ago.

13 There was (a, an) unusual sunset yesterday.

14 The stormy clouds cast a strange (hew, hue) over the water.

15 The (intents, intense) of the politicians were unclear to the audience.

16 She gazed at the view from the hill in an (intents, intense) manner.

Improve Keying Accuracy

Key each line with no more than one error.

1 An annual cantata was planned about a data bazaar.

2 At the bazaar a gala saga was arranged with an array of food.

3 Busy busboys blabbed about the probable, bragged about the bribe.

4 The circle club's change cycle caused new tactics to recycle crucial cutbacks in the scenic classic concert.

EXERCISE 2

Take two 2-minute timings.

Minimum goal: 23 wam with three or fewer errors 1.4 S.I.

Your speed is slowly improving. Very soon you will be keying faster than 25 words per minute. As you progress, your speed and accuracy will also increase. It is rewarding to learn a new skill. Your new skill in keyboarding will pay handsome returns for your efforts.

Persons with keyboarding skill and word-processing knowledge are in great demand. You will find it much easier to enter data into your computer now that you have a touch system of keying. The time you have spent in learning to keyboard will pay many dividends in the future.

EXERCISE 3

Take two 3-minute timings.

Minimum goal: 20 wam with five or fewer errors 1.6 S.I.

Try to exceed the minimum goal.

Silicon chips are the nervous system of the computer. The chips are covered with very fine pathways that form circuits. Small currents of electricity move along the pathways. Each of the circuits is designed to perform certain functions that allow the computer to execute various commands. The small pulses that race along the chip's circuits are called "bits." These bits add, subtract, compare, store, and do a variety of other tasks when the computer system is on. The circuits or designs in the chips are chemically bound onto silicon wafers.

The design of a microcomputer is amazing. The small computers of today can perform tasks that the largest computer of several years ago could not perform. What will the future hold in store in computer technology?

42

Improving Keying Accuracy and Skills

GOALS

- Build Language Arts Skills
- Improve Keying Accuracy
- Improve Keying Skills

REVIEW

Key each line two times.

1 any time/appears that/I would like/it is/it is not

2 Are you going on spring break with class in April?

3 A debate over global warming will begin on Friday.

4 January, June, July 4, 1997, December 1998, August

BUILD LANGUAGE ARTS SKILLS

WORD USAGE

Understand the correct usage of the following words.

A/An

A used before all words beginning with a consonant sound or a long *u* sound (for example, *union*, *unit*)
An used before all words beginning with a vowel sound (except for the long *u* sound) and before words beginning with a silent *h* (for example, *hour*, *heir*)

Hew/Hue

Hew chop or cut
Hue color; shade

Intense/Intents

Intense strong; earnest
Intents aims; purposes

Key each line.

1 A youth applied for the job.

2 Talk to a union representative before you join.

3 A computer is a very helpful tool.

4 An apple a day is good for health.

5 An eel is a slippery creature.

Learn to Double-Space and Triple-Space

Many documents and keyboarding projects require variable spacing between each line of copy. Standard between-line spacing is usually referred to as "single-space." The most popular alternative is called "double-space." Double-spacing leaves one blank line between each keyed line of copy; triple-spacing leaves two blank lines. If you are using the software that accompanies this textbook, follow these steps to double-space or triple-space copy.

Remember: F5 is the key that controls single- and double-spacing.

1. Changing line spacing can be done only when using the word-processor portion of this program.
2. When the word-processing screen first appears, a message on the format line indicates that the default setting is "Single-Space."
3. The prompt line at the bottom of the screen indicates that the F5 function key controls spacing.
4. To change to double-spacing, press the F5 key. The format message now changes to "Double-Space." All copy that you now enter will appear double-spaced on the screen and when you print copy.
5. To change to triple-spacing, press the F5 key. The format message changes to "Triple-Spacing." All copy that you now enter will appear triple-spaced on the screen and when you print.
6. To return to single-spaced copy, press F5 again until the format line reads "Single-Space."
7. Single-space, double-space, and triple-space are the options available in this word processor.

Practice Line Spacing and Review Center and Underline

Using the word processor, name the document LES24DC1. Key the following announcement. Double-space the copy. Center each line of the announcement (use the F6 key). Underline the last line (use the F8 key).

```
THE DESKTOP PUBLISHING CLUB

Cordially invites you to attend

A SOFTWARE DEMONSTRATION

on

Tuesday, January 15

at 12:15 p.m.

Computer Laboratory

RSVP 555-8923 by January 10
```

UNIT 7

TABLES

Proofread the copy on the screen. Use the editing keys to make corrections. Save and print the announcement.

Proofread the printout and mark any errors you may have missed. Pay close attention to capitalization, line spacing, centering, and underlining. Retrieve the document and make corrections as necessary. When satisfied, have the computer check your work. Save and print your corrected copy.

Composition Exercise

Using the word processor, compose two short paragraphs describing how you would respond to the following problem. Do not worry about errors on your first attempt. Name the document LES24CM1.

Problem: You and another person are being considered for a promotion. The supervisor has asked each of you to write about your personal characteristics and qualities that would qualify you for the promotion. What do you write about yourself?

When finished, proofread the document on the screen. Use the editing keys to make any corrections. Save and print the document.

Proofread the printout and mark any errors you may have missed. Retrieve the document and make corrections as necessary. Save and print your corrected copy.

Learn to Format Unbound Reports

A report is a written summary of an activity or a presentation of data and information concerning a specified topic. Reports are designed to communicate, in a concise format, the results of various activities such as projects, meetings, assignments, and research.

Reports may be classified as informal or formal. The informal report is often used in business to present factual information. Formal reports are used to present the results of a study or investigation and are usually presented in bound format.

Look at the sample one-page unbound report format on page 142. This report follows one acceptable format. Formats for reports vary depending on the style manual you are using. Always consult the appropriate manual before keying a report.

Follow these steps to layout a one-page informal report.

1. Leave a 2-inch top margin. Key the title centered and in all capital letters. Remember that the software automatically leaves a one-inch top margin, so press Enter until the cursor is on line 13 (two inches).
2. Turn on double-spacing.
3. Key the body of the report.

TO: Terrence Suarez
FROM: Juanita Mendoza
SUBJECT: Medical Coverage
DATE: May 2, 1996

I recently received the following information from R. U. Buehler & Company proposing the Advantage Choice plan for our employee group. Shown below is a comparison of those rates to the ExtendaCare rates for the last year.

Advantage Choice		ExtendaCare	
Single	$ 71.96	Single	$ 91.12
+ Minor	107.98	+ Minor	141.18
Family	190.80	Family	241.42

As you can see, there are substantial savings in changing this group over to the Advantage Choice plan. I propose that we make this change effective July 1 of this year. In order to make this conversion, I will need each person in your group to complete the Risk Fact Finder sheet, which is enclosed. (¶) If you can complete these documents and return them to me by May 29, we will move forward with a proposed starting date of July 1.

xxx/les41dc3
Attachment
c: Sarah M. Wade
Ashton E. Mulligan

End-of-Lesson Procedure

After completeing the activities for this lesson, follow the appropriate end-of-lesson procedure.

4. Indent each paragraph five spaces (to the first default tab).
5. Use the 1-inch default side margins and the 1-inch default margins for the bottom of the page.
6. Use automatic word wrap. Do not strike Enter at the end of each line. Strike Enter to end a paragraph.

Formatting Exercise

1. Using the word processor, name a document LES24DC2. Key the model unbound report on the next page using the layout directions you just learned.
2. Proofread your copy on the screen. Use the editing keys to make corrections. Save and print the document.
3. Compare your printed copy with the model. Mark any errors you missed. Save and print your corrected copy. Have the computer check your document when you are satisfied with your work.

End-of-Lesson Procedure

At the end of each lesson, you will have the following options:

1. To restart the same lesson, press the F1 function key.
2. To return to the Lessons Menu, press ESC. This action automatically will save the completed lesson.
3. To proceed to the next, or any other lesson, highlight your choice on the menu and press Enter.
4. To return to the Main Menu, press ESC again.
5. To print the lesson, select Print Activities.
6. To exit the program:
   a. Select the Exit option and press Enter.
   b. When the DOS prompt appears on the screen, remove your data disk.
   c. Turn off the monitor. (Your instructor also may ask you to turn off the computer and printer.)

Line 7 → MEMORANDUM

TS

Current Date

DS

TO: Distribution List

DS

Marshall Kinze ← Sender's Name and Title
Office Manager

DS

MEMO FORMAT ← Subject Line

TS

The NASOA Office Support Staff Task Force has completed its assignment to develop standardized forms for companywide use. This memo and those attached illustrate the newly adopted form for memorandums.

DS

All but one of the traditional guide words are no longer needed. However, double-spacing is maintained between the sections of heading information. The body begins on the third line after the capitalized subject line.

DS

Key lists of information as follows:

Tab →

* Use an asterisk, bullet, number, or letter to introduce each item.
* Single-space within the lists, but double-space above and below the lists.
* Indent lists one 5-space tab stop from the left margin.

Key reference initials a double-space after the body of the memo. After the reference intials, include a file name to ensure easy file retrieval.

DS

When a memo is being sent to more than one person, include an alphabetical distribution list either a double-space below the reference initials or a double-space below an attachment notation if used.

DS

xxx/les41dc2

DS

Attachment

DS

Distribution:
A. Anderson
S. Calver
K. Mai

2"

GREAT BRITAIN ← centered

England, Northern Ireland, Scotland, and Wales make up the United Kingdom of Great Britain and Northern Ireland. These four countries, under one government, are located in Northwestern Europe. Most people refer to the country as Great Britain, Britain, or the United Kingdom.

1" → The capital of Britain is London. English is the official language. The country is governed by a Prime Minister and Parliament. Great Britain is inhabited by about one percent of the world's total population and has few natural resources; yet it has been one of the world's most important countries. ← 1"

The British are credited with starting the Industrial Revolution. The revolution, which began in the 1700s, started in the cotton textile industry and later spread to other areas such as mining and transportation. The revolution evolved as machines gradually replaced hand labor, and factory systems were developed. For instance, people used to work at home spinning cotton into yarn and weaving yarn into material.

The Industrial Revolution made Britain one of the world's richest manufacturers and the world's greatest traders. During the eighteenth century, the British Empire began to crumble. There were then the two world wars and a series of economic crises. Today, the United Kingdom is no longer a leading world power. They have lost the huge empire and economic strength.

↑
1"

Learn to Format Simplified Memos

For speed and efficiency reasons, many companies are adopting the simplified memo format. The major difference between the simplified and traditional format is the limited use of the guide words—only the guide word TO: is used in the simplified format. To format a simplified memo on a plain piece of stationery, follow the guidelines below.

Learning Activity 2

1. Key the simplified memo on page 258. Use the default margins and tab stops.
2. Key the title MEMORANDUM centered and in all capital letters on line 7.
3. Key the date flush with the left margin. Do not precede the date with a guide word Double-space and key the guide word TO: in all capital letters. Strike Tab after keying the colon and key the heading information. Follow the style shown and key the remainder of the memo.
4. Indent enumerations and quotations 5 spaces from the left margin. Block indent continuation lines within an enumeration or quotation. Leave one blank line above and below indented copy, but single-space within the copy.
5. Double-space between the end of the body and reference initial/document code line. Double-space between any other special notations.

Learning Activity 3

1. Key the unarranged memorandum on page 259 in the blank-paper style. Follow the directions given in Learning Activity 1. Double-space before and after the column headings and listings.
2. This software has a decimal tab feature that will enhance the keying of numerical columns with decimals. To use the decimal tab feature, follow these steps.
   a. Key the key line for the table with 6 spaces between columns.
   b. Move the cursor to the positions where you want to set tabs. For a left tab, position the cursor under the first character of the column. For a decimal tab, position the cursor under the decimal point. Note the position where these tabs should be set. The left tab settings should be at 15, 20, and 46. The decimal tab settings should be at 37 and 63.
   c. Press F7 to move to the ruler line. Delete any existing tabs. Set any required left tabs in the normal way.
   d. To set a decimal tab stop, move the cursor to the decimal position. Strike "d" to set the tab. This is the spot where the decimal point should appear. When a decimal point is keyed in a column, the software automatically will align at the decimal.
   e. Study the table carefully before beginning to key. Note that between column spacing varies.

25 Skill Building and Formatting Business Letters

GOALS

- Reinforce Previous Learning
- Increase Keying Speed
- Improve Keying Accuracy
- Learn to Format Personal Business Letters

Remember the "Get Ready" checklist.

REVIEW

Key each line two times.

1 She quickly learned the skills of the zany clowns.
2 That quiet zoologist studies a variety of animals.
3 Get the new file! Hold the copy! Send a receipt!
4 Take a break! Go home early! Catch those horses!
5 The order was 2 doz. #3's $ $.02 ea. and 4 @ $.05.
6 This order should create >10% profit or >15% loss.
7 Marty said, "Dial this number, 706-483-9251, now!"

INCREASE KEYING SPEED

Key each line two times.

1 of at or in an it if is to te ti do id di my fa go ho lo got
2 how cut big put hot ten lie was per its eve cab dot cub spot
3 jars sale rain give fair its yours mine hers his ours theirs
4 use the/let her/off the/end the/was for/was he/did he/get it
5 head home now/dues paid count/very open sites/come home soon
6 send reply quick/took noon lunch/play her hunch/give a bunch
7 I cover the computer keyboard. Keying skill takes practice.
8 Quick fingers are a result of proper practice and technique.
9 Electronic mail lets you correspond with a lot of coworkers.
10 Use of an outline saves time when writing a business report.
11 Spreadsheets help people compute and diagnose business data.

1 to 1½ inches

MEMORANDUM

4 lines

To: Chakkris Siri, Data Processing Manager

From: Anh-thu Phan, Systems Analyst

Subject: System Passwords

Date: November 17, 1999

3 lines

1" margin

The system passwords are being changed for the third time since the system has been operational. I want to make absolutely certain that these passwords remain confidential with the persons who receive them.

1" margin

Under no circumstances are these to be given or received by any person other than Nancy Hawthorne or me. I also expect that if anyone is aware that password security is broken, this matter will be brought to my attention.

These passwords have been designed to control the integrity of the data in the system and are to be handled as a security measure and in a strictly confidential manner.

Thank you for your cooperation.

xxx/les41dc1

c: Estelle Bennett
Byron Hilderbrand
Jomo Rodreo

Improve Keying Accuracy

Key each of the following sentences concentrating on accuracy—no more than one error per sentence. If you do not reach the accuracy goal, repeat the sentence. Try to maintain your already achieved speed.

1 Mules were used for moving heavy dirt and plowing the field.
2 People wish to avoid dieting but decide not to give up food.
3 World golfers wallow in sorrow when missing short tee shots.
4 It is sad that exact spending quotas sparked a palace panic.
5 A zoo was not the best place to exhibit the valued elephant.
6 A lazy eagle soared over the majestic mountains and valleys.
7 Jet planes quickly break through foggy skies across borders.
8 Be sure that workers have exact ways to zero in on problems.
9 Get good results, which may amaze me, when you view options.
10 Simulated ivory is now used on pianos to save the elephants.

Measure Progress

Exercise 1

Minimum goal: 25 wam with one or fewer errors 1.8 S.I.

Try to exceed the minimum goal.

Take two 1-minute timings.

Computer-assisted instruction is when the computer actually performs teaching functions. The computer may present lessons, provide drill and practice, conduct assessment, and assign future lessons based on current skill levels. Good computer-assisted instruction requires student interaction and will adapt to the student's needs for enrichment or remedial instruction.

4. The order and placement of the guide words will vary from office to office. For instance, some organizations will put the date first. Some organizations will divide the guide words into two columns. Consult an organization's procedures manual to determine the appropriate style.

Example 1—
Memo keyed on preprinted form

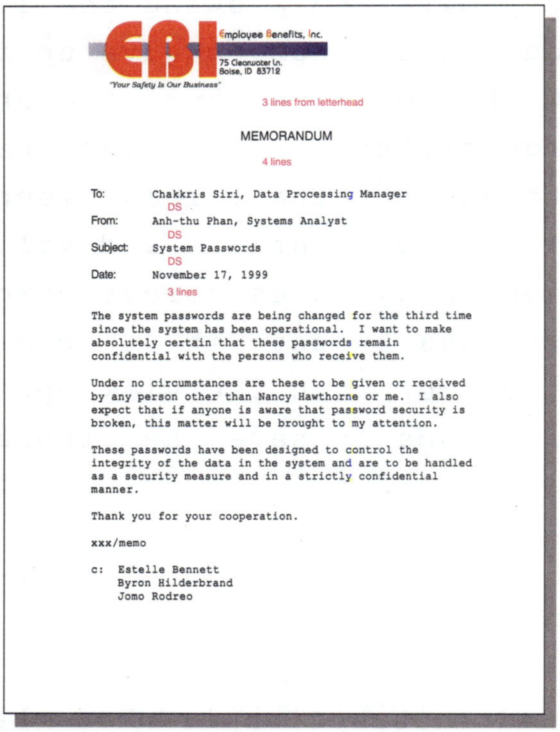
EBI Employee Benefits, Inc.
75 Clearwater Ln.
Boise, ID 83712
"Your Safety Is Our Business"

3 lines from letterhead

MEMORANDUM

4 lines

To: Chakkris Siri, Data Processing Manager
DS
From: Anh-thu Phan, Systems Analyst
DS
Subject: System Passwords
DS
Date: November 17, 1999
3 lines

The system passwords are being changed for the third time since the system has been operational. I want to make absolutely certain that these passwords remain confidential with the persons who receive them.

Under no circumstances are these to be given or received by any person other than Nancy Hawthorne or me. I also expect that if anyone is aware that password security is broken, this matter will be brought to my attention.

These passwords have been designed to control the integrity of the data in the system and are to be handled as a security measure and in a strictly confidential manner.

Thank you for your cooperation.

xxx/memo

c: Estelle Bennett
Byron Hilderbrand
Jomo Rodreo

Example 2—
Memo keyed on printed letterhead with headings aligned at the right

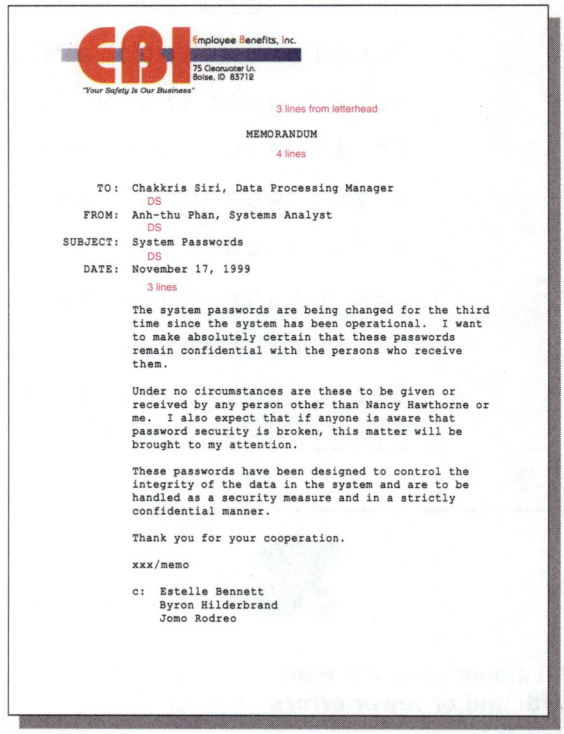
EBI Employee Benefits, Inc.
75 Clearwater Ln.
Boise, ID 83712
"Your Safety Is Our Business"

3 lines from letterhead

MEMORANDUM

4 lines

TO: Chakkris Siri, Data Processing Manager
DS
FROM: Anh-thu Phan, Systems Analyst
DS
SUBJECT: System Passwords
DS
DATE: November 17, 1999
3 lines

The system passwords are being changed for the third time since the system has been operational. I want to make absolutely certain that these passwords remain confidential with the persons who receive them.

Under no circumstances are these to be given or received by any person other than Nancy Hawthorne or me. I also expect that if anyone is aware that password security is broken, this matter will be brought to my attention.

These passwords have been designed to control the integrity of the data in the system and are to be handled as a security measure and in a strictly confidential manner.

Thank you for your cooperation.

xxx/memo

c: Estelle Bennett
Byron Hilderbrand
Jomo Rodreo

Learning Activity 1

1. Key the following memo in the blank-paper style as shown. Use the default margins. Center the word "Memorandum" in all capital letters 1½ inches from the top (begin keying on line 10). Key the guide words "To:," "From:," "Subject:," and "Date:" in all capital letters at the left margin. At the second tab (10 spaces from the margin) key the heading information. Double-space between each heading.
2. Proofread the copy on the screen and use the editing keys to make corrections. Reformat if necessary.
3. Print a copy. Compare the format with the model memorandum. Mark any uncorrected errors on the printout.
4. Press ESC to have the computer check your work.

Exercise 2

Minimum goal: 23 wam with three or fewer errors 1.7 S.I.

Try to exceed the minimum goal.

Take two 2-minute timings.

The central processing unit of a computer receives every instruction coming into the computer system and sends out all resulting messages. It processes all operations of the system. It controls all functions and stores various commands and operating programs. Some central processing units can perform computations and operations faster than a millionth of a second. The central processing unit is thought of as the brains of the computer.

Optical disk memory systems are now available. They have a greatly increased memory capacity. In the future, their storage capacity is expected to double. This will produce cost and space saving.

Exercise 3

Minimum goal: 20 wam with four or fewer errors 1.7 S.I.

Try to exceed the minimum goal.

Take two 3-minute timings.

The cathode ray tube is a large vacuum tube. Images are produced on the front of the tube by tiny charges of electricity hitting the phosphor on the screen, causing it to glow in the shape of letters, numbers, or graphics that you have keyed. These screens come in various sizes.

Each microcomputer brand has some different special function keys. Most are very similar, and the alphabetic keys are usually alike, as well as the numeric keypad. Your major task will be to learn the function keys for the various software packages. Each word-processing program is different. The differences, however, are not very great once you have mastered the basic word-processing concepts.

Measure Progress

Take two 3-minute timings.

Minimum goal: 30 wam with six or fewer errors

Messages to be sent outside the company generally use a letter format. For internal communications, the memorandum is used. Many offices have printed memorandum forms containing printed headings. If printed forms are not available, memorandums may be prepared on printed letterhead or plain paper. Some companies prefer to use half sheets of paper or stationery.

The formats of the memorandums may vary from office to office, but the information included in the heading is fairly standardized. The heading usually includes the name of the addressee, the name of the sender, a subject line, and the date.

When you go to work for a company or institution, you should consult the style manual to determine the format for memos. After determining that, you should use the style adopted by that organization.

Learn to Format Interoffice Memorandums

1. Study the information in the preceding Measure Progress section. A memorandum, usually called a memo, does not have to be centered vertically on the page like a letter. Whether you are using a preprinted form on letterhead or are keying your own heading, the heading, "Memorandum," appears near the top of the page.
2. On a preprinted memorandum form, the word "Memorandum" often is printed as a part of the letterhead as shown in Example 1 on the following page. On preprinted forms, set the margins to align with the printed guide words (To:, From:, Subject:, Date:).
3. On plain paper, key "Memorandum" in all capital letters 1 to 1½ inches from the top of the page. Leave four blank lines between the title and the heading. Set a tab ten spaces from the margin to align the heading information. Double-space the guide words. Single-space the paragraph copy. Most memorandums are keyed using the software's default margins.

Composition Exercise

Using the word processor, name a document LES25CM1. Compose a short report describing how you would respond to the following problem. Do not worry about errors on your first attempt.

Problem: You work in an office that needs to copy a great number of correspondence, invoices, and sales reports. However, your office area does not have a copy machine—you must use a copier located on another floor. Compose a draft of a short one-page report justifying the purchase of a copier for your department.

When finished, proofread the document on the screen. Use the editing keys to make any corrections. Save and print the document.

Proofread the printout and mark any errors you may have missed. Retrieve the document and make corrections as necessary. Save and print your corrected copy.

Learn to Format Personal Business Letters in Block Style

Refer to the example on page 148.

Study the personal business letter on page 148. Look carefully at the formatting directions and how the document is arranged on the page. Then read the following information for formatting and punctuation guidelines.

Block style is an efficient letter style because all lines begin at the left margin. The letter should be centered on the page, leaving approximately equal space at the top and bottom and in the left and right margins. When using automated equipment to key letters, the default margins are used by most operators. Proper placement of the letter is achieved by varying the space between some of the parts of the letter; for example, between the dateline and the inside address.

A note about punctuation: There are two punctuation styles commonly used in today's business world—standard and open. In **standard punctuation**, a colon follows the salutation and a comma follows the complimentary close. In **open punctuation**, no punctuation follows either the salutation or the complimentary close. Each business decides which format to use. The formats are not combined. Use one or the other.

A personal business letter contains the following parts:

1. **Return Address.** All letters should have a return address. Sometimes the company name and return address are preprinted on the stationery, so the return address does not need to be keyed. The preprinted name and address are called a **letterhead**. Most personal business letters are keyed on plain paper; therefore, the return address is keyed above the dateline. The return address should begin approximately 2 inches from the top of the page on line 13. This space may be adjusted if needed for shorter or longer letters. Leave two spaces between the two-letter state abbreviation and the ZIP code.

Key the following sentences, capitalizing as needed.

1 The meeting of the board of directors was scheduled for 1 p.m.

2 We enjoyed our trip to the empire state building when we visited new york city.

3 Her father, bob, was a cpa.

4 Was doctor hackler on duty monday?

IMPROVE KEYING SKILLS

Take two 1-minute timings on each paragraph. Set a speed or an accuracy goal. If you complete the paragraph before time runs out, start over.

EXERCISE 1

Recruiting good professional staff is a very demanding job. Many top organizations have professional full-time recruiters who visit the top universities and colleges across the nation. The major objective of these visits is to interview prospective employees who have potential.

EXERCISE 2

The recruiters look for top academic achievement and evidence of leadership activities. In other words, a well-rounded person who has been active in campus life and maintained above-average grades is the type of future employee that many organizations are seeking. Activity and grade balance indicate good time management.

2. **Dateline.** Key the dateline immediately below the return address. This line includes the month (spelled out), the day, and the year.
3. **Inside Address.** Key the inside address approximately 4 lines beneath the dateline. This space may vary, based on the length of the letter. If the letter is directed to a particular person, the inside address includes a courtesy title (such as Ms.) or professional title (such as Dr.) with the name, and the complete mailing address.
4. **Salutation.** Begin the salutation a double-space below the inside address. The salutation usually begins with "Dear," followed by the courtesy title or professional title and the addressee's last name. In standard punctuation, key a colon after the salutation. If the letter is directed to a company instead of a person, use the salutation "Ladies and Gentlemen."
5. **Body.** Begin the body of the letter a double-space below the salutation. The body is usually single-spaced, with a double-space between paragraphs.
6. **Complimentary Close.** Key the complimentary close a double-space below the body. In standard punctuation, key a comma after the complimentary close.
7. **Signature Block.** Key the name of the person writing the letter 3 lines below the complimentary close to allow space for the handwritten signature.

Formatting Exercise

1. Name a document LES25DC1. Key the model letter on page 148. Follow the format instructions above.
2. Proofread your copy on the screen. Use the editing keys to make corrections. Save and print the document.
3. Compare your printed copy with the model. Mark any uncorrected errors you may have missed. Pay attention to the spacing between parts of the letter.
4. Retrieve the document and make corrections as necessary. Save and print your corrected copy. When you are satisfied with your work, have the computer check you document. Press ESC and make the selection for checking.

41

Formatting Interoffice Memorandums

GOALS

- Build Language Arts Skills
- Improve Keying Skills
- Learn to Format Interoffice Memorandums

Review

Key each line two times.

1 Little zebras evolved from quaint, equine animals.
2 Did Marla take care of the new blue car yesterday?
3 Do you have these items--string, pliers, and wire?
4 The cost of the 3 items was $.76, $9.50 and $8.23.

Build Language Arts Skills

Capitalization

Study the following rules.

- Proper nouns (words that name a particular person, place or thing) are capitalized.
- Abbreviations are capitalized if the words they represent are capitalized.
- Professions, ranks, political offices, and family relationships are capitalized if they are used with names.

Key each line.

1 The train was scheduled to leave at 8 p.m.
2 The APA Style Manual was adopted for all papers.
3 Her degree was a B.S. from UNC.
4 When Father O'Malley arrives, bring him in.
5 Tell Senator Smith that he will receive my vote.
6 If Doctor Jenkins is scheduled to speak, I will attend.
7 The Duke of Kent was next in line for the honor.
8 The drive across the Chesapeake Bay Bridge Tunnel was exciting.
9 The Sears Tower is located in Chicago, Illinois.

2"

Return Address → 719 Cole Place
Birmingham, AL 35203

Dateline → May 22, 1995

4 blank lines

Inside Address → Microburst, Inc.
200 Innsbrook Place
Suite 800
San Diego, CA 92138

double-space

Salutation → Ladies and Gentlemen:

1" margin — double-space — 1" margin

Body →

On August 15 I purchased your new software package, "QuickType." The program disk loads properly, and the program runs. However, when I press the F1 key as indicated for "Help," the main menu appears on the screen. I have reloaded the program several times and am still unable to access the "Help" files when needed.

double-space

If you know of a solution to this problem, please send me instructions. If you do not know how to solve this problem, I would appreciate receiving a new copy of the program as my original may be defective or damaged.

double-space

Closing → Sincerely yours,

3 blank lines

Signature Block → Jason Hefler

3. Fold down the top third to approximately ½ inch from the first fold.
4. Insert the last fold made into the envelope first. The top edge of the paper is at the top edge of the envelope.

Learning Activity 3

Practice folding two letters you have printed previously. Insert one into a small envelope and one into a large envelope.

End-of-Lesson Procedure

At the end of each lesson, you will have the following options:

1. To restart the same lesson, press the F1 function key.
2. To return to the Lessons Menu, press ESC. This action automatically will save the completed lesson.
3. To proceed to the next, or any other lesson, highlight your choice on the menu and press Enter.
4. To return to the Main Menu, press ESC again.
5. To print the lesson, select Print Activities.
6. To exit the program:
   a. Select the Exit option and press Enter.
   b. When the DOS prompt appears on the screen, remove your data disk.
   c. Turn off the monitor. (Your instructor also may ask you to turn off the computer and printer.)

End-of-Lesson Procedure

At the end of each lesson, you will have the following options:

1. To restart the same lesson, press the F1 function key.
2. To return to the Lessons Menu, press ESC. This action automatically will save the completed lesson.
3. To proceed to the next, or any other lesson, highlight your choice on the menu and press Enter.
4. To return to the Main Menu, press ESC again.
5. To print the lesson, select Print Activities.
6. To exit the program:
   a. Select the Exit option and press Enter.
   b. When the DOS prompt appears on the screen, remove your data disk.
   c. Turn off the monitor. (Your instructor also may ask you to turn off the computer and printer.)

DR MARJORIE P OLIVER
9402 WEST PLATTE ST
OMAHA NE 68121-2947

FIRST CANADIAN NATIONAL BANK
903 MOUNTAIN HWY
CALGARY AB B4M 2J8
CANADA

Learn to Fold Letters

Folding Letters for Small Envelopes (#6-3/4)

To fold a letter to be placed in a small envelope, follow these steps.

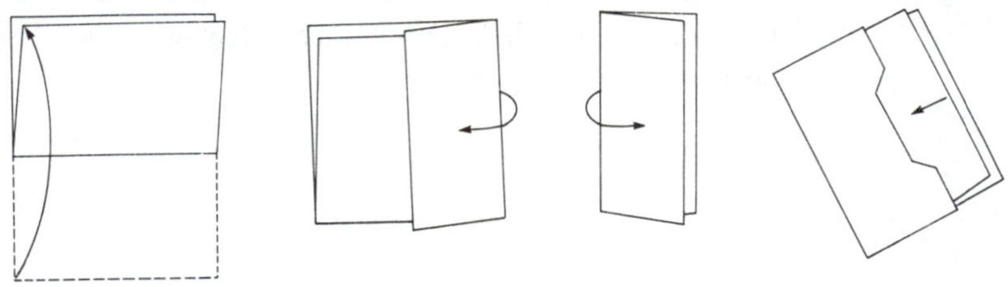

1. Fold up one half of the page so that the bottom edge is approximately ½ inch below the top edge.
2. Fold the right side over one third of the paper.
3. Fold the left third of the page over the right third so that the left edge is approximately ½ inch from the right fold.
4. Insert the page so that the left edge is at the opening of the envelope. The last crease made enters the envelope first.

Folding Letters for Large Envelopes (#10)

To fold a letter to be placed in a large envelope, follow these steps.

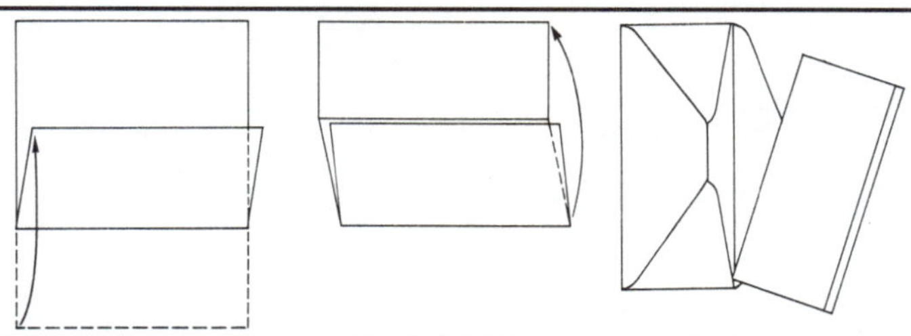

1. Place the letter with the printed side up.
2. Fold up the bottom third.

26 Skill Building and Formatting Tables

GOALS

- Reinforce Previous Learning
- Increase Keying Speed
- Improve Keying Accuracy
- Learn to Set Tab Stops
- Learn to Format Simple Tables

Remember the "Get Ready" checklist.

Review

Key each line two times.

1 The judge awarded six quotas at a zoology exhibit.
2 That lazy ox caused Quincy extra anxiety and envy.
3 All reports should be clear, concise, and correct.
4 Communication skills are critical for job success.
5 I think it is time for all of us to learn a skill.
6 Ken's grades were three A's, two B's, and two C's.
7 The meeting will be held at 8:30 a.m. on March 25.

Increase Keying Speed

Key each line two times.

1 move ahead soon/take the lead/take this list/wind blows hard
2 take your time/play fair now/quit your post/found extra room
3 If you want to be good at keyboarding, set up practice time.
4 Office procedures are vital to ensure compliance with rules.
5 Offices are becoming more involved with interactive systems.
6 An advanced workstation using a 32-bit processor is popular.
7 On the job, it is necessary to work promptly and accurately.
8 Correctly designed systems interface easily with technology.
9 Software entails application programs and operating systems.
10 Types of command languages involve the use of function keys.
11 There's a large increase in computer usage by the workforce.
12 Local area networks make it possible to use electronic mail.

Learning Activity 2

1. Practice keying envelopes for business letters. If your printer will not accommodate envelopes, key the addresses at the left margin; double-space between each address. You will not key a return address in this exercise, assuming that the envelopes would be preprinted. Use the U.S. Postal Service OCR style.
2. Have the computer check the document and print a copy. Note any marked errors on the printout.

```
MRS ANNETTE JACKSON
OFFICE MANAGER
REGAL CORPORATION
109 N MAIN ST
PEORIA IL  61643-0450

MR PIERRE DESALME BRANCH MANAGER
TELEPHONE INFORMATION SYSTEMS
600 BROAD ST
VANCOUVER BC  L8H 2H6
CANADA

MRS ELIZABETH R TOONE
VICE PRESIDENT
CITIZENS BANK
4280 S MAIN ST
BANGOR ME  04401-4398

COASTAL COMMUNITY COLLEGE
2890 TIDEWATER DR
SEATTLE WA  98164-8767

MS ANGELA I CRONINO
DISTRICT MANAGER
GENERAL TELEPHONE COMPANY
89302 VALDOSTA DR
MARIETTA GA  30074-7832

MR CARLITOS S BOLIVIA JR
LANDMARK REAL ESTATE INC
489 FERNCASTLE DR
SACRAMENTO CA  95880-4987

MS KATHRYN A MCINTYRE
THE COMPUTER COMPANY
75 MAIN ST
MILLBURN NJ  07041-3247
```

Improve Keying Accuracy

Both speed and accuracy are recorded.

```
1  Big brown bears barter for berries better than tiny bunnies.
2  Can credit cause cash to collapse?  Can it be a catastrophy?
3  Obnoxious odor in oceans is offensive to oysters and otters.
4  Perfect people prefer positive political posts and practice.
5  Quails are quite quick.  Conquer the quaint queasy quotient.
6  To excel Evan must exhibit extra excitement and not excuses.
7  Yummy yak yogurt and yoga yielded Yonil's youthful yearning.
8  The maze dazzled and dazed the zany, crazy, frizzy zoo gang.
9  Vacuums are vacant of various vapors.  Veto the verbal vote.
10 Wild waves washed away the wreckage.  Wan winds wailed west.
```

Learn to Set and Change Tab Settings

Note: Use the F7 key to change tab settings.

Most word processing software allows the user to set tab stops wherever they are needed. Variable tab settings are often needed when creating tables and other columnar applications. Until now, you have used only the default five-space paragraph indent tab stop. Your software does allow you to set tabs.

To set new tab stops or clear existing tab stops in this program, follow these steps:

1. Tabs may be set or cleared only at a word-processing screen.
2. At a blank word-processing screen strike F7 to display the "ruler" line near the top of the screen. The L on the ruler shows the location of the left margin. The R shows the location of the right margin. Each dot (.) indicates one space along the line and a small square appears every five spaces. A lower case t indicates any space where a tab is now set.
3. The cursor should be at the left margin. Use the Left- or Right-Arrow keys to move the cursor back and forth across the ruler line.
4. To set a new tab stop, move the cursor to the spot where you want a tab to appear. Once there, strike t. A t should now appear at that spot. A tab stop is set.
5. To remove (delete) an already set tab stop, move the cursor to an existing t. Once there, strike the DEL (delete) key. The t will be replaced with either a dot or a small square. The tab stop is cleared.
6. After setting or deleting tab stops, press Enter to start or resume a word-processing activity.

Learning Activity 1

1. All microcomputer printers may not have the capacity for loading envelopes. In many offices, envelopes may still be addressed on a typewriter, or mailing labels may be generated on the computer. Because of the diversity of the printers used, this exercise has been modified. If a typewriter is available or if your computer printer will handle envelopes, key the exercises. Use the appropriate size envelope and follow the preceding formatting directions.
2. If you are using the software and the printer will not accommodate envelopes, follow these directions to simulate addressing envelopes. Practice keying the addresses following. Clear all tabs; then set a tab at the center of the line. Key the return address for each envelope at the left margin; then double-space and key the address at the center tab. Double-space and key the next address. Use the U.S. Postal Service OCR style.
3. Have the computer check the document and print a copy. Note any marked errors on the printout.

Return Address	**Address**
JEFFREY MONTIELL 849 RIDGE LN PUEBLO CO 81004-2010	MR XAVIER GIBSON 1285 PARHAM RD SAN BERNARDINO CA 92437-5187
MRS SHERRY TURNER RT 1 BOX 2455 MADISON VA 22727-3929	MS MELINDA LEE TECHNICAL COMMUNITY COLLEGE 1458 N 60 ST PHOENIX AZ 85034-4428
CHARLES STEINBERG 8401 ASPEN WAY NEW YORK NY 10042-8932	MS KITA LIN TRAINING CONSULTANT SOLUTIONS UNLIMITED INC 4283 MAUNA DR HILO HI 96720-3056
JANE FOSTER 8592 WINDING RIDGE LN NAPERVILLE IL 61084-1132	DR LOUISA BARRONE RAMSEY CLINIC 120 E WATER ST CHICAGO IL 60018-5184

Practice Changing Tabs

Exercise 1

Set new tab stops.

Using the word processor, name a document LES26DC1. First remove the default tabs. Follow the steps for setting tabs and set a tab every ten spaces from the left margin.

Space	Strike	Space	Strike	Space	Strike	Space	Strike	Space	Strike	Press
10	T	10	T	10	T	10	T	10	T	↵

Key the following exercise. Key across the columns.

```
Kid(Tab)dim(Tab)fur(Tab)fun(Tab)guy(Tab)buy ↵
may      wet      gum      hut      pat      zip ↵
gun      quo      hut      jim      lot      fat ↵
tax      cue      red      cat      for      and ↵
```

Proofread your document on the screen and then print it. Proof the printout and mark any errors you may have missed. Make corrections if necessary. Save and print your corrected copy. When you are satisfied with your work, have the computer check your document.

Exercise 2

Now create a new document and name it LES26DC2. Clear the existing tab stops. Set the first tab at five spaces and tab stops every ten spaces after that. Key the following exercise. Key across the columns. Strike Tab before keying the first word and strike Tab after keying each word. Press Enter at the end of each line.

```
about   could   labor   place   spent   until
again   doubt   least   price   start   voice
begin   drive   leave   quick   store   water
carry   force   north   round   these   whose
color   happy   paper   south   trust   write
```

Proofread your document on the screen and then print it. Proof the printout and mark any errors you may have missed. Make corrections if necessary. Save and print your corrected copy. When you are satisfied with your work, have the computer check your document.

Large Envelopes (#10) 9½ inches by 4½ inches Plain Envelope

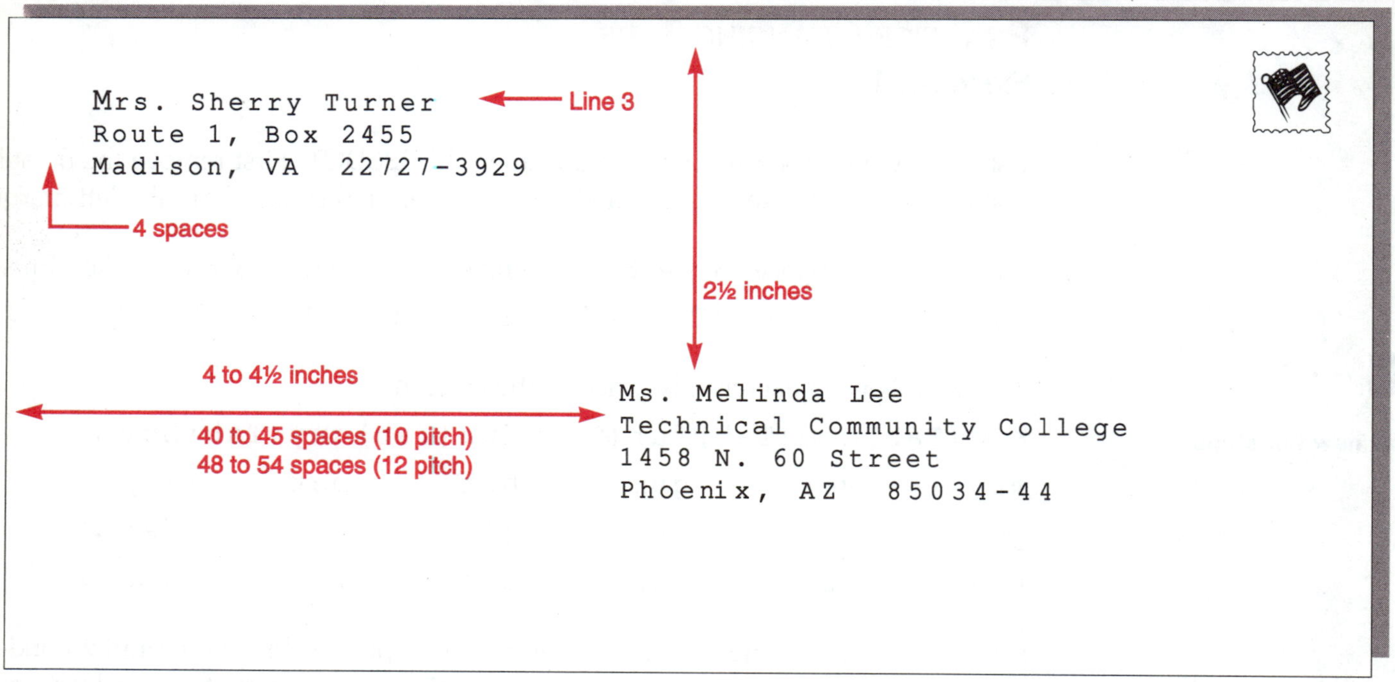

U.S. Postal Service OCR Style Printed Envelope

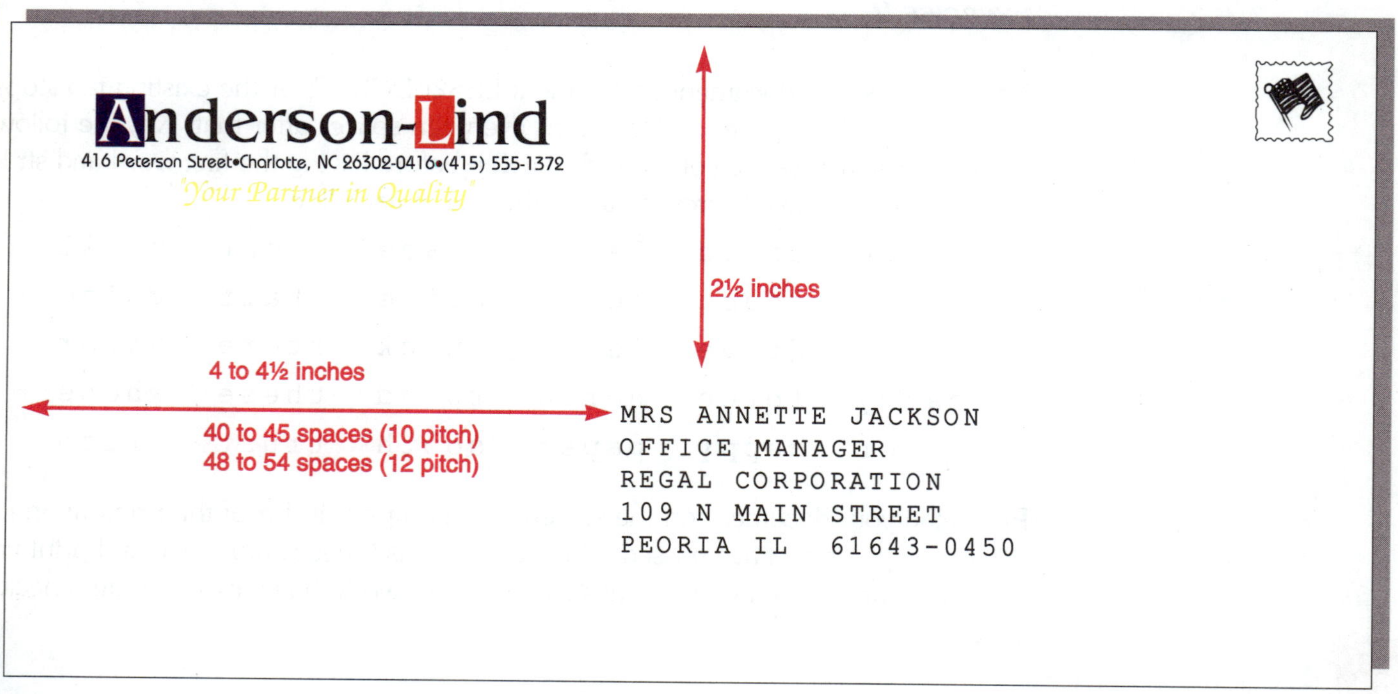

Measure Progress

Exercise 1

Minimum goal: 25 wam with one or fewer errors 1.3 S.I.

Take two 1-minute timings.

When you are distracted, it helps to concentrate on your copy. Some distractions can be eliminated with a little effort. When people are talking too loudly, a courteous request to talk a little quieter will usually accomplish your goal. If this does not work, you can buy a small set of soft ear plugs designed to block out noise.

Exercise 2

Minimum goal: 23 wam with three or fewer errors 1.4 S.I.

Try to exceed the minimum goal.

Take two 2-minute timings.

The types of pressure on the job will include time deadlines, noise, co-workers who distract you, and personal problems. Even when you are at work, things that are worrying you at home will often affect your job. It is not easy to concentrate in a distracting environment.

If you have good keyboarding skills and have mastered proper techniques and the touch method, one major source of distraction will be eliminated. The major source mentioned is having to look at the keys as you keyboard.

3. If a return address is not preprinted in the upper left corner of the envelope, one must be keyed. Key the return address in block style, single-spaced. Begin the address on line 3. Start 4 spaces from the left edge.
4. On small envelopes (#6-3/4), begin the address 2 to 2½ inches from the left edge (20 to 25 spaces for 10 pitch, 24 to 30 spaces for 12 pitch). Leave 2 inches (12 lines) of blank space above the address; key the address beginning on line 13.
5. On large envelopes (#10), begin the address 4 to 4½ inches from the left edge (40 to 45 spaces for 10 pitch; 48 to 54 spaces for 12 pitch). Leave 2½ inches (15 lines) of blank space above the address; key the address beginning on line 16.

Small Envelopes (#6-3/4)
6½ inches by 3-5/8 inches

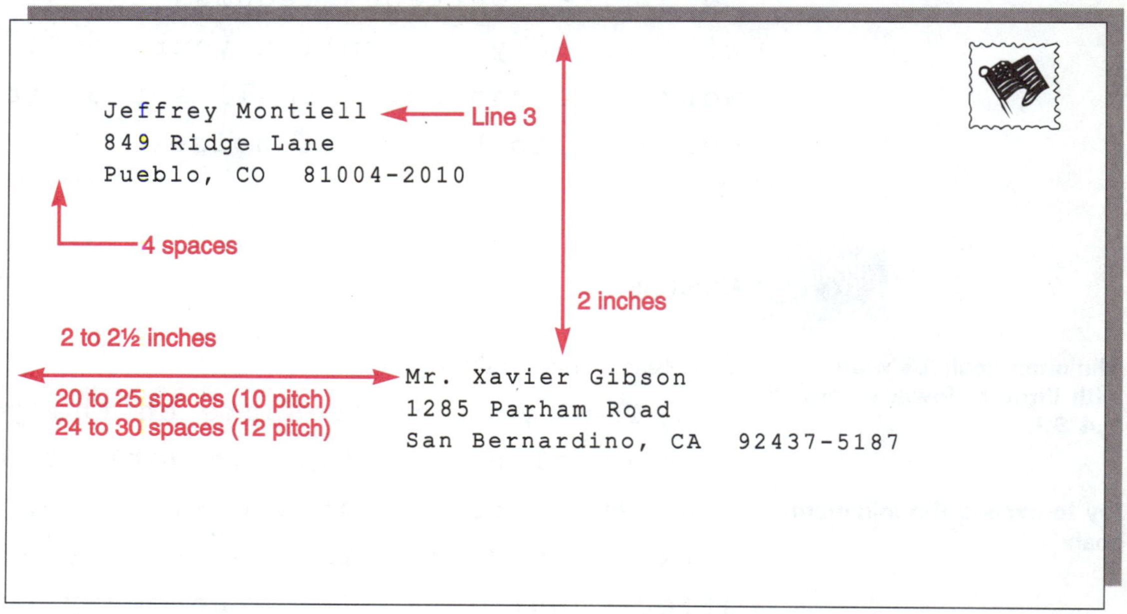

U.S. Postal Service OCR Style

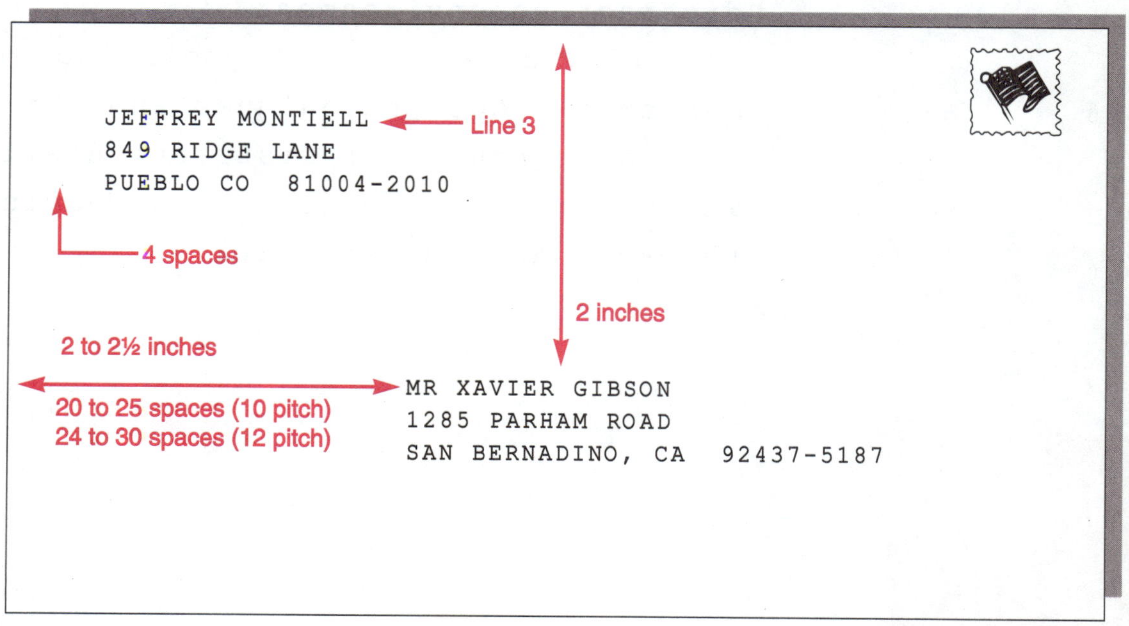

Exercise 3

Minimum goal: 20 wam with four or fewer errors 1.5 S.I.

Try to exceed the minimum goal.

Take two 3-minute timings.

At this point in your progress, you should be able to key at least 25 words a minute without looking at the keyboard. You should be exhibiting proper techniques and feel confident about your skills. Your new skills will be useful in keying programs, word processing, and correspondence.

People who have not acquired keyboarding skills will find less of a market when trying to find a job in business and industry. Many people who are already on the job will need to learn microcomputer keyboarding. Often change is threatening; however, in this case, it means greater efficiency and much improved copy.

As you continue to practice and observe proper techniques, your speed and accuracy will increase, and you will feel pride in knowing that you have acquired a new and marketable professional skill.

Composition Exercise

Using the word processor, name a document LES26CM1. Compose two or three short paragraphs describing how you would respond to the following situation. Do not worry about errors on your first attempt.

Situation: Describe in your own words why you think keyboarding is a valuable skill for everyone.

When finished, proofread the document on the screen. Use the editing keys to make any corrections. Save and print the document. Proofread the printout and mark any errors you may have missed. Retrieve the document and make corrections as necessary. Save and print your corrected copy.

Measure Progress

Minimum goal: 30 wam with six or fewer errors

Take two 3-minute timings.

There are two sizes of envelopes commonly used for business letters. They are called the "personal use," or small, envelope and the "business," or large, envelope.

The address of the sender, called the "return address," goes in the upper left corner. If this information is not preprinted on the envelope, it is keyed single-spaced in block style.

The address of the person or company receiving the letter is keyed in the lower right section of the envelope. Begin the address slightly to the left of the center of the envelope.

The U.S. Postal Service uses a high-speed optical character reader (OCR) to sort mail electronically. To avoid delays in sorting mail, use the recommended style.

In envelope style for OCR, addresses are keyed single-spaced, in all capitals, and with all punctuation marks omitted. The address should include the two-letter state abbreviation and the nine-digit ZIP code.

Learn to Format Envelopes

1. Study the information in the Measure Progress section above. For general correspondence, some companies still prefer that the inside address on the letter and the address on the envelope be identical in style. Many companies, however, have adopted the U.S. Postal Service recommendations for optical character reading (OCR). Using this recommended style will speed the mail service because mail can be sorted by machine. In OCR style, key items in all capitals and omit all punctuation marks.
2. Study the illustrations in this lesson. Both address styles are shown for small and large envelopes. Note the formatting instructions.

Learn to Format Simple Tables

Tables are a concise way of presenting complex data. They may range in complexity from simple two-column tables with a main heading to those with several levels of headings and many columns. Tables should be centered vertically (top to bottom) and horizontally (left to right) on the page. Tables may be presented alone on a page or incorporated into letters, reports, and memorandums.

Study the two-column table on page 157. Follow these general guidelines for formatting.

1. Center tables horizontally and vertically on the page. (If a table is to be incorporated into another document such as a letter or report, center it horizontally and leave two blank lines above and below the table.)
2. Center the main heading. Key it in all capital letters. Double-space after the title.
3. Format the body of the table in columns. The body may be single- or double-spaced, depending on the layout.
4. Center the columns horizontally, leaving a constant amount of space between each column. This space usually ranges from 4 to 8 spaces.
5. Align word columns on the left and numerical columns on the right or at the decimal point.

Determine the Vertical Center

To center text vertically on a page, determine how many blank lines to leave at the top before you begin keying. Follow these steps to center the table vertically:

1. Know the number of vertical lines available on the paper you are using. Standard 8½ by 11-inch paper has 66 vertical lines (11 inches x 6 lines per inch).
2. Determine the number of printed and blank lines in the copy to be keyed. For the table on page 157:

   Count the number of lines, including blank lines, to be keyed. In this case, the number is 15.

   Subtract the lines to be keyed from the total lines available on the page.

Available	66
Used	-15
Unused	51

   Divide the unused lines by 2 to determine the number of blank lines to leave for the top margin. Disregard any fraction. Add 1 line to the number of lines calculated and begin keying on this line.

   $51 \div 2 = 25\frac{1}{2}$ Drop fraction: $25 + 1 = 26$

   Begin keying on line 26.

Improve Keying Skills

Take two 1-minute timings on each paragraph. Set a speed or an accuracy goal. If you complete the paragraph before time runs out, start over.

Exercise 1

Many computer users become frustrated when the software packages they have purchased do not perform as desired. A good practice is to at least try out a program before purchasing it or make sure that it can be returned if it does not perform satisfactorily. Quite often the sales claims do not match the actual performance of a package.

Exercise 2

Another problem with some software packages is the amount of training required to understand the program's functions. Some programs require a great deal of skill to operate. Obviously, one who cannot keyboard will be at a great disadvantage when it comes to operating a software program that requires a large amount of input from the user.

3. Some microcomputer software leaves a set amount of space at the top before printing begins. Check the software you are using and include those lines as a part of your count from the top. Remember: This software automatically leaves 6 blank lines in the top margin.

Determine Horizontal Placement of Columns

You can use the automatic features of your software to simplify the horizontal centering of a table. Using the word processor, name a document LES26DC3. Follow these step-by-step directions to key the model table on page 157 using automatic features.

1. Determine the vertical center. Press Enter until you reach that line. Press the F5 key to change to double-spacing. Remember, if you have set the software for double-spacing, the cursor will move two lines each time you press Enter. On the correct line key the title and press F6 to center it. Press Enter.
2. Key the longest entry from each column. This is called the "key line." In this table, the longest lines in each column are:

   ```
   Volunteers for Literacy (8 spaces) Ms. Bettye Peoples
                                ↑
   ```

   (Add 8 spaces for between column spacing.)
3. Notice that the line is centered because the centering key, F6, is still activated.
4. Note the position where the first column, Volunteers for Literacy, starts. It should be at position 18. Note the position where the second column, Ms. Bettye Peoples, starts. It should be at position 49.
5. Press the F7 key to bring the ruler line to the screen. Clear all existing tabs. Set a tab for column 1 at position 18 and a tab for column 2 at position 49. Press Enter to return to the document.
6. Delete the key line. Press F6 to turn off the centering.
7. Key the table. Key across the columns. Press Tab before keying the first column and then to move to the second column. Press Enter at the end of each line.
8. Proofread the document on the screen. Use the editing keys to make any corrections. Save and print a copy. Compare it with the model. If the table is not properly centered vertically and horizontally, key it again making adjustments as necessary. Save and print your corrected copy. When you are satisfied with your work, have the computer check your document.

Follow the appropriate end-of-lesson procedures.

Now key each of the following sentences, adding correct capitalization.

1 Representatives from the math department will interview the new candidate.

2 The manager of the bank of the southwest will hire the new trainees.

3 The department of education will institute the new guidelines.

Word Usage

Understand the correct usage of the following words.

Leased/Least

Leased rental contract for a period of time
Least littlest or smallest

Lessee/Lessor

Lessee a person who agrees to a lease
Lessor a person who grants a lease

Key each line.

1 The property has been leased for a five-year period.

2 We should strive for the least amount of overhead possible.

3 The lessee has agreed to keep the grass mowed.

4 The lessor will remove the garbage and repair the roof.

Now key each of the following sentences, choosing the correct word.

1 Did the company approve the (leased, least) amount of construction delay?

2 Which of the plans caused the (leased, least) amount of construction delay?

3 As the owner of the property, the (lessee, lessor) will be liable for constructing the new porch.

4 As the renter of the house, the (lessee, lessor) must keep the grass cut.

Line 26 → PROGRAM ADVISORY COMMITTEE

double-space

Literacy Foundation	Dr. Ed Jones
Volunteers for Literacy	Mr. John Smith
United Way, Inc.	Ms. Bettye Peoples
State Literacy Director	Dr. Lynn James
Governor's Office	Ms. Joyce Booth
Ford Foundation	Dr. Milton Hirsh
State University	Dr. Paul Simeon

↑ 8 spaces

↑ Position 18

↑ Position 49

40

Formatting Envelopes and Folding Letters

GOALS

- Build Language Arts Skills
- Improve Keying Skills
- Learn to Format Envelopes
- Learn to Fold Letters

Review

Key each line twice.

1 for your/you will a/you did/will it/of it/all but/

2 The wind caused the waves that wash away the weak.

3 His expenses were $198 for food and $295 for rent.

4 The processes of scheduling, reviewing, planning, implementing, and changing can all be managed.

Build Language Arts Skills

Capitalization

Study the following rules.

- Capitalize principal words in the names of all organizations.
- Capitalize the official title of a division or department within an organization.

Key each line.

1 The United Fund conducts an extensive drive each year.

2 The manager of the Bank of the James left a message for you.

3 The Admissions Office sent you a complete set of forms.

4 Our contract is with the Department of Defense.

5 A representative from the Collections Department called.

UNIT 5

WORD PROCESSING AND BASIC FORMATTING

APEX Computers, Inc.

1200 Energy Drive ○ Oklahoma City, OK 45332

July 17, 1998

Dr. Kaneesha P. Rice
9402 West Platte Street
Omaha, NE 68121-2947

APEX COMPUTER SERVICE

We apologize for any inconvenience caused by the malfunction of our Apex computer. The Apex computer has an outstanding performance record. Occasionally, however, a computer does not function properly. It is our policy to always correct malfunctions.

We are asking our service personnel to contact you this week to repair the computer. Be assured that if the computer cannot be repaired, we will replace it with a new unit.

We are enclosing a list of Apex computer dealers in your area. If you have any service requirements in the future, please call one of them. They respond to any service call within 24 hours.

MS. ANGELA DEANGELO, CUSTOMER SERVICE

cag/les39dc3

Enclosure

copy: Customer Service

27 Skill Building

GOALS

- Build Language Arts Skills
- Increase Keying Speed
- Improve Keying Accuracy
- Improve Keying Skills

Review

Key each line two times.

```
1 and but for the are was pay two buy met net you it
2 That icy quake zone caused extra anxiety for them.
3 Place an extra order for #4389 & #9876 & 302, Tim.
4 All people should be ready for a new airplane test
  tomorrow.
```

Build Language Arts Skills

Efficient and accurate document production requires good keyboarding skills and strong language arts skills. The Build Language Arts Skills section of a lesson reviews basic punctuation, capitalization, and word usage guidelines that should be mastered. Follow these steps to complete each Build Language Arts Skills section:

1. Read the guidelines and rules presented in the textbook.
2. Refer to the sample sentences for the application of the guidelines.
3. Key the sample sentences as prompted by the program.
4. Key the application sentences as prompted by the program. In the application sentences, key the correct punctuation, capitalization, or usage as required. The sentences automatically will be checked for correct application of the guidelines.
5. Repeat any sentences that contain errors.

Punctuation: Comma

Study the following rules.

- Use a comma to separate two or more adjectives preceding a noun when *and* is omitted.
- Use a comma to set off an appositive or appositive phrase from the rest of the sentence. An appositive is a word or phrase that renames or explains previously mentioned nouns or pronouns and usually immediately follows that noun or pronoun.

Learn to Format Formal Business Letters in Simplified Style

Over the past few years, many organizations have adopted the AMS simplified business letter style. AMS refers to the Administrative Management Society, the organization that created the format. Like the full-block format, all parts and lines of the simplified letter format start at the left margin. The simplified format, however, does not include a salutation or a complimentary close. Instead, a subject line replaces the salutation. Each of these lines is keyed in all capital letters. All other parts of the simplified letter are keyed the same as in block format and the same sequence. To further simplify formatting, this letter style accepts a default side margin setting of 1-inch and a default tab setting of five spaces for continuation lines in an enumeration.

Learning Activity 3

1. Start document LES39DC3. Key the simplified style letter on the next page.
2. Space down to line 13. Key the date. Strike Enter and space down six lines to the inside address.
3. Leave two blank lines above and below the subject line. After the last line of the letter, press Enter four times and key the signature block.
4. Key the reference initials, enclosure notation, and copy notation at the left margin.
5. Proofread the document on the screen. Use the editing keys to make corrections. Pay close attention to the placement of the dateline, complimentary close, and signature block.
6. Press ESC when you are finished and follow the prompts to have the program check your document. Save and print a copy of your document.
7. Proofread your printout and mark any additional errors you may have missed. Compare the format with the model letter.
8. Retrieve your document and make corrections as necessary. Save and print your corrected copy.

End-of-Lesson Procedure

After completing the activities for this lesson follow the appropriate end-of-lesson procedure.

Key each line.

1 Brandy was a sweet, gentle dog.

2 The children have a wonderful time playing in the cool, salty ocean.

3 Elizabeth was elected president of the organization because she was a logical, organized thinker.

4 Last summer we visited Virginia, the Cavalier State.

5 The Mississippi, the mightiest river in the United States, influences the lives of many people.

6 Jim LaGrange, the governor of Iowa, gave an outstanding inaugural speech.

Now key each of the following sentences, adding the correct comma punctuation.

1 We anticipated a terrible storm after viewing the dark swirling clouds.

2 My uncle Juan DeSilva won the marathon last year.

3 Michael Washington our best runner finished the meet in first place.

4 The sailboat sliced through the choppy wavy water.

Increase Keying Speed

Key each line twice. Try to increase your keying speed as you repeat the line.

Balanced Hand Words

1 land hand halt then sign hang dish disk hair risk soak pairs

2 paid pane lens than halt lake half fish idle foam laps maids

3 angle fight shake gland tight digit giant blend bible flames

4 island height signal emblem problem title amble disown spent

Trudeux and Trudeux, Inc.

900 Rue Montague, Portland, OR 90120-3332

May 24, 1998

Attention Auditing Department
First Canadian National Bank
903 Mountain Highway
Calgary, AB B4M 2J8
CANADA

Ladies and Gentlemen:

ACCOUNT #533-7895

In connection with our annual audit, our auditors have requested the following additional information:

1. monthly bank statements and all paid checks

2. names of persons authorized to sign checks

3. list of all securities held by your bank

Please forward this information directly to our auditors as soon as possible. Send the information to the following address: Trudeux and Trudeux, Inc., 900 Rue Montague, Portland, OR 90120-3332.

Sincerely yours,

William R. Manley, President

avb/les39dc2

Letter Combinations

1 le let left lest leaf lend lead lean less level letter leach
2 sa sat sack safe sails said sake saddled sallow salty salons
3 th the that then than them that this there their think theft
4 an and ant any apex answer antler angry angle animal ancient
5 we wet wed weed were weary weak wealthy weasel weigh welders

Improve Keying Accuracy

Key each line with no more than one error. If you do not reach the accuracy goal, repeat the line.

Double-Letter Words

1 need teen tall hall knee miss sell fell keen deed feel stall
2 feel glee shall little sheet assist stiff sniff skill allies
3 sleek rabbit fiddle hook pool roof moon root mood tool skill
4 install falling settling needle gobble pebble hobby irritate
5 shipping happen slipping endless gallant seeing knitting add

Longer Words

1 elephant minimum rhythm telegram familiar eliminate athletes
2 registrar elaboration ambition leniency estimating retrieval
3 negotiate delights alkaline imagination diligent acknowledge
4 rational legislation essential delegates negative advertises
5 observation wholesale negligent rational residence primitive

Improve Keying Skills

The Improve Keying Skills sections in the remaining lessons are designed to improve your straight-copy speed and accuracy skills. Regular practice will help your fingers move quickly to the correct keys.

Your practice will be more effective if you concentrate on a specific goal. Set either a speed or an accuracy goal for each exercise and concentrate only on that goal.

Learn About Attention and Subject Lines

Attention and subject lines are sometimes used in business letters to draw attention to a special person, department, or subject.

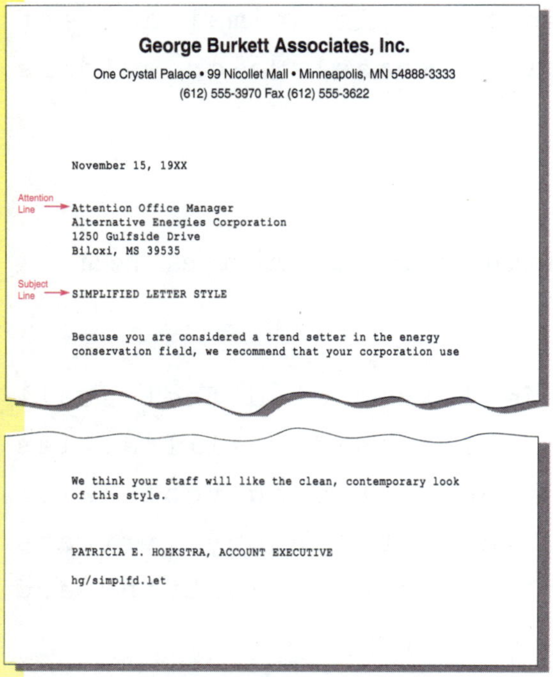
George Burkett Associates, Inc.

One Crystal Palace • 99 Nicollet Mall • Minneapolis, MN 54888-3333
(612) 555-3970 Fax (612) 555-3622

November 15, 19XX

Attention Office Manager
Alternative Energies Corporation
1250 Gulfside Drive
Biloxi, MS 39535

SIMPLIFIED LETTER STYLE

Because you are considered a trend setter in the energy conservation field, we recommend that your corporation use

We think your staff will like the clean, contemporary look of this style.

PATRICIA E. HOEKSTRA, ACCOUNT EXECUTIVE

hg/simplfd.let

1. ***Attention Line***. This line is used when a letter is addressed to an organization rather than a particular person. It is used to direct the letter to a specific department, individual, or position within an organization.

   The attention line is keyed at the left margin as the first line of the inside address. The attention line may include a person's name or simply a job title or department name.

   ```
   Attention Karin Peterson
   Attention Editorial Director
   Attention Personnel Department
   ```

2. ***Subject or Reference Line***. This line is used to draw the reader's attention to the main subject of the correspondence. The subject line generally is keyed a double-space below the salutation. The subject line is keyed in all capital letters. In a simplified letter style, the subject line replaces the salutation. This provides a choice when writing to groups or to people whose names you do not know. This style does not use a complimentary close.

The letter shown here demonstrates how these lines might be handled.

Learning Activity 2

1. Start document LES39DC2. Key the letter on the next page in modified block style with standard punctuation.
2. Using the default tabs, indent the enumerations five spaces from the left margin. After keying the number, Tab to the second stop to key the copy. Single-space the paragraph copy. Double-space the enumerations.
3. Proofread the letter on the screen. Use the editing keys to make corrections.
4. Press ESC when you are finished and follow the prompts to have the program check your document. Save and print a copy of your document.
5. Proofread your printout and mark any additional errors you may have missed. Pay attention to formatting as well as keying errors.
6. Retrieve the document and make corrections as necessary. Save and print your corrected copy.

If you are working on speed development, don't worry about errors. Key as quickly as you can. If you are working on accuracy development, attempt to key the drill within the error limit. Minimum goals are established for each lesson. You may not set a lower goal, but you are encouraged to set higher goals.

To determine whether your practice goal should be for speed or accuracy, you can select from the following procedures:

1. Take a 1-minute timing on the paragraph. Key at a controlled rate and determine your speed and the total number of errors. Compare your performance to the minimum goal. Determine your practice goal.
2. Analyze your performance for the "Measure Progress" section of the last lesson. Set a practice goal based on that performance.
3. Concentrate on speed development for several lessons until you reach a new speed level. Ignore errors during this speed development. Then concentrate on accuracy for several lessons. Try to maintain the new speed rate while reducing errors to within the error limit.
4. Ask your instructor to assist you in determining appropriate practice goals.

Take two 1-minute timings on each paragraph. Set either a speed or an accuracy goal. Remember, strike the Tab key once to indent a paragraph. If you complete the paragraph before time runs out, start over again.

Remember: For best results, all practice should have a specific goal. You should concentrate on either speed or accuracy. Do not attempt to do both in the same drill.

Exercise 1

```
     The use of desktop publishing software has
enabled many businesses to prepare their brochures
in-house.  Using this software is quite easy.  Once
the text is entered, you can alter the layout of the
document by pressing a few keys.  The margins and
type styles can be changed and the newly formatted
document can be viewed on the screen.
```

Exercise 2

```
     The text can be arranged in newspaper-style
columns, if desired.  The document can be enhanced
using graphic art that is available with the
software.  Just select the design that you like and
move it into the text.  The size and placement of the
graphic design easily can be altered.
```

Key at Horizontal Center (43) → September 23, 1999

Ms. Kathryn A. McIntyre
The Computer Company
75 Main Street
Millburn, NJ 07041-3247

Dear Ms. McIntyre:

The meeting with you last Thursday was most enjoyable. I talked with our president, Ms. J. R. Lohmann, about your training needs; and she asked me to assure you that we are committed to working with new industry in our area.

As we discussed, we would like very much to make our services available to your client. Our staff is experienced in planning training programs that meet the needs of business and industry.

We offer a variety of courses and programs as outlined in the brochure I am enclosing. These programs can be adapted to the needs of your client. In addition, we can design courses and training programs to meet their specific needs.

I look forward to meeting with you on October 8. Please let me know if you desire any additional information before that meeting.

Key at Horizontal Center

Sincerely yours,

Dustin M. Monahan
Training Director

iff/les39dc1

Enclosure

Measure Progress

Take two 2-minute timings.

Minimum goal: 24 wam with four or fewer errors

Demands on today's businesses and workers are different than in the past. Traditional jobs are changing; new jobs are created every day. Employees must be adaptable and possess the ability to learn. Statistics show that today's workers will have seven different jobs.

To be best prepared to face the changes in the work force, you need to develop a set of competencies and foundation skills. The SCANS Report, issued by the U.S. Department of Labor, identifies factors that lie at the heart of job performance. The competencies involve the productive use of resources, interpersonal skills, information systems, and technology. The foundation identified in the SCANS Report consists of basic skills, thinking skills, and the personal qualities of individual responsibility, self-management, and integrity.

End-of-Lesson Procedure

At the end of each lesson, you will have the following options:

1. To restart the same lesson, press the F1 function key.
2. To return to the Lessons Menu, press ESC. This action will automatically save the completed lesson.
3. To proceed to the next, or any other lesson, highlight your choice and press Enter.
4. To return to the Main Menu, press ESC again.
5. To print the lesson, select Print Activities.
6. To exit the program:
   a. Select the Exit option and press Enter.
   b. When the DOS prompt appears on the screen, remove your data disk.
   c. Turn off the monitor. (Your instructor also may ask you to turn off the computer and printer.)

Measure Progress

Minimum goal: 29 wam with six or fewer errors

Take two 3-minute timings.

The modified block style for business letters is generally selected by companies that desire to project a more conservative or traditional image.

This letter style is a modification of the block style, hence the name modified block. The major difference is that the date and the closing lines start at the center point of the paper.

In letters keyed in this style, paragraphs may be indented, depending on the preference of the writer. Letters keyed in modified block style require a tab at the center point. If paragraphs are indented, a tab is set for the indentation.

Because more formatting is required, this style is not as efficient as the block style, which is preferred by most operators.

Learn to Format Business Letters in Modified Block Style

Review the information in the Measure Progress section above. Study the modified block-style letter on page 237. Notice that the date, complimentary close, and signature block, start at the horizontal center of the page.

Learning Activity 1

1. Start document LES39DC1. Key the modified block-style letter on the next page.
2. Delete any existing tab stops other than the tab at 15. Set a second tab stop at the horizontal center of the line. Space down to line 13. Press Tab twice and key the date.
3. After keying the body of the letter, use the Tab key to place the complimentary close and signature block at the horizontal center of the page.
4. Key the reference initials and the enclosure notation at the left margin.
5. Proofread the document on the screen. Use the editing keys to make corrections. Pay close attention to the placement of the dateline, complimentary close, and signature block. Press ESC to have the computer check your work.

28

Skill Building

GOALS

- Build Language Arts Skills
- Increase Keying Speed
- Improve Keying Accuracy
- Improve Keying Skills

Review

Key each line two times.

1 use the/let him/off the/end the/was for/was she it

2 The total trip transforms Tony into a trailblazer.

3 Her new room number was A-1568 rather than B-3456.

4 Most companies keep accurate financial records on disk.

Build Language Arts Skills

Study the following rules.

Use a comma after an introductory infinitive, a participial phrase, or a prepositional phrase. An **introductory infinitive** is a verb preceded by *to*. A **participial phrase** is a verb form used as an adjective. A **prepositional phrase** is a group of words containing a preposition and an object.

Infinitive To make a decision about a career, Kim met with the guidance counselor.

Participial Phrase Hoping to be given a scholarship, Jonah studied every afternoon.

Prepositional Phrase During the board meeting on Wednesday, the trustees will vote on the referendum.

Key each line.

1 Required to work overtime for three Saturdays to meet production, the workers were glad to finally have a free weekend.

2 Upon receiving the report from the geological crew, the research company invested in the desert land.

3 To do well in school, Tyronne found it necessary to improve his keyboarding skills.

Now key each of the following sentences, choosing the correct word.

1 Please bring all of the textbooks (here, hear).

2 Did you (here, hear) about the new regulations?

3 The action of the mob (insighted, incited) a riot.

4 She has perceptive (insights, incites) into the solution of the problem.

5 The keyboard was broken; (its, it's) keys were gone.

6 (Its, It's) very disheartening to (here, hear) about people who do not have enough to eat.

IMPROVE KEYING SKILLS

Take two 1-minute timings on each paragraph. Set a speed or an accuracy goal. If you finish the paragraph before time runs out, start again.

EXERCISE 1

Job safety is usually an on-going training concern. New employee orientation is a continuing training function in most large organizations. It's important to gain insight as to which safety programs are of greatest worth.

EXERCISE 2

"Time Management" and "Communication Skills" are popular workshop and seminar topics. Most training and employee development programs require someone in the organization to be responsible for designing, managing, and evaluating staff activities.

Now key each of the following sentences, adding necessary commas.

1 After reading about the approaching storm the family decided to head home early.

2 To best plan for the upcoming meeting the committee organized into small planning groups.

3 While learning a new song the band added five new percussion members.

4 Judging by the amount of food that was gone the parents knew the teenagers had guests.

INCREASE KEYING SPEED

Key each line twice. Try to increase your keying speed as you repeat the line.

UP REACHES

1 lawyer away outlaw straws choose sawing awaken sequel baking

2 ordeal garden hazard rabbit severe seized kidney shirts skin

3 edited junior jump kite edict educated kitty letter juvenile

4 Those lawyers chose to practice law with profound adherence.

DOWN REACHES

1 avoid naval saved avid avenue starve paves carts cable cargo

2 cards carton carpet cake ballot bacon bakery back bang balmy

3 back cracks vacant actual canvas invade vanish knight knocks

4 A naval carton knocked from the canvas cargo cable vanished.

JUMP REACHES

1 song only into sings much mute must muddy common bonus prone

2 induce regain filing index muddle museum minimum wave active

3 faces cereal notice excite exam flexed verify notice honored

4 Notice many muddled faces going quickly into the wax museum.

39 Formatting Business Letters in Alternate Styles

GOALS

- Build Language Arts Skills
- Improve Keying Skills
- Learn to Format Formal Business Letters in Modified Block Style
- Learn About Attention and Subject Lines

REVIEW

Key each line two times.

```
1 of at or in an it if is to te ti do id di my fa go
2 Grants get greater each year and go out gradually.
3 The officer said, "Ticket #693 was issued Friday."
4 Electronic filing systems must be properly set up.
```

BUILD LANGUAGE ARTS SKILLS

WORD USAGE

Understand the correct usage of the following words.

Hear/Here
Hear to perceive through the ears
Here at this point in place

Incite/Insight
Incite to provoke
Insight revelation or understanding

Its/It's
Its possessive form of *it*
It's contraction of *it is*

Key each line.

```
1 Her speech was designed to incite the audience.
2 Their insight into the problems was practical.
3 The computer has its memory increased.
4 It's evident word processing increases production.
5 Did you hear the machine, Anne?
6 Place the manuscript here when it is finished.
```

Improve Keying Accuracy

Key each line with no more than one error. If you do not reach the accuracy goal, repeat the line.

1 Dinner was served aboard the fancy yacht with much flourish.
2 Kathy visited Mexico during the normal examination vacation.
3 Was the census canvas a burden or ordeal to the tax workers?
4 A lawyer vanished in the snow storm in that scenic valley.
5 A border guard seized all the toxic and hazardous chemicals.

Improve Keying Skills

Take two 1-minute timings on each paragraph. Set either a speed or an accuracy goal. If you complete the paragraph before time runs out, start again.

Key quickly

Exercise 1

We descended into the scenic canyon to get a view of the winding river. Many rafts were spotted trying to navigate the rapids. The view from the cliff was breathtaking. We wondered how many others had viewed the beauty in awe. As the sun was setting over the beautiful canyon, we slowly made our way back to the camp.

Exercise 2

Have you ever tried the sport of white-water rafting? It is thrilling to go zipping down the rapids in a raft. It seems as if it is a dangerous sport, but the experienced guides know how to take precautions to remove much of the danger. After a day of white-water rafting, you are quite tired but eagerly anticipate the next event.

pay these agents the commission that is due on their lease throughout the life of the lease, including renewals. (¶) Special accounting is required to handle the payout of these commissions on the owner's statement for Mullins Medical Park. We will show only two percent as the commission rate for management. (¶) Please review these arrangements and advise me of the procedure that can be used to best accomplish this with the least amount of administrative effort./Sincerely yours/Ms. Sim Lin Hanni/Regional Sales Manager/cmg/les38dc3/c: Olaf R. Stranberg

End-of-Lesson Procedure

At the end of each lesson, you will have the following options:

1. To restart the same lesson, press the F1 function key.
2. To return to the Lessons Menu, press ESC. This action automatically will save the completed lesson.
3. To proceed to the next, or any other lesson, highlight your choice on the menu and press Enter.
4. To return to the Main Menu, press ESC again.
5. To print the lesson, select Print Activities.
6. To exit the program:
   a. Select the Exit option and press Enter.
   b. When the DOS prompt appears on the screen, remove your data disk.
   c. Turn off the monitor. (Your instructor also may ask you to turn off the computer and printer.)

Measure Progress

Take two 2-minute timings.

Minimum goal: 24 wam with four or fewer errors

Travel in this country could be revolutionized by the proposed use of high-speed trains. These trains exceed speeds of 200 MPH. Two experimental systems are being proposed for the Orlando, Florida, area and a Dallas-to-Houston route.

These high-speed trains are quite expensive. They are modeled after similar trains in Europe. If the two experimental lines are built and prove to be cost beneficial, other lines will be proposed.

One proposal is to link Boston to Washington. Another includes a network linking Chicago with cities that it serves. Another could be built for the Los Angeles area, and another to join Portland and Seattle. These high-speed trains could be beneficial by eliminating thousands of cars and improving the environment.

End-of-Lesson Procedure

At the end of each lesson, you will have the following options:

1. To restart the same lesson, press the F1 function key.
2. To return to the Lessons Menu, press ESC. This action will automatically save the completed lesson.
3. To proceed to the next, or any other lesson, highlight your choice and press Enter.
4. To return to the Main Menu, press ESC again.
5. To print the lesson, select Print Activities.
6. To exit the program:
   a. Select the Exit option and press Enter.
   b. When the DOS prompt appears on the screen, remove your data disk.
   c. Turn off the monitor. (Your instructor also may ask you to turn off the computer and printer.)

LEARN TO ADJUST SPACING IN LONGER LETTERS

If possible, business correspondence should not exceed one page. Longer letters tend to lose the reader's interest. If a letter appears as if it will exceed one page, some placement adjustments may be made. For longer letters, the space between the letterhead and the dateline and between the dateline and the inside address can be decreased. Adjustments also can be made by single-spacing between the reference initials, enclosure notation, and copy notation.

LEARNING ACTIVITY 3

1. Start document LES38DC3. Key the following unarranged letter in block style with open punctuation. Use the 1-inch default side margins and assume a 1½-inch letterhead (nine lines).
2. Key the dateline on line 11.
3. Start the inside address five lines below the dateline.
4. Single-space between the reference initials and the copy notation.
5. Proofread the copy on the screen. Use the editing keys to make corrections.
6. Press ESC when you are finished and follow the prompts to have the program check your document. Save and print a copy of your document.
7. Proofread your hard copy and mark any additional errors that you may have missed. Pay close attention to the top, bottom, and side margins as well as spacing between the parts of the letter.
8. Retrieve the document and make corrections as necessary. Save and print your corrected copy.

```
April 12, 1997/Mr. Jeffrey S. Constine, Jr./Landmark
Real Estate, Inc./489 Ferncastle Drive/Sacramento, CA
95880-4987/Dear Mr. Constine/We have been advised
that the management commission for the Mullins
Medical Park project is to be two percent for all
tenants of the property.  This rate will become
effective at the time of the purchase in May of this
year.  (¶) For the rent commission due to outside
agents and to internal agents, Ms. Bowman has advised
that we are to continue to make payments from
Commercial Rent Commission throughout the term of the
lease and any lease renewals.  We will continue to
```

29 Vertical and Horizontal Spacing and Setting Margins

GOALS

- Build Language Arts Skills
- Improve Keying Skills
- Learn Vertical and Horizontal Spacing
- Learn to Set Margins

REVIEW

Key each line two times.

1 as it is/all of the/call me ask/the for hers/is it
2 The underwriter unfolded the uneven managing plan.
3 He had 37 quarters, 456 dimes, and 12,500 pennies.
4 Many unique spreadsheet programs are available.

BUILD LANGUAGE ARTS SKILLS

PUNCTUATION: COMMA

Study the following rules.

- Use a comma to separate items in a series. When the last item in the series is preceded by a conjunction, a comma is placed before the conjunction.
- Use a comma to separate parts within an address.

Key each line.

1 I will bring a tent, sleeping bags, stove, and fuel.
2 Order some staples, tape, paper clips, and paper.
3 You may bring a salad, vegetables, or cake.
4 Her new address is 9428 Berkley, Washington, D.C.
5 He will visit Los Angeles, California.
6 Send my gifts to Dr. James Forrest, Route 1, Box 2455, Rockville, Maryland 24156.

Now key each of the following sentences adding correct comma punctuation.

1 Please bring me the book paper and folders.
2 When will you visit Chicago Illinois?
3 Please send it to Sewell Street Portland Oregon.
4 We will need official transcripts three reference letters and a completed application for our files.

August 2, 1997

Ms. Paula I. Cronin
District Manager
General Telephone Company
89302 Valdosta Drive
Marietta, GA 30074-7832

Dear Ms. Cronin:

Effective January 1, 1998, General Telephone Company will implement a spelling test in addition to the current operator telephone ability battery.

Employment candidates at the time of implementation who are required to take and pass the spelling test will be informed. The only candidates for the operator job who will be exempt from passing the spelling test are those who have met current test standards on the operator tab and spelling test.

Implementation guidelines have been forwarded to the General Employment Office. Mr. C. Crist, vice president personnel, will be glad to discuss any questions the union may have concerning the new test battery.

Sincerely yours,

Julia J. Parrish
Personnel Manager

xxx/les38dc2

c: Mr. C. Crist
Ms. R. Aigner
Ms. I. Marshall

Improve Keying Skills

Take two 1-minute timings on each exercise. Set either a speed or an accuracy goal. If you complete the paragraph before time runs out, start again.

Exercise 1

Sales are the heart of a business. Nothing happens until someone sells something, either a product or a service. Essential components of selling are motivation, knowledge, and persistence.

Exercise 2

Motivation can be internal and self-directed or external and provided by others. One of the first principles in sales is to believe in your product. It is very difficult to sell something in which you do not believe.

Measure Progress

Minimum goal: 25 wam with four or fewer errors

Take two 2-minute timings.

The computer is used for creative activities in graphics, design, art, music, and writing. The recent development of devices that create graphics puts many new features at the fingertips of users. This new type of input device does not require the user to memorize commands or learn a programming language to create new graphics, sounds, or designs.

Using these new devices greatly simplifies the process of preparing creative documents. In the past, combining graphics, design, and text was work that only could be performed by professionals. Now the home and office computer user can prepare sophisticated copy without enlisting the services of a professional.

Coastal Community College
2980 Tidewater Drive
Seattle, WA 98164

January 16, 1996

Central Hi School
8637 Escher Dr.
Seattle, WA 98161-2137

Ladies and Gentlemen:

The Society for Educational advancement is soliciting nominations of scholarship awards the next school year. Since we maintain currant scholarship awards, additional awards will not exceed 1000.

Eligibility requirements include:

1. desire to further education in afield

2. record of academic excellence

3. evidence of need

Should your school have qualified candidates, that you wish to nominate, please have them complete the enclosed application. And mail it to the appropriate address. Thank you for your support of our program.

Sincerely yours,

Tito G. O'Neal
Scholarship Chair

xxx/les38dc1

Enc.

Learn Vertical and Horizontal Spacing

All documents you prepare should be attractively arranged on a sheet of paper. Equal margins create a balanced look for the entire document. To produce attractive and balanced documents, study the following information.

Vertical Spacing Standard Paper Size

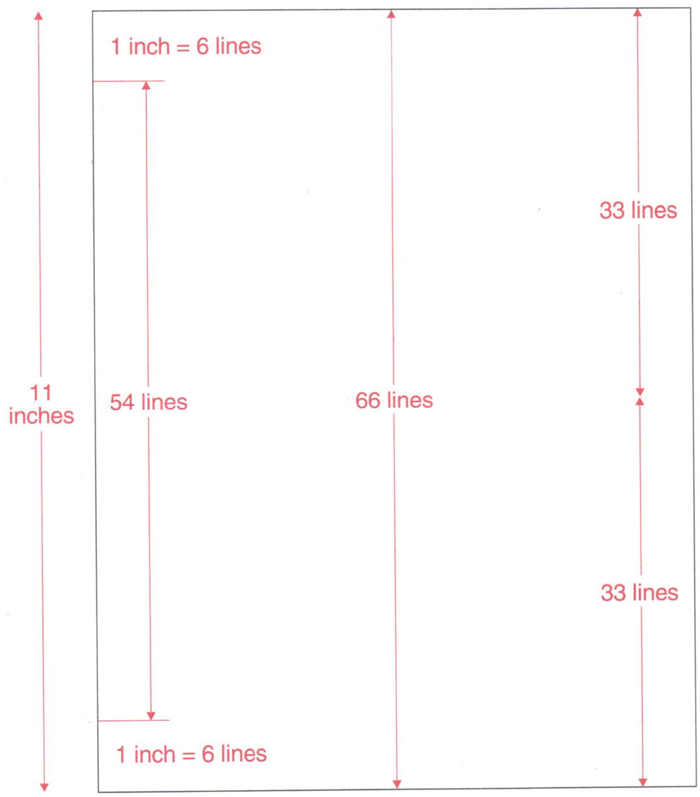

The vertical length (top to bottom) of a standard sheet of paper is 11 inches. Computer printers usually are set to print 6 lines of copy per vertical inch. That means there could be 66 lines of copy on each sheet of paper (11 x 6 = 66). However, most documents require at least a 1-inch margin at both the top and bottom of a page. With 6 blank lines for the top margin and 6 blank lines for the bottom margin, only 54 lines are actually available for printed copy (2 x 6 = 12 and 66 - 12 = 54).

Many software programs, including the one that accompanies this textbook, are preset to automatically allow for 1-inch top and bottom margins. When keying a document, the status line at the top of the word-processing screen indicates the line where the printed copy will appear on the printout. If the status line indicates "Line 7," for example, the printer will automatically start printing 1 inch from the top of the page. Any copy keyed starting on "Line 13" will print 2 inches from the top of the page.

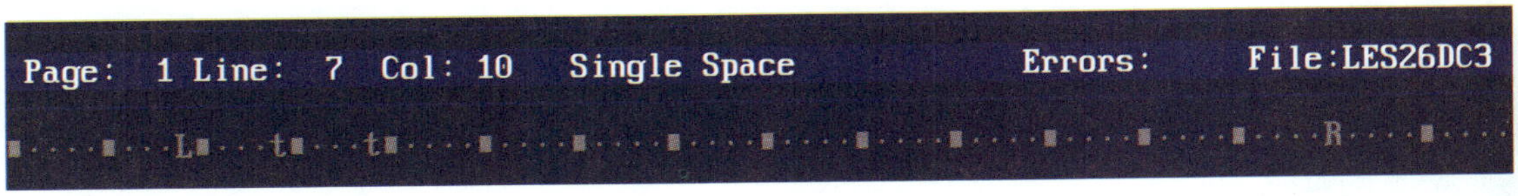

Learn to Format Formal Business Letters in Block Style From Edited, Handwritten, and Unarranged Copy

Learning Activity 1

1. Start document LES38DC1. Key the formal business letter on the next page in block style using standard punctuation. Use the 1-inch default side margins and assume a 1½ inch letterhead (nine lines). Make any corrections indicated by proofreader's marks.
2. Using the default tabs, tab the enumerations five spaces from the left margin. After keying the number, indent to the second tab stop to key the copy. Single-space the paragraph copy. Double-space the enumeration copy.
3. Proofread the letter on the screen. Use the editing keys to make corrections.
4. Press ESC when you are finished and follow the prompts to have the program check your document. Save and print a copy of your document.
5. Proofread your printout and mark any additional errors you may have missed. Pay attention to formatting as well as keying errors.
6. Retrieve the document and make corrections as necessary. Save and print your corrected copy.

Learning Activity 2

1. Start document LES38DC2. Key the handwritten letter on page 231 in block style with standard punctuation. Use the 1-inch default side margins and assume a 1½ inch (nine lines) letterhead.
2. Single-space copy within a paragraph. Use the editing keys to make corrections.
3. Proofread the copy on the screen. Use the editing keys to make corrections.
4. Press ESC when you are finished and follow the prompts to have the program check your document. Save and print a copy of your document.
5. Proofread your printout and mark any additional errors that you may have missed. Pay attention to formatting as well as keying errors.
6. Retrieve the document and make corrections as necessary. Save and print your corrected copy.

This software program uses 10-pitch type.

Horizontal Spacing Standard Paper Size

Horizontal spacing is measured from left to right across a page. The spot where each character or space appears is referred to as a **column**. The number of columns available for printed copy depends upon the pitch setting of the printer. Although many printers can be adjusted to a variety of pitches, the most commonly used settings are 10 pitch and 12 pitch. The number refers to the number of characters per inch. A higher numbered pitch will print more characters per inch than a lower numbered pitch. The lower the pitch size, the larger the print.

```
10 pitch = 10 characters per inch (cpi)
12 pitch = 12 characters per inch (cpi)
```

A standard sheet of paper is 8 ½ inches wide. If all spaces were filled with print, there would be room for 85 characters when using 10-pitch type and 102 characters when using 12-pitch type. However, most documents require at least a 1-inch margin on both the left and right edges of the page. Thus, the actual space available for printed copy will be at least 2 inches less than the width of the page. This print area is referred to as the **writing line** or the **text length line**. When using 10-pitch type, the text length line will be no longer than 65 spaces. When using 12-pitch type, the text length line will be no longer than 78 spaces. Automatic word wrap features on most word processors prevent copy from extending into the margins.

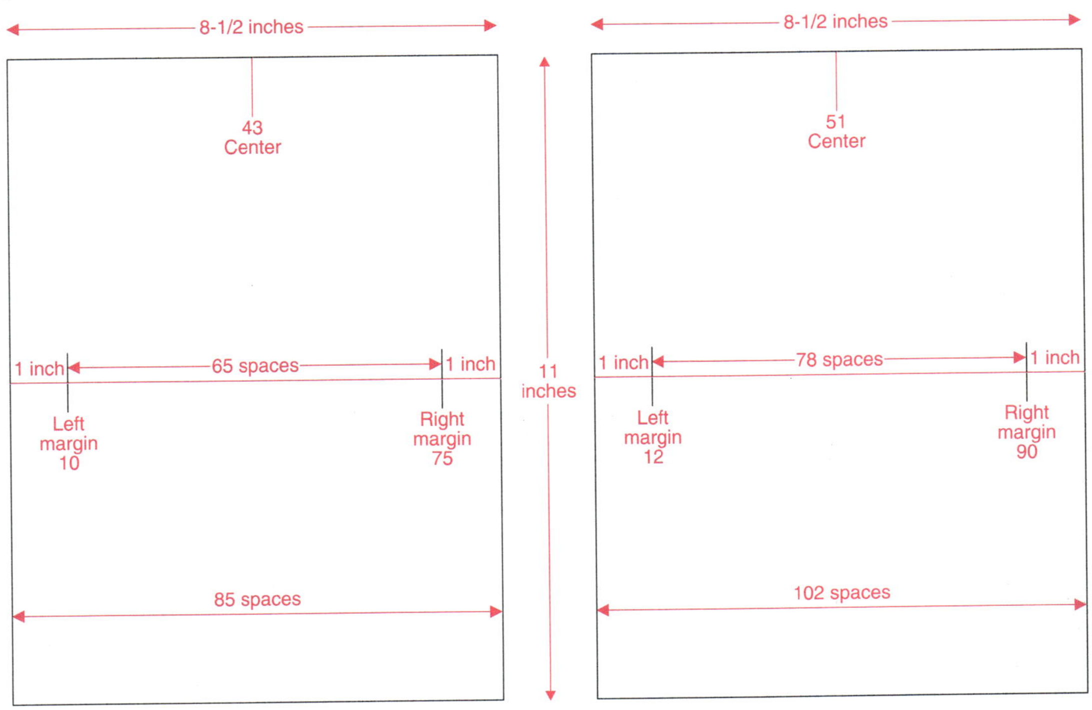

10 Pitch 12 Pitch

Measure Progress

Minimum goal: 29 wam with six or fewer errors

Take two 3-minute timings.

Effective communication skills are essential for the person who wishes to succeed in business. Many executives report that the ability to communicate is the single most important factor in their career development.

The ability to communicate is a valuable job asset. A review of the job descriptions for college graduates indicates communication ability is high on the list of requirements.

Managers spend the majority of their time directing other people. Persons who have not developed their communication skills may find themselves in low-paying, dead-end positions.

If you wish to advance in your career, take the time to perfect your oral and written communication skills. You will have an advantage over many of the other people in your company.

Learn About Special Features of Business Letters

When copies of correspondence also are sent to individuals other than the addressee, a copy notation should be keyed at the bottom of the letter. This notation is keyed a double-space below the enclosure notation (if used) or a double-space below the reference initials. If copies are sent to more than one individual, the names are listed by rank or in alphabetical order. The following are examples of common styles:

```
copy:  Ms. Barbara Hall
copies:   Jorge Tiller
          Anna Menuca
c:  Accounting Department Staff
C:  Mrs. Virginia Joyner
copy to Mr. Michael Hughes, Treasurer, Merit Company
pc:  Lynda R. DeAngelo, M.D.
```

(pc refers to personal copy)

Setting Side Margins

Most documents are keyed with equal left and right side margins. When using the word processor that accompanies this textbook, a default margin of 1 inch (using 10-pitch type) already is set. The "ruler line" at the top of the screen shows the column position of the left (L) and the right (R) margins as well as the position of any existing tab stops (t). The "status line" at the top of the screen indicates the present line and column location of the cursor according to the text line length. Since there is a 1-inch left margin default, column 10 is the column where the text line begins.

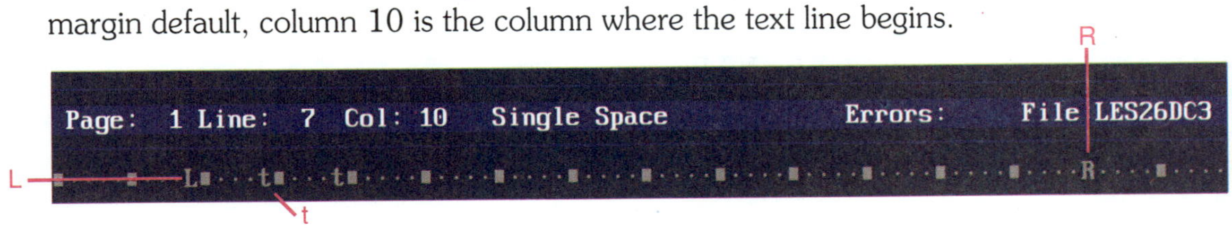

For efficiency, most operators accept the default margins and create a balanced look for the document by adjusting the top and bottom margins. You can change the default side margins whenever a document format requires it by following these steps:

1. Determine the width, in inches, for the side margins.
2. Multiply the number of desired inches by the pitch size (characters per inch) to determine the left margin (LM) setting. For example:

1-inch side margin using 10 pitch	1 x 10 = 10 (default)
1-inch side margin using 12 pitch	1 x 12 = 12 (set LM at 12)
2-inch side margin using 10 pitch	2 x 10 = 20 (set LM at 20)
2-inch side margin using 12 pitch	2 x 12 = 24 (set LM at 24)

3. If the right margin is to be equal to the left margin, determine the right margin setting (RM) by subtracting the left margin from the total spaces available across the page and set the RM at that point. For example:

1-inch side margin using 10 pitch	85 - 10 = 75 (default)
1-inch side margin using 12 pitch	102 - 12 = 90 (set RM at 90)
2-inch side margin using 10 pitch	85 - 20 = 65 (set RM at 65)
2-inch side margin using 12 pitch	102 - 24 = 78 (set RM at 78)

4. If the left margin and right margin are not equal, determine the setting for the left margin first. Determine the right margin by subtracting the number of spaces needed for the margin from the total number of spaces available across the page. The following table will help you make the determination.

Margin Chart

	10 pitch		**12 pitch**	
	LM	RM	LM	RM
1 inch	10	75	12	90
1 ½ inches	15	70	18	84
2 inches	20	65	24	78

The actual number of spaces will be determined by the pitch of the type.

Now key each of the following sentences, choosing the correct word.

1 He ran (farther, further) than I possibly could.

2 Before we (can, may) complete this application, we must have (farther, further) information.

3 Please send me the tuition money so that I can (farther, further) my education.

4 The team came (fourth, forth) with the skills needed to win.

5 They now rank (fourth, forth) in the overall standings.

Improve Keying Skills

Take two 1-minute timings on each paragraph. Set a speed or an accuracy goal. If you complete the paragraph before time runs out, start again.

Exercise 1

In order to develop an organization's staff, a training and education program is needed. This program will include a variety of growth opportunities for the various types of employees. Some programs are designed to further employee qualifications for higher positions.

Exercise 2

The training opportunities can include workshops, conferences, seminars, and classes. These can be offered both on- and off-site. In addition to the off-the-job types of training, various on-the-job skills can be taught. A fourth of the available opportunities also offer college credit upon completion.

Changing the Side Margin Settings

Side margins can be changed only in the word processor of the program. If you wish to change the default margins, follow these steps:

1. Be sure that you are at a word-processor screen.
2. From the prompts at the bottom of the screen select F7-ruler. When F7 is pressed, the cursor will move to the first column on the ruler line.

3. Use the Right- or Left-Arrow key to move the cursor to the column where you would like to set the left margin. Remember, the number that appears after "Column" will indicate the column position of the cursor.
4. When you are at the column where you would like to set the left margin, press L on the keyboard. An L will now appear on the ruler line at that position.

5. Use the Right- or Left-Arrow key to move the cursor to the column position where you would like to set the right margin and press R. An R will appear on the ruler line at that position.
6. If you wish to set new tab stops, use the Right- or Left-Arrow keys to move to the position where you would like to set new tab stops. Press T to set a left tab at that position. Tab stops that are to the left of the left margin or to the right of the right margin will not be recognized by the software. Tab stops must be located between the margin settings. To delete an existing tab stop, move to that position and press the DEL (delete) key. The T will be replaced with a small square. (Remember: Setting tabs was introduced in Lesson 26.)
7. When both margins and all tab stops are set, press Enter to return to the body of the document.

Learning Activity 1

1. Start document LES29DC1. Key the following paragraph. Refer to the preceding steps for setting margins and tab stops.
2. Change both the left and right margins to 2 inches. Refer to the Margin Chart if necessary.
3. Set one tab stop five spaces from the left margin for the paragraph indent.
4. Allow word wrap to format the lines. Press Enter only at the end of the paragraph.

Now key each of the following sentences, adding correct use of quotation marks and correct placement of other punctuation marks.

1 We will begin our vacation after the job is completed said Mrs. Melnekov

2 We will begin our vacation said Mrs. Melnekov after the job is completed

3 When will we go on vacation asked Mikado

4 When asked Mikado will we go on vacation

5 What a wonderful day yelled Stephen

6 Were you able to read the article The Death of the Dinosaurs in this month's magazine

Word Usage

Understand the correct usage of the following words.

Farther/Further

Farther a larger or greater distance

Further additional; to help forward

Forth/Fourth

Forth forward

Fourth a numeric term denoting rank; one of four equal parts

Key each line.

1 The building site was farther from town than I originally thought.

2 The clerk requested further information.

3 The loan will be used to further my education.

4 He brought forth his new ideas with creativity.

5 The team ranks fourth in the league standings.

5. Proofread the copy on the screen. Use the editing keys to make corrections. Press ESC to have the computer check the document. Save and print a copy of the document.
6. Proofread the printout and note any errors you may have missed. Measure the printout to be sure there are 2-inch left and right margins.
7. Retrieve the document and make corrections as necessary. Save and print your corrected copy.

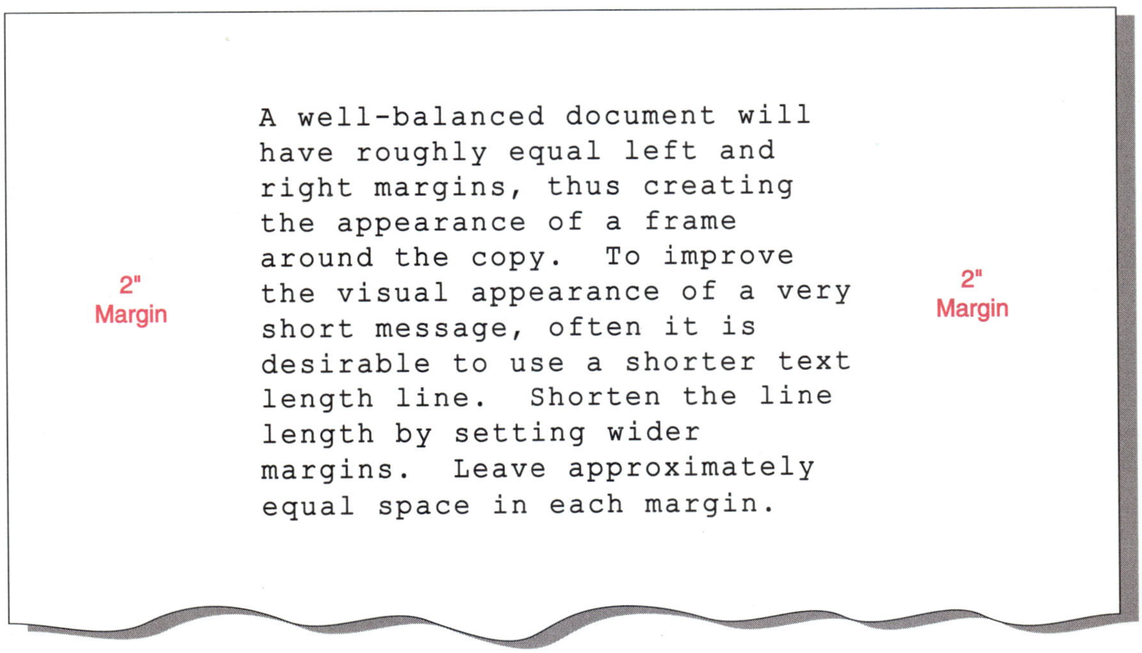

A well-balanced document will have roughly equal left and right margins, thus creating the appearance of a frame around the copy. To improve the visual appearance of a very short message, often it is desirable to use a shorter text length line. Shorten the line length by setting wider margins. Leave approximately equal space in each margin.

Learning Activity 2

1. Start document LES29DC2. Key the paragraph on the next page.
2. At a new word processor screen, reset the side margins for 1½ inches. Refer to the Margin Chart if necessary.
3. Remove any existing tab stops and set one tab stop five spaces from the left margin for the paragraph indent.
4. Press Enter only at the end of the paragraph.
5. Proofread the copy on the screen. Use the editing keys to make corrections. Press ESC to have the computer check the document. Save and print a copy of the document.
6. Proofread the printout and note any errors you may have missed. Measure the printout to be sure there are 1½ inches.
7. Retrieve the document and make corrections as necessary. Save and print your corrected copy.

38

Problem Solving: Business Letters

GOALS

- Building Language Arts Skills
- Improve Keying Skills
- Learn About Special Features of Business Letters
- Learn to Format Formal Business Letters in Block Style from Edited, Handwritten, and Unarranged Copy
- Learn to Adjust Spacing in Longer Letters

REVIEW

Key each line two times.

1 he in on so or of it at if be by ti do ha la it or

2 Foundations find funds frequently from financiers.

3 Marita's phone number was changed to 703-555-9821.

4 Computers occasionally malfunction, but most often it is operator error.

BUILD LANGUAGE ARTS SKILLS

PUNCTUATION: QUOTATION MARKS

Study the following rules.

- Always place periods and commas inside quotation marks.
- Place semicolons and colons outside quotation marks.
- Place exclamation points, question marks, and dashes inside quotation marks when they apply to the quoted material. Place them outside when they apply to the entire sentence.

Key each line.

1 Did you read my recent article, "Office Automation," in this month's news bulletin?

2 Mr. O'Brien said, "Please complete the report today."

3 Did someone say, "Today is my birthday"?

4 Barbara said, "Where is my umbrella?"

5 The speaker said, "I have completed my talk"; then he continued to talk for another ten minutes.

1½" Margin

A well-balanced document will have roughly equal left and right margins, thus creating the appearance of a frame around the copy. To improve the visual appearance of a medium-length message, it is often desirable to use a text length line slightly longer than for a short message. Increase the line length by setting narrower margins. Leave approximately equal space in each margin.

1½" Margin

End-of-Lesson Procedure

At the end of each lesson, you will have the following options:

1. To restart the same lesson, press the F1 function key.
2. To return to the Lessons Menu, press ESC. This action will automatically save the completed lesson.
3. To proceed to the next, or any other lesson, highlight your choice and press Enter.
4. To return to the Main Menu, press ESC again.
5. To print the lesson, select Print Activities.
6. To exit the program:
   a. Select the Exit option and press Enter.
   b. When the DOS prompt appears on the screen, remove your data disk.
   c. Turn off the monitor. (Your instructor also may ask you to turn off the computer and printer.)

Learning Activity 3

1. Name the document LES37DC3. Key the following unarranged formal business letter in correct format using block style with standard punctuation. Use the 1-inch default side margins.
2. To complete the activity, follow the same directions as for Learning Activity 1 on page 221.

December 5, 1998/Ms. Elizabeth R. Toone/Vice President/Citizens Bank/4280 S. Main Street/Bangor, ME 04401-4398/Dear Ms. Toone:/Enclosed is your copy of the audited financial statement for our company dated December 3, 1998. Should you have any questions regarding this report, please do not hesitate to give me a call. (¶) Also enclosed is a copy of the statement that we paid with our check number 7753 in the amount of $704.32. I have asked our accounting department to send copies of your invoice with all future checks. (¶) As soon as our accounting department validates the statement from your company, all charges will be paid. Please let me know if you need any further information./Very truly yours,/James L. Gregory/Vice President and Treasurer/sjv/les37dc3/Enclosures

End-of-Lesson Procedure

At the end of each lesson, you will have the following options:

1. To restart the same lesson, press the F1 function key.
2. To return to the Lessons Menu, press ESC. This action automatically will save the completed lesson.
3. To proceed to the next, or any other lesson, select your choice on the menu.
4. To return to the Main Menu, press ESC again.
5. To print the lesson, select Print Activities.
6. To exit the program follow the appropriate procedures.

30 Review Line Spacing and Learn to Indent

GOALS

- Build Language Arts Skills
- Improve Keying Skills
- Review Line Spacing
- Learn to Indent

Review

Key each line twice.

1 will he/ask the/for her/the women/one of them/call

2 Earnest excess could not be exclaimed and exalted.

3 Numbers quantify things; 764, 343, 124 + 236 = 360

4 Simulations on the computer allow you to experience events.

Build Language Arts Skills

Punctuation: Comma

Study the following rules.

- Use a comma to set off introductory words, phrases, and clauses from the main part of a sentence.
- Use commas within sentences to set off phrases and clauses that could be omitted without changing the meaning.

Key each line.

1 At the gong, the time will be one o'clock.

2 When the sun rises, all the birds begin to sing.

3 Our guide, looking French in his beret, led us through the castles.

4 The lake, however, was stormy and windblown.

5 That is my daughter, the one in the dark green car.

Micro-Logic Sales Ltd.
Computer Supplies
14 Plaza Place
Salt Lake City, Utah 84106-9220
(801) 555-5984

July 30, 1997

Note address format for Canada.

Mr. Pierre DeSalme, Branch Manager
Telephone Information Systems
500 Broad Street
Vancouver, BC L8H 2H6
CANADA

Dear Mr. DeSalme

I thought you would like to know about the most recent problem with our new telephone system. During the last month, I have had numerous complaints from our sales agents about the phones ringing as many as 15 or 20 times without being answered when a call is received through our switchboard.

On two separate occasions today, we observed this occurring with a call that came in to our main number (555-5984) and was extended from the switchboard to the sales agent's telephone number. The call rang several times and never returned to the switchboard for coverage. When testing this immediately following that occurrence, the call came back to the switchboard in the appropriate manner. Later in the afternoon, there was a second occurrence of the same situation but with a different agent.

I am at a loss to explain this situation to you, since the problem seems to come and go. We placed a trouble call on this problem today; however, I wanted to keep you advised of the problems with the system.

Very truly yours

Ashley S. Barnes
Administrative Manager

es/les37dc2

Now key each of the following sentences, adding the correct comma punctuation.

1 When the sun rises we will go fishing.

2 My father who is often late will pick me up after school today.

3 We will therefore need to be at the office at 5 p.m.

4 Since we enjoy going to the theme park we go whenever we can find the time.

5 Well it's about time you arrived!

Improve Keying Skills

Concentrate on your goal

Take two 1-minute timings on each paragraph. Set either a speed or an accuracy goal. If you complete a paragraph before time runs out, start again.

Exercise 1

Most large corporations have a logo or symbol. This provides instant public recognition of the corporation and its products. When designed properly, a logo will help create a particular image of a company.

Exercise 2

A corporate image, good or bad, may depend on many factors. It is important to create a good image for a business and its products and services. This is usually accomplished through advertising and other public relations activities.

Exercise 3

In the final analysis, every employee is a public relations contact. Persons who come in contact with employees form an opinion about the business based on the service or treatment they receive.

Business Forms, Inc.
Towers Complex • Suite 427 • Richmond, Virginia 23220-2022 • 807-555-6293

Dateline — February 28, 1996 — Line 13 or 2 lines below letterhead

4 to 8 lines

Inside Address —
Ms. Annette Jackson
Office Manager
Regal Corporation
109 N. Main Street
Peoria, IL 61643-0450

DS

Salutation — Dear Ms. Jackson:

DS

Body —
This letter illustrates a business letter keyed in block style with standard punctuation. This style is similar to the personal business letter style, except it is usually keyed on a company's printed letterhead stationery.

DS

The business letter also includes the writer's title in the signature block. The operator's reference initials are keyed at the left margin a double-space below the signature block.

DS

If additional items are to be sent with the letter, an enclosure notation should be included. The enclosure notation is keyed at the left margin a double-space below the reference initials.

DS

A booklet that illustrates the block-style business letter is enclosed. Please let me know if you need additional information on letter styles.

DS

Complimentary Close — Sincerely yours,

4 lines

Signature Block — John Small, Consultant

DS

Reference Initials — kbo/les37dc1

DS

Enclosure Notation — Enclosure

Measure Progress

Take two 2-minute timings.

Minimum goal: 25 wam with four or fewer errors

Many software programs are designed to be educational. Using a tutorial approach, the computer actually teaches content and can bring in drill and practice if needed. These programs measure progress and provide practice activities as necessary.

Large numbers of these programs are available in almost every subject area. A trend among software publishers is to develop programs related to the required courses in public schools and colleges.

This keyboarding software is an example of a tutorial program. There are many activities the computer can perform efficiently, but your instructor is still the most important element of the learning process.

Review Line Spacing

Lesson 23 presented detailed instruction about single- and double-spaced formatting. If necessary, review that information. Exercises keyed in the word processor can be in single- or double-spaced format. Double-spacing leaves a blank line between each keyed line. The F5 key controls line spacing. The status line at the top of the screen displays the current setting. If you wish to change from one format to the other, press F5 before keying the material that requires the changed format.

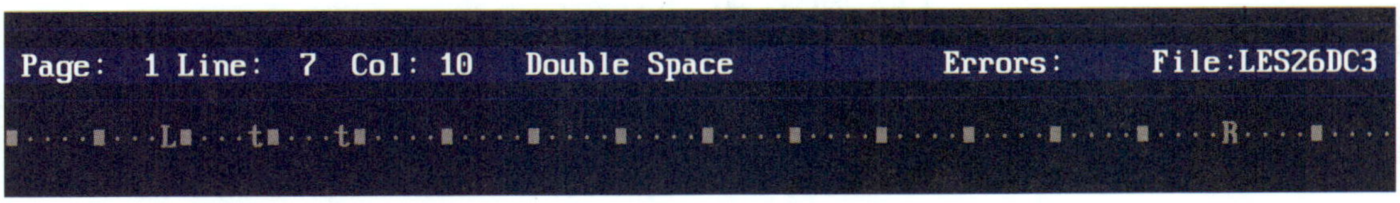

5. **Reference Initials**. The initials of the operator who keyed the letter appear in lowercase letters at the left margin a double-space below the last line of the signature block.
6. **Document Code**. Many companies no longer keep printouts of their correspondence. Instead all documents are stored on disks. In order to quickly recall stored documents, a document code is included. It is keyed on the same line as the reference initials and separated from the initials by a slash.
7. **Enclosure Notation**. This is a reminder if additional items are enclosed with the letter. Often, the type of enclosure also is included. There is no standard enclosure notation, but some widely used formats include:

```
Enclosure                   Enclosures
Enc.                        Enclosures:   Check
                                          Invoice
Enclosure:     Check        Enclosures 2
Enc. 2
```

Learning Activity 1

1. Start document LES37DC1. This will also be the document code used for this letter. Key a copy of the model formal business letter on the next page in correct format. Use standard punctuation. Follow the directions carefully. Use the 1-inch default side margins.
2. Proofread the copy on the screen. Use the editing keys to make corrections.
3. Press ESC when you are finished and follow the prompts to have the program check your document. Save and print a copy of your document.
4. Proofread your printout and mark any additional errors that you may have missed. Pay close attention to the spacing between parts of the letter.
5. Retrieve the document and make corrections as necessary. Save and print your corrected copy.

Learning Activity 2

1. Start document LES37DC2. Key a copy of the model formal business letter on page 223 in correct format. Use open punctuation. Follow the directions carefully. Use the 1-inch default side margins.
2. Proofread the copy on the screen. Use the editing keys to make corrections.
3. Press ESC when you are finished and follow the prompts to have the program check your document. Save and print a copy of your document.
4. Proofread your printout and mark any additional errors that you may have missed. Pay close attention to the spacing between parts of the letter.
5. Retrieve the document and make corrections as necessary. Save and print your corrected copy.

Learn to Indent

Quotations, listings, and numbered lists are indented.

Most word-processing programs include an indent feature that allows the operator to set a temporary left margin for indented blocks of text. This time-saving feature is useful when keying lengthy quoted material, listings, and enumerations (numbered lists). When using the indent feature, it is not necessary to set a new left margin for the block of indented material. The following information and directions refer to the software program that accompanies this textbook. If you are using a different word-processing program, check the user's manual for that software.

The indent feature can be used only when working in the word processor and only when tab stops are already set. Each time the Indent key is pressed, the left margin of the text is temporarily set at the next tab stop. As long as the indent is active, all lines of text will wrap to the indent location. Striking Enter cancels the indent command and moves the text to the originally set margin.

To activate indent, press the F4 function key. (See the prompt line at the bottom of the word processor screen.) A small arrow on the screen shows where the temporary left margin is now located. The left margin will stay at that spot until Enter is pressed. Indent affects only the left margin. Remember, the indent feature will work only when tab stops are already set on the ruler line.

```
F3-Help  F4-Indent  F5-Spacing  F6-Center  F7-Ruler  F8-Underline  F9-Block
```

Learning Activity 1

1. Start document LES30DC1. Key the following exercise. Set tab stops at five and ten spaces from the left margin. Press F5 to select double-spacing.
2. Paragraph indent the first line of the first paragraph by striking the Tab key once. Indent all of the text in the second paragraph using the indent feature. Before keying the paragraph, press F4. An arrow should appear on the screen. To further indent the first line of the paragraph, strike Tab once. When you are finished keying the second paragraph, press the Enter key to return to the original left margin. Key the remaining text material.
3. Correct keying errors as you enter the copy. Proofread the copy on the screen. Use the editing keys to make any corrections.
4. Press ESC when you are finished and follow the prompts to have the program check your document. Save and print a copy of your document.
5. Proofread your printout and note any additional errors you may have missed.
6. Retrieve the document and make corrections as necessary. Save and print your corrected copy.

Measure Progress

Minimum goal: 28 wam with six or fewer errors

Take two 3-minute timings.

The salutation used in a business letter should be in agreement with the name in the inside address. The most common form is to use a courtesy title and the last name. The following are commonly used forms of salutations: Dear Mr. Everett, Dear Mrs. Steinbeck, Dear Ms. DeAngelo, or Dear Miss Ward.

If the letter is addressed to a company and the name of the individual is not known, the preferred salutation is Ladies and Gentlemen or Gentlemen and Ladies. If the organization is composed entirely of men, the salutation Gentlemen is appropriate. For an organization composed of all women, Mesdames or Ladies is appropriate.

Learn to Format Formal Business Letters in Block Style

A business letter contains essentially the same parts as a personal business letter, with some minor modifications. Formal business letters usually use letterhead paper, thus there is no need for a return address. Review the material in the Measure Progress section above. Then refer to the business letter on page 222. Read and carefully study the formatting directions and the document placement on the page.

Parts of a Formal Business Letter

1. **Letterhead**. Stationery with the company name and address printed on it. Replaces the return address.
2. **Dateline**. The first keyed line. Key on line 13 (2 inches from the top of the page) or two lines below the letterhead.
3. **Inside Address, Salutation, Body, and Complimentary Close**. Use the same format as for the personal business letter.
4. **Signature Block**. Key the business title of the person who wrote the letter as part of the signature block. Standard formats are:

Short name and title:

Rocio Salcedo, Manager

Long name and title:

Crystal Taylor
Executive Director

Most word-processing software programs have an indent feature that allows the operator to indent blocks of text to a temporary left margin. Subsequent lines automatically wrap to the temporary margin. The indent feature differs from a regular tab because a tab will indent only one line of text. The indent feature indents all lines of text until you strike Enter.

> To use the indent feature, you must first set a tab at the point where you wish to have a temporary left margin. To begin the first line of indented copy, first press the Indent key. If the first line is to be indented further, press the Tab key once. Each subsequent line automatically will wrap to the new temporary margin. To return to the original left margin, press the Enter key.

Some word-processing software has a double indent feature that allows you to indent from both margins. With the double indent feature, you do not have to reset the right margin to indent it. Indent features make the keying of blocks of indented text within a document much easier.

Learning Activity 2

This software also has a feature that will indent both the left and right margins. To indent both left and right margins, hold the Shift key while you press F4.

1. Rekey the above exercise to create document LES30DC2. This time, when you reach the indented section, hold down the Shift key while you press F4. Do not paragraph indent the paragraph.
2. Proofread the copy. Check to be sure that the correct paragraph is indented on both the left and right margins. Make any necessary corrections.
3. Press ESC to have the computer check your work.

End-of-Lesson-Procedure

After completing the activities for this lesson, follow the appropriate end-of-lesson procedure.

4 The program was designed to (elicit, illicit) responses from the class.

5 Please be (explicit, implicit) in your instructions to the students.

6 The need for the structural renovations was (explicit, implicit) in the building design.

Improve Keying Skills

Take two 1-minute timings on each paragraph. Set a speed or an accuracy goal. If you complete the paragraph before time runs out, start over again.

Exercise 1

Most of our top management positions are filled from within the organization. We have a very small turnover rate, which indicates the employees' satisfaction with their positions. We devised a policy that whenever new positions open we search our own pool of qualified workers first.

Exercise 2

Our staff of recruiters visits all the major universities and schools within our geographic area that prepare potential recruits for our organization. Brochures and job descriptions are available in the placement office. At least twice a year, potential recruits may visit directly with our personnel representatives.

31

Learning Proofreader's Marks

GOALS

- Build Language Arts Skills
- Improve Keying Skills
- Learn Proofreader's Marks
- Key Edited Copy

Review

Key each line two times.

1 or as us he an at so of in it to on be do go lo if

2 is and run get yet sit pay hot him are won let out

3 in lime effect number annual carbon bright brought

4 The dance at school happens to be informal attire.

Build Language Arts Skills

Punctuation: Comma

Study the following rules.

- Use a comma before the conjunction to separate two independent clauses in a compound sentence.
- Do not use a comma between compound verbs that have the same subject.

Key each line.

1 John will ride his bicycle on the touring path, and I will jog behind him.

2 You should take the old car to the mechanic, and Joy will drive the new car.

3 She reached the city before dark and spent an hour looking for the hotel.

4 William went to the park and exercised until dark.

Now key each of the following sentences, adding correct comma and colon punctuation.

1 `Please send me the following supplies 20 tents 10 gas stoves 15 awnings and 12 sleeping bags.`

2 `The new position required the following traits on time neat in dress and accurate.`

Word Usage

Understand the correct usage of the following words.

Device/Devise

Device a mechanism or means
Devise plan or make

Elicit/Illicit

Elicit bring out
Illicit unlawful

Explicit/Implicit

Explicit indicate clearly
Implicit implied or alluded to

Key each line.

1 `The device often malfunctioned.`

2 `She will devise a way to solve the problem.`

3 `A good computer program will elicit proper responses from the user.`

4 `He engaged in many illicit business practices.`

5 `The plan for the new process was very explicit.`

6 `The need for additional funding was implicit in the presentation.`

Now key each of the following sentences, choosing the correct word.

1 `The new (devise, device) required much skill to operate it.`

2 `We must (devise, device) a plan to ensure that we meet our quota.`

3 `The operation involved (elicit, illicit) practices.`

Now key each of the following sentences, adding correct comma punctuation.

1 Today I will go to the beach and go swimming in the blue ocean.

2 Jamie wants to play soccer and Jilleen would rather play volleyball.

3 You need to take all the files to the copy center and be sure to have each one copied.

4 Wong Le is the best swimmer at our school and Julio is the best basketball player.

Improve Keying Skills

Take two 1-minute timings on each paragraph. Set a speed or an accuracy goal. If you complete the paragraph before time runs out, start again.

Exercise 1

Employee morale is an essential consideration in any successful business. Happy employees create a desirable work environment and they usually produce superior products and services. Happy employees often ensure happy customers.

Exercise 2

Telemarketing is a sales concept that is being used successfully with a number of products. Businesses find it to be an efficient and cost-effective marketing tool. Some consumers, however, view it as an unwanted intrusion into their privacy.

Exercise 3

Most banks have computer programs that allow instant access to computers' accounts. A problem develops, however, when the computer is down or when a customer has to wait because of insufficient telephone access lines.

37

Formatting Formal Business Letters in Block Style

GOALS

- Build Language Arts Skills
- Improve Keying Skills
- Learn to Format Formal Business Letters in Block Style

REVIEW

Key each line two times.

1 he of or on be by my no up at as do in or so oz at

2 Your ears encode many series of serious sequences.

3 The date on invoices #8769 and #8548 was 12/30/97.

4 Decision-making skills will become more important as greater use of computers occurs.

BUILD LANGUAGE ARTS SKILLS

PUNCTUATION: COLON

Study the following rule.

- Use a colon after a complete thought that introduces a formal listing or enumeration.

Key each line.

Use two spaces after a colon.

1 We ordered the following items: one dozen pencils, four dozen folders, three dozen rulers, and three dozen staplers.

2 Job interview techniques include the following: appropriate dress, prompt arrival, and accurate applications.

Measure Progress

Minimum goal: 26 wam with four or fewer errors

Take two 2-minute timings.

With the current explosive growth of computers in the office, the need for fluent keyboarding skills by all levels of office employees is more important than ever. People who have not needed to keyboard will be required to operate computer terminals. Also, because computers are available in many homes, students may need keyboarding skills long before they can enroll in a formal course.

Many schools are now implementing keyboarding courses during the middle-school years. These courses will be required for all students and will come at a very crucial time--the time when students are beginning to use the computer for writing. These students will develop a skill they can use in all of their future education and careers.

Learn Proofreader's Marks

Authors, editors, proofreaders, and office workers use a standard set of marks to indicate desired changes in printed copy. The marks may be used in pairs. If so, one mark is placed in the margin closest to the change, and one in the text where the change is to be made.

Study the proofreader's marks that follow.

Mark Meaning	Example	Revised Copy
Transpose or	Run the program computer. or Second, turn on the CPU. First, insert the disk.	Run the computer program. or First, insert the disk. Second, turn on the CPU.
Insert ^ ∨	Turn the monitor and ENTER. (on, strike)	Turn on the monitor and strike ENTER.
Close up space	Key boarding is fun.	Keyboarding is fun.
Add space #/	Quality work is apriority.	Quality work is a priority.

department. I am pleased to have him as a peer and reluctant to see him leave. I recommend him without reservation for your position./Sincerely yours,/Rose Munoz, Ed.D.

Learning Activity 3

Following the directions given in Learning Activity 2, key this unarranged letter in proper format. However, use open punctuation.

75932 Gordon Road/Montgomery, AL 36121-8932/Current Date/Coordinator of Scholarships/State University/901 W. Franklin Street/Atlanta, GA 30384-5281/Ladies and Gentlemen/Ms. Latoya Matthews is a student in the Business Administration program at Montgomery Community College. She plans to graduate next spring. (¶) Ms. Matthews' academic excellence is demonstrated by her selection to the President' s Honor Roll during each quarter that she has been enrolled. Her cumulative grade point average is 3.9. She was awarded an Educational Foundation Scholarship this year. This scholarship is awarded to the highest ranking student in the Division of Business. (¶) Ms. Matthews has been employed part time as a bank teller while attending school. She served as night supervisor at the bank. (¶) All of these accomplishments are outstanding. In addition, she has a wonderful personality. She is a sincere individual and exhibits a positive image. She is comfortable with people. I recommend her for this scholarship./Cordially yours/Robert J. Ellis, Ph.D.

End-of-Lesson Procedure

After completing the activities for this lesson follow the ppropriate end-of-lesson procedure.

Delete or	Computers are very dependable. or Some computers havve disks.	Computers are dependable. or Some computers have disks.
Lowercase lc or /	Every Programmer is accurate. or Learning Machine language is difficult.	Every programmer is accurate. or Learning machine language is difficult.
Uppercase uc or ≡	come to the computer display. or come to the software show.	Come to the computer display. or Come to the software show.
Move left [	[Planning your work is fun.	Planning your work is fun.
Move right]	]Unplanned work is chaotic.	Unplanned work is chaotic.
Single-space SS	Make more income. SS Try hard and succeed.	Make more income. Try hard and succeed.
Double-space DS	The lazy usually fail. DS Turn off the computer.	The lazy usually fail. Turn off the computer.
Triple-space TS	Turn off the color monitor. TS You are learning very fast.	Turn off the color monitor. You are learning very fast.
Move as shown	The computer basic system	The basic computer system
Let stand stet	Three major components	Three major components
Spell out sp	The U.S. is a great place to live.	The United States is a great place to live.
New paragraph ¶	¶ It is best if you learn proofreader's marks.	It is best if you learn proofreader's marks.
Underline	The title was How to Keyboard More Effectively.	The title was How to Keyboard More Effectively.
Run in	Long-range planning is necessary for effective planning.	Long-range planning is necessary for effective planning.
Bold	Knowing how to use a computer is very important.	Knowing how to use a computer is **very important**.
Center] [	]Heading Are Centered[	Headings Are Centered
Hyphen	You did a first rate job.	You did a first-rate job.

LEARNING ACTIVITY 2

When keying unarranged materials, you must make the decisions about placement and formatting of the document. Whenever unarranged copy is presented, the slash mark (/) indicates a line break. The paragraph mark (¶) indicates the start of a new paragraph. You must make decisions as to which lines belong to which part of the document. For personal business letters, refer to the table on page 207 and the model letter on page 208. Be sure to follow the required punctuation style.

1. Start document LES36DC2. Key the following unarranged personal business letter in correct format using *standard* punctuation. Use the 1-inch default margins.
2. Proofread the copy on the screen. Use the editing keys to make corrections.
3. Press ESC when you are finished and follow the prompts to have the program check your document. Save and print a copy of your document.
4. Proofread your printout and mark any additional errors that you may have missed. Pay close attention to the spacing between parts of the letter.
5. Retrieve the document and make corrections as necessary. Save and print your corrected copy.

```
8592 Winding Ridge Lane/Fort Myers, FL 33963-
3912/Current Date/Dr. Lena Barrone/Dean, School of
Business/State University/Waterloo, IA 50722-
5184/Dear Dr. Barrone:/Dr. Mark Esposito has asked me
to send you a letter of recommendation for him for an
accounting position at your school.  Dr. Esposito
joined our faculty in 1990 as an instructor in the
Accounting Department.  Since 1993 he has served as
department head.  (¶) Dr. Esposito teaches all levels
of accounting courses, including cost, tax auditing,
and computer accounting.  He was responsible for the
development of a videotape lecture series in
accounting that has been broadcast over cable
television.  (¶) The work experience that he had
prior to joining our faculty also has contributed to
his classroom expertise.  Dr. Esposito has a CPA
certification.  He completed his doctorate in 1989.
He was an honor student in all academic work.  (¶) In
summary, Dr. Esposito is a valuable member of our
```

Key Edited Copy

Learning Activity 1

1. Start document LES31DC1. Key the following document. Make the changes indicated by the proofreader's marks. Use the default margins.
2. Press the ESC key when you are finished. The computer will check your document and highlight errors.
3. Save and print the document. Proofread the printout and note any additional errors you may have missed.
4. Retrieve the document and make corrections as necessary. Save and print your corrected document.

Make the required corrections as you key the document.

```
] Learn to Save Documents [
# In most programs software, documents are not
permanently saved unless you give a command to so do.
Until you store or SAVE a Document, it exists only in
the active memory of the micro computer. If you trun the
microcomputer off, the document is lost. to save the
document to disk for later use, you need to tell the program
to file the document before turning off the
microcomputer. ¶ In morst software programs, once you
have keyed a ducment you will have an opportunity to
SAVE or store it. the software will prompt you to
name the document. After assigning the document a
Name, following the on naming documents restrictions
for that software, you can then respond toany
additional prompts that appear on the screen. Turn
off the monitor.
```

Learning Activity 2

Edited Copy with Enumeration

1. Start document LES31DC2. Key the following document, making changes as indicated. Accept the 1-inch default margins. Set tab stops five and ten spaces from the left margin.
2. Single-space the document, but double-space between the enumerations.

Learn to Format Personal Business Letters From Handwritten and Unarranged Copy

Learning Activity 1

1. Start document LES36DC1. Key the following handwritten personal business letter. Use the model letter on page 208 as your guide for spacing. Use standard punctuation and the 1-inch default side margins.
2. Proofread the copy on the screen. Use the editing keys to make corrections.
3. Press ESC when you have finished and follow the prompts to have the program check your document. Save and print a copy of your document.
4. Proofread your printout and mark any additional errors you may have missed. Pay close attention to the line spacing between parts of the letter.
5. Retrieve the document and make corrections as necessary. Save and print your corrected copy.

8401 Aspen Way
New York, NY 10042-8932
Current Date
Mrs. Marcia Hubbard
Training Consultant
Solutions Unlimited, Inc.
4283 Mauna Drive
Hilo, HI 96720-3056
Dear Mrs. Hubbard:
All the arrangements have been made for my speaking engagement with your company. I will arrive in Hilo on March 11 at 4:45 p.m. and stay at the Hilo Inn.
An overhead projector and a large screen will be needed for my presentation. A handout of my talk will be presented to all participants. By February 15, please give me an idea of the approximate number of people who will be attending the presentation.
Please let me know if you need any additional information from me. I am looking forward to meeting with you and visiting your beautiful island.
Cordially yours,
Charles Steinberg

3. At the enumerated listing, strike Tab once, then key the number and period. Press the F4 key to set a temporary left margin at the next tab stop. Key all of the copy of that item. Press Enter only at the end of that copy. For the next enumerated item, follow the same procedure.
4. Proofread the copy on the screen. Use the editing keys to make additional corrections. Press ESC to save and check the document. Print the document.
5. Proofread the printout and mark any additional errors you may have missed.
6. Retrieve the document and make corrections as necessary. Save and print your corrected document.

```
] Goals of efficient office systems [

     For office systems to be efficient they need to
possess components that allow for the product of
information quickly and accurately.  Some specific
requirements are:

     1.  Quality--All equipment used must be of
superior quality free from defects and requiring very
low maintenance

     2.  Speed--The systems must allow for a high
production rate.  equipment and software should be
designed in a manner to achieve this goal.

     3.  Cost--The components of the system should
be available at a reasonable cost.  Cost studies
should be conducted to be sure the highest products
are purchased at the most reasonable cost.
If these goals are followed the company should
operate at a high level of production within our cost
guidelines.
```

END-OF-LESSON PROCEDURE

After completing the activities for this lesson, follow the appropriate end-of-lesson procedure.

Exercise 2

The opportunity to learn from colleagues always should be encouraged among employees. Quite often a peer will have the answer to a work problem that you are trying to solve. Opportunities for networking should be encouraged.

Exercise 3

The various opportunities to network should always be taken. The informal communications and contacts made at conferences and social events can be very valuable to sales personnel and managers. Many resources and opportunities are discovered through informal channels.

Measure Progress

Take two 2-minute timings.

Minimum goal: 28 wam with four or fewer errors

Educational researchers have repeatedly told us that it is important to vary instructional methods in order to focus attention, maintain motivation, and increase learning. Using the computer in a computer-managed instructional mode allows one to accomplish this goal.

Programmers are able to control several media with the computer. For example, a video disk can be controlled by the computer to present single images like a slide projector or a sequence of images like a motion video.

32

Keying Edited Copy

GOALS

- Build Language Arts Skills
- Improve Keying Skills
- Review Format Changes in Edited Copy

Review

Key each line twice.

1 to be as is in the and are put que dog bee wax bag

2 red ear dye six race gift pond long hive fact text

3 Police Academy, Texas, Dr. J.B. Kirk, Richmond, VA

4 Her dress looked like it had been worn many times.

Build Language Arts Skills

Punctuation: Comma

Study the following rules.

- Use commas in dates to separate the day from the year and in addresses to separate city from state.
- Use a second comma after the year or the state name when it appears in the middle of a sentence.

Key each line.

1 The report that was due on July 10, 1995, was not received until July 30.

2 On Tuesday, February 3, 1995, the order was received by the shipping department.

3 Do you live in San Francisco, California, in the winter months?

4 The professor can be reached in Dallas, Texas, after June 20, 1996.

4 Bill can load the computer for you.
5 You may take the rest of the day off.
6 Sacramento is the capital of California.
7 Our capital investment was over $1.2 million.
8 The meeting was held in the capitol building.
9 Congress meets in the Capitol.

U.S. Capitol is always capitalized.

Now key each of the following sentences choosing the correct word.

1 We develop the (biennial, biannual) plan to cover the next two-year period.
2 We must pay our taxes based on a (biennial, biannual) cycle April 15 and October 15.
3 You (can, may) take all the children to the theme park.
4 Jackie (can, may) use the spreadsheet software effectively.
5 Our senate meets in the (capital, capitol) building.
6 How much (capital, capitol) is required for the investment?

Improve Keying Skills

Take two 1-minute timings on each paragraph. Set a speed or an accuracy goal. If you complete the paragraph before time runs out, start again.

Exercise 1

The importance of the informal communication network must not be overlooked. When corporate personnel eat lunch together or discuss business during coffee breaks, the informal communication network can be in full operation.

Now key each of the following sentences, adding the correct comma punctuation.

1 The date of the meeting was changed to January 15 1995 in Little Rock Arkansas.

2 The family will move to Boston Massachusetts in February.

3 Next Wednesday June 15 1995 we will attend the fashion show.

Improve Keying Skills

Take two 1-minute timings on each paragraph. Set a speed or an accuracy goal. If you complete the paragraph before time runs out, start again.

Concentrate on your goal.

Exercise 1

Quality performance is usually rewarded by an organization. The knowledge, however, that you have completed a job or assignment to the best of your ability is often enough reward.

Exercise 2

Unhappy employees with low morale usually have high turnover and absentee rates. In addition to those problems, the products and services provided by disgruntled workers are usually inferior.

Exercise 3

Individual responsibility for one's actions is a sign of maturity. Often in large organizations the individual is immersed in the corporate image and does not feel responsible for inferior performance.

36

Problem Solving: Personal Business Letters

GOALS

- Build Language Arts Skills
- Improve Keying Skills
- Learn to Format Personal Business Letters from Handwritten and Unarranged Copy

Review

Key each line two times.

```
1 if up is or no an so in as at me up no en an of on
2 Drunk driving displays dumb, degenerate decisions.
3 Your 10:30 corporate meeting didn't start on time.
4 The future paperless office will need trained office
  workers who understand computer applications.
```

Build Language Arts Skills

Word Usage

Understand the correct usage of the following words.

Biannual/Biennial

Biannual twice a year
Biennial once every two years

Can/May

Can ability to perform an act
May granting permission

Capital/Capitol

Capital official seat of government; the assets of a company
Capitol a building

Key each line.

```
1 Your biannual billing will be computed on January 15
  and June 15 of each year.
2 You will be billed on a biennial basis in 1995, 1997,
  and 1999.
3 Jean can keyboard very effectively.
```

Measure Progress

Minimum goal: 26 wam with four or fewer errors

Take two 2-minute timings.

```
     The use of computers in teaching keyboarding
also has many advantages for the teacher because
computers can assist the teacher in managing
instruction.  Much of the burden of paper grading and
recordkeeping can be performed by computers, thus
freeing the teacher for individual tutoring and
counseling.
     Computers can be used to analyze each student's
work and provide other assignments.  The effective
use of computers in instruction can be a timesaving
device for both teachers and students.
```

Review Format Changes in Edited Copy

Learning Activity 1

1. Start document LES32DC1. Key the following exercise. Double-space the copy. Make corrections as indicated by the proofreader's marks. Correct any keying errors as you enter the document.
2. Proofread the document on the screen. Use the editing keys to make any additional corrections. Press ESC to save and check the document. Print the document.
3. Proofread the printout and note any additional errors you may have missed.
4. Retrieve the document and make corrections as necessary. Save and print your corrected document.

```
                    AGENDA
The administrative services committee is planning a
special meeting on February 21, 1995, at 3 p.m.  The
agenda for the meeting will include discussion of the
following items:
New Budget Procedures
Cost Saving Plans
Staffing Needs
Vacation Coverage
```

Route 1, Box 2455
Madison, VA 22727-3929
Current Date

Ms. Melinda Lee
Technical Community College
1458 N. 60th Street
Phoenix, AZ 85034-4428

Dear Ms. Lee

Mrs. Pamela Bassette has informed me that you are speaking at the workshop session I will be coordinating. According to my records, your session will be on Friday, April 17. It is scheduled from 2:45 to 3:45 p.m.

At this time, I do not have the room scheduled. When you arrive, please check to see where the session will be held. So that I might have an opportunity to clarify any last-minute details, please contact me when you have checked in to the hotel.

I would like to meet with you 30 minutes prior to your session in the assigned room. Please send me your biographical information by April 1 so that I can use it in preparing the introduction. I look forward to meeting you and hearing your informative session.

Cordially yours

Ms. Sherry Turner

Learning Activity 2

1. Start document LES32DC2. Key the following document, making changes as indicated. Correct any keying errors as you enter the document.
2. Proofread the document on the screen. Use the editing keys to make any additional corrections. Press ESC to save and check the document. Print the document
3. Proofread the printout and note any additional errors you may have missed.
4. Retrieve the document and make corrections as necessary. Save and print your corrected document.

```
Learn to Retrieve Documents
An advantage to using work-processing is the ability
to recall retrieve a document to revise it.  One
documents have been saved, they can be retrieved at
any time.
It is important to give documents an name identifying
that can be used to retreve them at a later time.
Different software programs may use procedures to
retrieve a document, but the process is basically the
same.
Once the document has been revised, the new document
may be stored in place of the old one.  If it is
desirable to keep both the original and revised
documents, most software programs have a procedure
that allows this. In that case, be sure to give each
document a different name.
```

End-of-Lesson Procedure

After completing the activities for this lesson, follow the appropriate end-of-lesson procedure.

Learning Activity 2

1. Start document LES35DC2. Key the model personal business letter on the next page. Follow the preceding formatting instructions for each part of the letter. Use the 1-inch default margins.
2. Correct any keying errors as you enter the text.
3. Proofread the copy on the screen. Use the editing keys to make any changes. Be sure to pay attention to spacing and format.
4. Press ESC when you have finished and follow the prompts to have the program check your document. Save and print a copy of your document.
5. Proofread your printout and mark any additional errors you may have missed. Pay close attention to the spacing between parts of the letter.
6. Retrieve the document and make corrections as necessary. Save and print your corrected copy.

End-of-Lesson Procedure

At the end of each lesson, you will have the following options:

1. To restart the same lesson, press the F1 function key.
2. To return to the Lessons Menu, press ESC. This action automatically will save the completed lesson.
3. To proceed to the next, or any other lesson, highlight your choice and press Enter.
4. To return to the Main Menu, press ESC again.
5. To print the lesson, select Print Activities.
6. To exit the program:
   a. Select the Exit option and press Enter.
   b. When the DOS prompt appears on the screen, remove your data disk.
   c. Turn off the monitor. (Your instructor also may ask you to turn off the computer and printer.)

33 Review Format Changes in Edited Copy

GOALS

- Build Language Arts Skills
- Improve Keying Skills
- Review Formatting Changes in Edited Copy

Review

Key each line two times.

1 for him/for the/and the/but all/had she/and all of

2 Jake joined John in joshing Joe and Jill jovially.

3 Reports #5986 and #4127 highlighted all the flaws.

4 Computers will not replace the worker but will ease stress.

Build Language Arts Skills

Punctuation: Semicolon

Study the following rules.

- Use a semicolon to separate two independent clauses not joined by a conjunction.
- When one or more of the elements in a series contains commas, use semicolons to separate the items.

Key each line.

1 We are going to the movie; Ed is not going with us.

2 Our coach, Mr. Olsen, will be presenting the awards; Joni is receiving the first one.

3 Attending the conference were Mr. James, our science teacher; Ms. Ruthers, our principal; and Mrs. Vail.

Now key each of the following sentences, adding correct semicolon punctuation.

1 Natasha is going to the prom on Saturday she has a new turquoise dress.

2 Bonner likes to go surfing and scuba diving.

3 The new officers for the organization are Samantha Adams president Antonio Romano secretary and Patrick McKenzie treasurer.

2 inches (12 blank lines)

Return Address
849 Ridge Lane ← Line 13
Pueblo, CO 81004-2010

Dateline
February 13, 1995

4 to 8 lines

Inside Address
Mr. Xavier Gibson
1285 Parham Road
San Bernardino, CA 92437-5187

DS

Salutation
Dear Mr. Gibson:

DS

1" margin | Body | 1" margin

You asked me to send you information regarding the formats for a personal business letter. The personal business letter style is generally used by individuals.

DS

Because these individuals usually do not have printed letterhead stationery, a return address must be keyed. This return address is keyed above the dateline.

DS

The parts of a personal business letter include the return address, dateline, inside address, salutation, body, complimentary close, and signature block.

DS

A personal business letter may use standard or open punctuation. In standard punctuation, a colon follows the salutation and a comma follows the complimentary close. In open punctuation, no mark of punctuation follows the salutation or complimentary close. This letter is an example of a personal business letter in block style with standard punctuation.

DS

Complimentary Close
Sincerely yours,

4 lines

Jeffrey Montiell

Signature Block

Word Usage

Understand the correct usage of the following words.

Aid/Aide

Aid act of helping or the help given
Aide person who acts as an assistant

Key each line.

1 Many students have completed their education with financial aid packages.

2 Many teachers benefit from having a student aide.

3 Ask the aide if you do not know how to load the disk.

Now key each of the following sentences, choosing the correct word.

1 The doctor's (aid, aide) led the patient to the examination room.

2 When the economy is depressed, many people may need (aid, aide).

Improve Keying Skills

Take two 1-minute timings on each paragraph. Set a speed or an accuracy goal. If you complete the paragraph before time runs out, start over again.

Exercise 1

Advertising is the art of persuading consumers to buy a certain service or product. Advertising involves motivating a buyer by creating a need for the service or product. A good advertising program is an important aid for a salesperson.

Letter Part	Placement	Line Spacing	Punctuation
Return Address	Line 13 (2 inches)	single	address style
Dateline	Immediately below return address	single	date style
Inside Address	4 to 8 lines below return address	single	address style
Salutation	2 lines below inside address	double before double after	colon after (standard) none (open)
Body	2 lines below salutation	single double between paragraphs	
Complimentary Close	2 lines below body	double before 4 lines after	comma after (standard) open (none)
Signature Block	4 lines below complimentary close	single	name style

Learning Activity 1

1. Start the document LES35DC1. Key the model personal business letter on page 208. Follow the preceding formatting instructions for each part of the letter. Use the 1-inch default margins.
2. Check the line position on the status line at the top of the screen. Remember, there is a 1-inch top margin default, so to begin at line 13 (2 inches from the top) press Enter six times (in single-spacing).
3. Word wrap is on automatically. Press Enter only to end a short line or to end a paragraph. Double-space between paragraphs.
4. Correct any keying errors as you enter the text.
5. Proofread the copy on the screen. Use the editing keys to make any changes. Be sure to pay attention to spacing and format.
6. Press ESC when you have finished and follow the prompts to have the program check your document. Save and print a copy of your document.
7. Proofread your printout and mark any additional errors you may have missed. Pay close attention to the spacing between parts of the letter.
8. Retrieve the document and make corrections as necessary. Save and print your corrected document.

Exercise 2

Many things happen in business when a product is sold. Selling is persuading people that they should buy a product or service. Competition for the products requires a company to explain the advantages of their particular products. Salespeople often rely on aides to contact potential customers.

Measure Progress

Take two 2-minute timings.

Minimum goal: 26 wam with four or fewer errors

Computer-based learning has potential for providing a flexible system of instruction that some people consider to be superior to traditional group instruction. This instruction can be self-paced and provide maximum provision for student learning.

Pacing, feedback, and knowledge of results are important factors in learning to keyboard. A well-designed computer software program can provide these factors. Because the learning process in computer-based instruction is student-controlled, the learning environment may be less threatening.

Review Format Changes In Edited Copy

Learning Activity 1

1. Start document LES33DC1. Key the following document, making changes as indicated. Leave a 2-inch top margin and 1-inch side margins. Correct any keying errors as you enter the document.
2. Proofread the document on the screen. Use the editing keys to make any additional corrections. Press ESC to save and check the document. Print the document.
3. Proofread the printout and note any additional errors you may have missed.
4. Retrieve the document and make corrections as necessary. Save and print your corrected copy.

Measure Progress

Minimum goal: 28 wam with four or fewer errors

Take two 2-minute timings.

```
     The trend in both business and personal correspondence is to use the block letter style.  In block letter style, all lines begin at the left margin.

     This letter style frequently is used by businesses that wish to project a modern, efficient image.  Many word-processing operators also prefer this letter style because it can be keyed faster.

     Some individuals and companies prefer to use the modified block or simplified letter styles.  Letter style is often chosen based on the image the company wishes to project.
```

Review Personal Business Letters in Block Style

The block style format for Personal Business Letters was covered in the optional portion of Lesson 25. If you did not complete that assignment, or if you need to review details, study the information in Lesson 25 before continuing with this lesson.

For further information about the block letter style, read the text of the preceding Measure Progress exercise. Then refer to the following table while studying the model letter on page 208. Look carefully at the formatting instructions and how the document is arranged on the page.

A note about punctuation style: There are two punctuation styles commonly used in today's business world—standard and open. In **standard punctuation**, a colon follows the salutation and a comma follows the complimentary close. In **open punctuation**, no punctuation follows either the salutation or the complimentary close. Each business decides which format to use. In no case, however, should the two formats be combined. Use one or the other.

BELIEFS, ATTITUDES, AND OPINIONS

In every usage, beliefs, attitudes, and opinions are very close together in meaning. Often they are used interchangeably. There are, however, distinctions between them:

A belief is the acceptance of a statement or proposition without requiring any evidence or proof. An attitude is an emotional attachment for or against an event, object, or person and is closely related to an opinion. An "opinion" is a judgment or generally held view not necessarily based on fact.

You may have an opinion about anything and it is usually the result of some activity. Attitudes are usually positive or negative. In practice, the distinction among these words is not very important. Most beliefs, attitudes, and opinions are closely linked and affected by a persons culture. A persons culture consists of customs and traditions which influence attitudes and beliefs that in turn color beliefs.

Individuals are influenced constantly by social class, social groups, schools, family, friends, and so on. All of these environmental factors shape our attitudes, beliefs, and opinions. Because of this, people from different environments will have different attitudes, beliefs, and opinions.

Among the cultural forces influencing an individual, the family is one of the most important. Parents are products of the culture and greatly shape the formation of the childs attitudes, beliefs, and opinions. It is not surprising that parents and childrens attitudes, beliefs, and opinions are closely related.

Now key each of the following sentences, choosing the correct word.

1 The (cite, sight, site) from the rim of the Grand Canyon was spectacular.

2 The (cite, sight, site) of the next Olympic games was announced yesterday.

3 It is important to (cite, sight, site) all references in your paper.

4 Death Valley is a southwestern (desert, dessert).

5 Do not (desert, dessert) your beliefs and you will be happier.

6 What is your favorite (desert, dessert)?

Improve Keying Skills

Take two 1-minute timings on each paragraph. Set a speed or an accuracy goal If you complete the paragraph before time runs out, start again.

Exercise 1

It is a paradox that so many organizations in a democratic society are operated in a dictatorial manner. Some organizations use a vertical top-down management style that discourages employee input. This type of management style is often cited as a cause of high turnover rates and low morale.

Exercise 2

Employee motivation is often difficult. It is, however, the joint responsibility of the employee and the employer. Employers need to learn what factors in the work environment are essential to employee motivation. No two people are motivated by the same set of items. Employers should not desert policies that encourage motivation.

End-of-Lesson Procedure

At the end of each lesson, you will have the following options:

1. To restart the same lesson, press the F1 function key.
2. To return to the Lessons Menu, press ESC. This action will automatically save the completed lesson.
3. To proceed to the next, or any other lesson, highlight your choice and press Enter.
4. To return to the Main Menu, press ESC again.
5. To print the lesson, select Print Activities.
6. To exit the program:
    a. Select the Exit option and press Enter.
    b. When the DOS prompt appears on the screen, remove your data disk.
    c. Turn off the monitor. (Your instructor also may ask you to turn off the computer and printer.)

Now key each of the following sentences, adding semicolon and comma punctuation.

1 The school-year opening sessions were scheduled for August 17 and Dr. Overby our dean was responsible for the program.

2 All students of course are requested to attend the graduation ceremony however some students received permission to be absent.

3 Ms. Angier our principal was present at the reception and she of course did not leave until it was over.

Word Usage

Understand the correct usage of the following words.

Cite/Sight/Site

Cite mention or quote
Sight see; a view
Site location

Desert/Dessert

Desert a sandy, barren area (noun); abandon (verb)
Dessert course served at the end of a meal

Key each line.

1 Did you cite the author in the list of references?

2 Did you sight the first eclipse?

3 He was quite a sight with his new hairstyle.

4 The site of the next conference was announced yesterday.

5 The Sahara is a very large and barren desert.

6 Did the employee desert the company during the strike?

7 The dessert was chocolate mousse with a pecan topping.

34

Formatting Edited Copy

GOALS

- Build Language Arts Skills
- Improve Keying Skills in Numeric Tabulation
- Improve Keying Skills

REVIEW

Key each line two times.

1 as it is/at my by/go to do/to no by/it is at go in

2 It is nice and novel to nearly nominate neophytes.

3 My recipe uses 2 cups of flour and 3 of margarine.

4 Teleconferences allow people in diverse areas to communicate.

BUILD LANGUAGE ARTS SKILLS

PUNCTUATION: SEMICOLON AND COMMA

Study the following rule.

- Use a semicolon to separate two independent clauses joined by a transitional expression.
- Use a comma after a transitional expression.

Transitional expressions include:

accordingly	however	so
consequently	nevertheless	therefore
furthermore	otherwise	yet

Key each line.

1 I wish I could go to the party; however, I must stay home and study.

2 The new budget director has not arrived; consequently, the audit cannot be completed today.

3 New catalogs will be shipped tomorrow; therefore, the sale can start on Monday.

35 Formatting Personal Business Letters in Block Style

GOALS

- Build Language Arts Skills
- Improve Keying Skills
- Review Personal Business Letters in Block Style

REVIEW

Key each line two times.

1 an is he at me go no as of it an am co to if at it

2 Hurry home, Hela and Hal deserve hours of harvest.

3 The operator said the new number was 919-555-4831.

4 A data bank is group of databases with files of information.

BUILD LANGUAGE ARTS SKILLS

PUNCTUATION: SEMICOLON

Study the following rule.

- If either part of two independent clauses that are separated by a conjunction contains commas, a semicolon is generally used before the conjunction.

Key each line.

1 Several new people were added to our staff; and Mr. Burton, our personnel officer, was responsible for their training.

2 You are, of course, invited to the graduation; but the reception is limited to current students.

Now key each of the following sentences, adding correct semicolon and comma punctuation.

1 We wanted to go to the concert however we could not purchase tickets.

2 The new items will be delivered tomorrow and we will be able to complete the renovations.

3 We wanted to attend the movie however we were not allowed to do so.

4 The new quotations are out we will be able to make an offer soon.

5 The test booklets did not arrive on time consequently the exams could not be given on February 21.

WORD USAGE

Understand the correct usage of the following words.

Among/Between

Among in or through the midst of; use if more than two
Between in the time, space, or interval that separates two things

Appraise/Apprise

Appraise estimate
Apprise notify or inform

Ascent/Assent

Ascent rise
Assent agree

Key each line.

1 The computers were distributed among the various departments.

2 You must choose between the two options.

3 The dealer will appraise the value of my car.

4 She wanted to appraise the condition of the house.

5 Please apprise us of the latest developments.

6 The recent ascent of meat prices created a demand for vegetables.

7 The lawyer had to assent to the changes in the contract.

UNIT 6

BUSINESS CORRESPONDENCE

Now key each of the following sentences choosing the correct word.

1 The choice was (among, between) the two major parties.

2 The food supplies were distributed (among, between) the four needy countries.

3 Please (appraise, apprise) the committee of your decision today.

4 The estimator will (appraise, apprise)the value of the property.

5 The (ascent, assent) in stock market prices caused an evaluation of the investing plans.

6 Did all parties (ascent, assent) to the changes in the document?

Improve Keying Skills In Numeric Tabulation

Multiple tab stops can be set when using the word processor. To change settings, follow these steps:

1. At a clear word processor screen, press the F7 key.
2. Use the Left- or Right-Arrow key to move to the position where you want to set or remove a tab. Existing tab settings appear as a t.
3. To set a new left tab, strike the T key.
4. To remove a tab, strike the Delete key when the cursor is on a tab setting.
5. After all desired tabs are set or deleted, press Enter to return to the document.

Start document LES34DC1. Follow the preceding steps to first remove all default tabs. Next, set tabs every ten spaces. Key the following exercise. Key across the columns, pressing Tab to move to the next column. Press Enter at the end of each line.

Remember: F7 will allow you to set tab stops.

Remember the number-reading rules.

7891	4832	4321	8731	2562	3671
0161	0451	7891	0150	4972	0596
6427	8395	7984	0510	2132	4624
8987	8332	6380	1836	4923	9243
5126	9842	9243	7426	6985	0479
9357	2598	1693	1492	9036	5018

PAPERLESS OFFICES

Computers and electronic mail both for internal and external use will speed communications and provide instant feedback on proposals, sales agreements, quotes, inventory, supplies, calendars, and itineraries. The paperless electronic office is becoming a reality.

Currently many offices are in the hybrid stage where they are using parts of both systems--paper and electronic mail. In the near future, most transactions and correspondence will occur electronically.

Offices may decide to use shared workstations or go to a centralized word processing. There are advantages and disadvantages to each of these approaches. The centralized word-processing center allows individuals to specialize in preparation of certain high-volume documents and the software packages required to produce them. A disadvantage of centralized word-processing cents is that the operators are often isolated from the people they serve.

End-of-Lesson Procedure

At the end of each lesson, you will have the following options:

1. To restart the same lesson, press the F1 function key.
2. To return to the Lessons Menu, press ESC. This action will automatically save the completed lesson.
3. To proceed to the next, or any other lesson, highlight your choice and press Enter.
4. To return to the Main Menu, press ESC again.
5. To print the lesson, select Print Activities.
6. To exit the program:
   a. Select the Exit option and press Enter.
   b. When the DOS prompt appears on the screen, remove your data disk.
   c. Turn off the monitor. (Your instructor also may ask you to turn off the computer and printer.)

Repeat the drill until you can key it at a comfortable rate.

1. Proofread your document on the screen. Use the editing keys to make any additional corrections. Press Esc to check the document. Print the document.
2. Proofread the document and note any additional errors you may have missed.
3. Retrieve the document and make corrections as necessary. Save and print your corrected copy.

Improve Keying Skills

Take two 1-minute timings on each paragraph. Set a speed or an accuracy goal. If you complete the paragraph before time runs out, start again.

Exercise 1

Quite often decisions involving important changes in policy and organizational structure are announced without employee involvement. Usually these changes meet resistance or are never successfully negotiated between management and employees.

Exercise 2

Participatory planning is on the ascent as an important management tool. Managers who apprise their employees about important planning decisions usually will gain the support of the employees in implementing the change.

Exercise 3

The image an organization projects is very important. Each employee is a public relations contact for the organization. Even when employees are not at work, they still represent their employer. Persons who are loyal to their employers should not criticize the organization publicly.

Measure Progress

Minimum goal: 27 wam with four or fewer errors

Take two 2-minute timings.

Computer simulations have great teaching potential. They are one of the more powerful teaching modes utilized by computers. A simulation may attempt to closely approximate reality. Sometimes a simulation designs a fantasy situation in which the learner must make decisions based on presented data and then cope with the consequences. Many of the popular arcade games are fantasies.

A simulation is an excellent approach to teaching logical thinking and problem solving. It provides the user the opportunity to learn essential skills and acquire knowledge for decision making.

Formatting Edited Copy

Learning Activity 1

1. Start document LES34DC2. Key the following report. Follow the proofreader's marks and make corrections as you key the document. Use the 1-inch default margins and a 2-inch top margin.
2. Correct any keying errors as you enter the text.
3. Proofread the copy on the screen. Use the editing keys to make any changes. Be sure to pay attention to spacing and format.
4. Press ESC when you have finished and follow the prompts to have the program check your document. Save and print a copy of your document.
5. Proofread your printout and note any additional errors you may have missed. Pay close attention to the spacing between parts of the letter.
6. Retrieve the document and make corrections as necessary. Save and print your corrected copy.